Fifty Lectures for Mathcounts Competitions

Volume 1

http://www.mymathcounts.com/index.php

ACKNOWLEDGEMENTS

We would like to thank the following math contests:

The Mathcounts Competitions, the nation's premier middle school math enrichment, coaching, and competition program.

The AMC 8, an examination in middle school mathematics designed to promote the development and enhancement of problem solving skills.

The AIME (American Invitational Mathematics Examination).

The China Middle School Math Competition.

We would like to thank many students and parents who participated in the "50 Mathcounts Lectures 2011 Summer Program." Without their support and trust, this program would not be possible. Thanks go to these parents and students who reviewed the draft of the lectures, made corrections to some errors, and provided excellent insights to some solutions.

Contributors

Jane Chen, Author.
Sam Chen, Author.
Yongcheng Chen, Ph.D., Reviewer.
Guiling Chen, Owner, mymathcounts.com, Typesetter, Editor

ISBN-13: 978-1461172710
ISBN-10: 1461172713

Please contact mymathcounts@gmail.com for suggestions, corrections, or clarifications.

Table of Contents

This page is intentionally left blank.

BASIC KNOWLEDGE

Statements

A statement is any sentence that is either true or false, but not both.

> **Examples:**
> Boston is a city in USA.
> $1 + 1 = 3$
> A spider does not have six legs.

The following sentences are not statements:

Do your homework.	(a command)
How do you solve this math problem?	(a question)
Mathcounts contest is harder than the AMC 8 contest.	(an opinion)
This sentence is false.	(a paradox)

Negations

The sentence "AMC 8 contest consists of 25 problems" is a statement; the negation of this statement is "AMC8 contest does not consist of 25 problems".

The negation of a true statement is false, and the negation of a false statement is true.

Statement	Negation
All do	Some do not (Not all do)
Some do	None do (All do not)

Examples: Form the negation of each statement:

The moon is not a star.	$\Rightarrow$	The moon is a star.
The moon is a star.	$\Rightarrow$	The moon is not a star.
A spider does not have six legs.	$\Rightarrow$	A spider has six legs.
Some rabbits have short tails.	$\Rightarrow$	No rabbit has a short tail.
Some rabbits do not have short tails.	$\Rightarrow$	All rabbits have short tails.
No rabbit has a short tail.	$\Rightarrow$	Some rabbits have short tails.

Converse, Inverse, and Contrapositive

Direct statement	If p, then q.
Converse	If q, then p.
Inverse	If not p, then not q.
Contrapositive	If not q, then not p.

Direct statement	If I live in Boston, then I live in USA.
Converse	If I live in USA, then I live in Boston.
Inverse	If I do not live in Boston, then I do not live in USA.
Contrapositive	If I do not live in USA, then I do not live in Boston.

Rectangle of logical equivalent

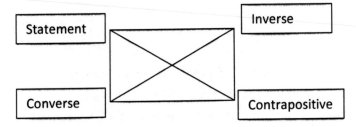

Logically equivalent pair of statements (diagonally opposite):

    A statement and its contrapositive

    The inverse and converse of the same statement

Not logically equivalent pair of statements (adjacent):

    A statement and its inverse

    A statement and its converse

    The converse and contrapositive of the same statement

    The inverse and contrapositive of the same statement

Examples:

Statement:	A square is a rectangle	(true)
Converse	A rectangle is a square	(false)
Inverse	A figure that is not a square is not a rectangle	(false)
Contrapositive	A figure that is not a rectangle s is not a square	(true)

2

Euler Diagram

Deductive reasoning consists of three steps as follows:
     (1). Making a general statement (major premise).
     (2). Making a particular statement (minor premise).
     (3). Making a deduction (conclusion).

Example:
     (1). The major premise is: All cats are animals
     (2). The minor premise is: Jerry is a cat.
     (3). The conclusion is: Jerry is an animal.

Procedures to draw the diagram:
     (1) Draw a big circle to represent the first premise. This is the region for "animals".
     (2) Draw a second circle to represent "all cats". Since all cats are animals, the second circle goes inside the first big circle.
     (3) Put Jerry inside where it belongs. The second premise stated that Jerry is a cat. Put Jerry inside the region marked "Cats".

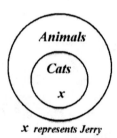

x represents Jerry

Example: Is the following argument valid? An argument is valid if that the premises are true and these premises force the conclusion to be true.
     All apple trees have green leaves
     That plant has green leaves.
     That plant is an apple tree.

3

Solution: we draw the Euler Diagram. We see that "that plant" can go either inside the small circle or outside it. So the argument is not valid.

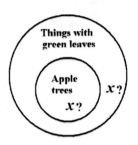

Some Problem Solving Skills

(a) Find the contrapositive of the statement.

Example 1: Each card has either a circle or a star on one side and either a triangle or a square on the other side. In order to verify the statement "every card with a star on it also has a triangle on it," which numbered card(s) must be turned over? (Mathcounts)

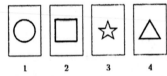

Solution: two cards (cards 2 and 3).

We introduce in this section a two-step method. This method can be used to solve any similar problems.

Step 1. We verify the statement first:

One side   Other side

Every card with a star on it also has a triangle on it.

We must turn over every card with a star on it (card 3) to make sure it has a triangle on the other side.

Step 2. We then verify the contrapositive of the statement:

Every card without a triangle on it also does not have a star on it.

We must turn over any card without a triangle on it (in this case, card 2 with a square as shown in the figure on the left) to make sure it doesn't have a star on the other side).

4

(b) *Find two statements that are contradicted to each other*

Example 2: There are three boxes with different colors: red, yellow and blue. One apple is in one of the three boxes.
Only one of the following statements is true, and the others are false.

I: Apple is in the red box; II Apple is not in the yellow box, and III: Apple is not in the red box.

Which box is the apple in?

Solution: First we find the two statements that are contradicted to each other. There must be a true statement between these two. Other statements left are all false.

Statement I and Statement III are two contradicted statements. We are sure that the true statement is one of these two statements, although we do not know which one. So we conclude that the statement II is false. Then we know the apple is in the yellow box.

(c) *Focus on the step before the last.*

Example 3: A turtle crawls up a 12 foot hill after a heavy rainstorm. The turtle crawls 4 feet, but when it stops to rest, it slides back 3 feet. How many tries does the turtle make before it makes it up the hill?

Solution: 9.
We look at where the turtle was just before the last try. Since the turtle can crawl 4 feet each time, $12 - 4 = 8$. Every try the turtle goes up 1 foot. It takes the turtle 8 tries when it reaches the 8 feet location. The turtle needs one more try to reach the top. Note when it reaches the top, there is no sliding back.

(d). *Dividing into three groups.*

When you need to weigh a number of coins with counterfeit coin, divide the coins into three groups with the number of coins in each group: *m, m, m*, or *m, m, m* – 1 or *m, m, m* + 1.

Example 4: A jeweler has four small bars that are supposed to be gold. He knows that one is counterfeit and the other three are genuine. The counterfeit bar has a slightly different weight than a real gold bar. Using a balance scale, what is the minimum number of weighings necessary to guarantee that the counterfeit bar will be detected? (Mathcounts)

Solution: 2.

We divide the four bars into three groups: 1, 1, and 2. We weight two bars, say, bar A and bar B, first.

Case I: If their weights are different, we remove one, say, bar A, and put a third bar, say bar C. If B and C are the same, and then bar A is the counterfeit. If bar B and bar C are different, bar B is the counterfeit (since it's weight is different from both A and C).

Case II: If their weights are the same, then we remove one, say, Bar A, and put a third bar, say Bar C. If B and C are the same, then Bar D is the counterfeit. If Bar B and Bar C are different, Bar C is the counterfeit.

So two weighings are necessary.

(e). Drawing Solid and Dash Lines

Example 5: Three friends – math teacher Mr. White, science teacher Mr. Black, and history teacher Mr. Redhead – met in a cafeteria. "It is interesting that one of us has white hair, another one has black hair, and the third has red hair, though no one's name gives the color of their hair" said the black-haired person. "You are right," answered White. What color is the history teacher's hair?

Solution: The history teacher's hair is black.
If the relationship of two things is certain, we draw a solid line between them. Otherwise, we draw a dash line.

We know that no one's name gives the color of their hair. So we draw the dash lines as shown on the right:

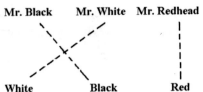

6

We know that Mr. White answered the black-haired person. So he has no black hair. We draw a dash line between Mr. White and "black hair".

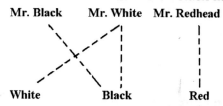

So Mr. White must have red hair. We draw a solid line to indicate that Mr. White has red hair.

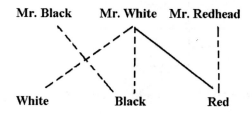

Mr. Black cannot have black hair, so he must have white hair. We draw a solid line for that.

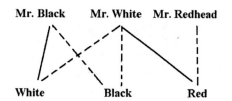

We know for sure that the history teacher's hair is black.

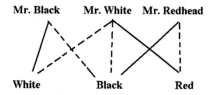

(f). Making a chart

Example 6: Each of three marbles *A*, *B*, and *C*, is colored one of the three colors. One of the marbles is colored white, one is colored red, and one is colored blue. Exactly one of these statements is true:

      1) A is red.   2) B is not blue.   3) C is not red.
What color is marble B? (Mathcounts Competitions).

Solution:

Case I: 1) is true.

Since exactly one of the three statements is true, so both 2) and 3) must be false.
Therefore B is blue and C is red. We know that only one marble is colored red, so
1) is not true.

		Red	White	Blue
True	A	√		
False	B			√
False	C	√		

Case II: 2) is true and both 1) and 3) are false.

We know that B can be red or white.

If B is red, C is also red. Contradiction!

		Red	White	Blue
False	A			
True	B	√		
False	C	√		

If B is white, C is red and A is blue. Works!

		Red	White	Blue
False	A			√
True	B		√	
False	C	√		

Case II: 3) is true and both 1) and 2) are false.

We know that C can be blue or white.

If C is white, B is blue. A is not red. So A must be white or blue. Contradiction!

8

		Red	White	Blue
False	A		?	?
False	B			√
True	C		√	

If C is blue, then B is blue. Contradiction!

		Red	White	Blue
False	A			
False	B			√
True	C			√

The answer is that B is white.

is in front of me," says the second. "Two ants are ahead of me and one other is behind," says the third ant. How can this be possible?

Problem 18. A centipede crawl a tree 75-inches high, starting from the ground. Each day it crawls 5 inches, and each night it slides down 4 inches. When will it first reach the top of the tree?

Problem 19. There are 4 cards on the table with the symbols a, b, 4, and 5 written on their visible sides. What is the smallest number of cards we need to turn over to find out whether the following statement is true: "If an even number is written on one side of a card then a vowel is written on the other side?

Problem 20. On an island, the inhabitants are either "knights" who always tell the truth or "knaves" who always lie. Person M said "I am a liar." Is he an inhabitant of the island?

Problem 21. On an island, the inhabitants are either "knights" who always tell the truth or "knaves" who always lie. What one question you must ask an islander in order to find out where a road leads to the city of knight or to the city of knaves?

Problem 22. A traveler has a straight gold chain with 7 links. She plans to stay at an inn that is willing to accept one link as payment for one night's lodging. She doesn't know when she'll want to leave, so she wants to pay on a daily basis. She'll have to cut some of the links in her chain of course; the inn is perfectly willing to accept cut links as payment. What is the smallest number of links she is forced to cut in order that she is able to pay every night (possibly getting change in the form of links paid earlier) for up to a week? Which link(s) should she break?

Problem 23. Each of the cards shown below has a number on one side and a letter on the other. How many of the cards must be turned over to prove the correctness of the statement: Every card with a vowel on one side has a prime number on the other side.

| A | B | E | 4 | 5 | 6 | 8 |

ANSWER KEYS

Problem 1. 2.   **Problem** 2. Saturday.   **Problem** 3. Bread

Problem 4. A and D   **Problem** 5. Mr. Eye.   **Problem** 6. 3.

Problem 7. 42.   **Problem** 8. Circles   **Problem** 9. Five children

Problem 10. 13 days.   **Problem** 11. Carol.   **Problem** 12. Ed.

Problem 13. Card 3.

Problem 14: Solution: Wrong. Her statement is invalid.

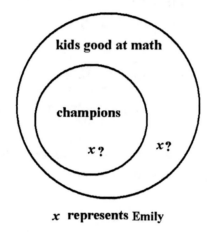

x represents Emily

Problem 15: Solution:

Method 1: Ann can pay a 15-chip coin to cover the fee for the ride. Other two can pay by giving Ann a 15-chip coin and receiving a 10-chip coin in return.

Method 2: Ann can pay a 15-chip coin to cover the fee for the ride. Other two can pay by giving Ann a 20-chip coin and receiving a 15-chip coin in return.

Method 3: Ann can pay a 15-chip coin to cover the fee for the ride. Other two can pay by giving Ann a 10-chip coin and a 15-chip coin and receiving a 20-chip coin in return.

Method 4: Ann can pay a 15-chip coin to cover the fee for the ride. Other two can pay by giving Ann two 10-chip coins and receiving a 15-chip coin in return.

Problem 16. Solution: No.

A statement and its converse are not logically equivalent pair of statements.

Problem 17. Solution: The third ant lied.

Problem 18. The caterpillar will be on the top of the tree at the end of the 71st day.

Problem 19. Two cards need to be turned over (Cards "4" and "b")

Problem 20. Solution: Person M is not an inhabitant of the island. If she is a knight, she would not say that she is a liar. If she is a liar, she would say that she is not a liar.

Problem 21. The question to ask: is this the road leading to your home? If the answer is "yes", the road is the way to the city of knights. If the answer is "no", the road is leading to the city of knaves.

Problem 22. Solution: Just one: the third.

Problem 23. Solution: We must overturn five cards.
We verify the statement first:
Every card with a vowel on one side has a prime number on the other side.
We must turn over every card with a vowel (cards A and E) to make sure it has a prime on the other side.
We then verify the contrapositive of the statement:
Every card without a prime number on one side does not have a vowel on the other side.
We must turn over any card with a composite number (cards 4, 6, and 8) to make sure it doesn't have a vowel on the other side).

1. BASIC KNOWLEDGE

Properties

Commutative Property:

The order in which numbers are added does not change the sum.

$4 + 7 = 7 + 4$ $a + b = b + a.$

$278 + 163 + 522$
$= 278 + 522 + 163$

Associative Property (grouping property)

$(4 + 3) + 7 = 4 + (3 + 7)$ $(a + b) + c = a + (b + c).$

$123 + 458 + 877 + 542$
$= (123 + 877) + (458 + 542)$

Distributive Property:

$3 \times (4 + 3) = 3 \times 4 + 3 \times 3$ $a(b + c) = ab + ac.$

$(15 + 4) \times 5 = 15 \times 5 + 4 \times 5$

Operation Skills

Examples:
(1) Thirty-seven people took a bus. Twelve got off. Then 5 got off. How many people are on the bus now?

Solution:
Method 1: $37 - 12 - 5 = 20$

Method 2: We calculate the total number of people that got off: $12 + 5 = 17$.
$37 - 17 = 20$

From example (1), we see that the following expressions are the same:
$37 - (12 + 5) = 37 - 12 - 5 = 20$.

(2).
(a). $128 - (28 + 10)$
$= 128 - 28 - 10 = 100 - 10 = 90$. $a - (b + c) = a - b - c$.

(b). $483 - (183 - 47)$
$= 483 - 183 + 47 = 300 + 47 = 347$. $a - (b - c) = a - b + c$.

(c). $(138 + 753 + 112) - 253$
$= (138 + 112) + (753 - 253)$ $(a + b + c) - d = a + (b - d) + c$.
$= 250 + 500 = 750$

(d). $(354 + 189) - (154 + 89)$
$= (354 - 154) + (189 - 89)$ $(a + b) - (c + d) = (a - c) + (b - d)$.
$= 200 + 100 = 300$.

2. DIFFERENT WAYS OF CALCULATIONS

2.1 When numbers are close to ten or one hundred

If the last digit of a number is close to ten or zero, make the number end in zero.

$9 = 10 - 1$	$8 = 10 - 2$	$7 = 10 - 3$
$11 = 10 + 1$	$12 = 10 + 2$	$13 = 10 + 3$
$19 = 20 - 1$	$18 = 20 - 2$	$17 = 20 - 3$
$101 = 100 + 1$	$199 = 200 - 1$	

Examples:

(1). Calculate: $276 + 199$
$= 276 + 199 + 1 - 1 = 276 + 200 - 1 = 476 - 1 = 475$.

(2). Calculate: $443 + 59$
$= 440 + 3 + 60 - 1 = (440 + 60) + (3 - 1) = 500 + 2 = 502$

16

(3). Calculate: 69 + 14 + 205 + 48 + 17
= (70 + 10 + 200 + 50 + 20) + (4 + 5 − 1 − 2 − 3) = 350 + 3 = 353.

(4). Calculate: 423 − 98
= 423 − 100 + 2 = 323 + 2 = 325.

(5). Calculate: 500 − 297 − 49
= (500 − 300 − 50) + (3 + 1) = 150 + 4 = 154.

(6). Calculate: 31 + 58 + 69
= (31 + 69) + 58 = 100 + 58 = 158.

2.2. Find a reference number.

Examples:

(1): Alex's father bought five bags of apples. They weighted 51, 52, 48, 47, and 53 lbs. What is the total weight of the apples?
Solution: We let the number 50 be the reference number.
51 + 52 + 48 + 47 + 53
= 50 + 1 + 50 +2 + 50 − 2 + 50 − 3 + 50 + 3
= (50 + 50 + 50 + 50 + 50) + (1 + 2 − 2 − 3 + 3) = 250 + 1 = 251.

(2): Bob's mother bought 10 bags of rice with the weights of 101, 102, 100, 106, 98, 103, 94, 99, 107, and 95 lbs. Find the total weight of the 10 bags of rice.

Solution: We let the number 100 be a reference number.
101 + 102 + 100 +106 + 98 + 103 + 94 + 99 + 107 + 95 = (100 + 100+ 100 + 100 + 100 + 100 + 100 +100 +100 +100) + (1 + 2 + 0 + 6 − 2 + 3 − 6 − 1 + 7 − 5)
= 1000 + 5 = 1005.

2.3. Using addition instead of subtraction.

Examples:

(1). Calculate: 1,200 − 230 − 450 − 270

Solution: 250.

$1,200 - (230 + 450 + 270) = 1,200 - [(230 + 270) + 450] = 1,200 - (500 + 450) = 1,200 - 950 = 1,200 - 1000 + 50 = 200 + 50 = 250.$

(2). Calculate: $4,000 - 5 - 10 - 15 - \ldots - 95 - 100$

Solution: 2950.

$4000 - 5 - 10 - 15 - \ldots - 95 - 100$

$= 4000 - (5 + 10 + 15 + \ldots + 95 + 100)$

$= 4000 - (5 + 100) \times (20 \div 2)$ (look at lesson 2.5 for the formula)

$= 4000 - 105 \times 10 = 4000 - 1050 = 4000 - 1000 - 50 = 3000 - 50 = 2950.$

(3). Evaluate the expression: $100 - 81 + 64 - 49 + 36 - 25 + 16 - 9 + 4 - 1$.

Solution: 55.

Method 1:

$100 - 81 + 64 - 49 + 36 - 25 + 16 - 9 + 4 - 1$

$= 100 + 64 + 36 + 16 + 4 - (81 + 49 + 25 + 9 + 1)$

$= 100 + (64 + 36) + (16 + 4) - (80 + 1 + 50 - 1 + 20 + 5 + 10)$

$= 100 + 100 + 20 - (80 + 20 + 50 + 10 + 5)$

$= 100 + 100 + 20 - (100 + 20 + 40 + 5) = 100 - 40 - 5 = 60 - 5 = 55$

Method 2:

$100 - 81 + 64 - 49 + 36 - 25 + 16 - 9 + 4 - 1$

$= 19 + 15 + 11 + 7 + 3 = (19 + 11) + (7 + 3) + 15 = 30 + 10 + 15 = 55.$

Method 3: Observe: $10^2 - 9^2 = 10 + 9$. $8^2 - 7^2 = 8 + 7$. We have:

$10^2 - 9^2 + 8^2 - 7^2 + 6^2 - 5^2 + 4^2 - 3^2 + 2^2 - 1^2$

$= 10 + 9 + 8 + 7 + 6 + 5 + 4 + 3 + 2 + 1 = 55.$

2.4. Find two numbers that will add to ten or hundred.

$1 + 9 = 10; 2 + 8 = 10; 3 + 7 = 10; 4 + 6 = 10; 5 + 5 = 10.$

Examples:

Compute:

(1). $31 + 57 + 69$

$= (31 + 69) + 57 = 100 + 57 = 157$

(2). $325 + 27 + 675$

$= (325 + 675) + 27 = 1,000 + 27 = 1,027.$

(3). $7,474 + 846 + 526 + 154$

$= (7,476 + 524) + (846 + 154) = 8,000 + 1,000 = 9,000$

2.5 Addition of consecutive positive integers

2. 5. 1 The following formula can be used to compute the sum of consecutive integers, or sum of consecutive odd/even integers or the sum of a series of integers that have a common difference.

$$S = \frac{(a+b)n}{2}$$

Where a is the beginning number and b is the ending number. n is the number of terms in the addition.

Common difference d:

For the list of numbers: 1, 2, 3, 4,…, the common difference is $d = 2 - 1 = 3 - 2 = 4 - 3 = 1$.

For the list numbers: 1, 3, 5, 7,…, the common difference $d = 3 - 1 = 5 - 3 = 7 - 5 = 2$.

For the list of numbers: 1, 5, 9, 13,…, the common difference is $d = 5 - 1 = 9 - 5 = 13 - 9 = 4$.

The number of terms n (with the common difference is d):

$$n = (\text{last term} - \text{first term}) \div d + 1$$

Examples:

(1). How many terms are there in the sequence $1 + 2 + 3 +.. + 100$?

Answer: $n = 100 - 1 + 1 = 100$

(2). How many terms are there in the sequence $11 + 12 + 13 + .. + 100$?

Answer: $n = 100 - 11 + 1 = 90$

(3). How many terms are there in the sequence $2 + 4 + 6 + .. + 100$?

Answer: $n = (100 - 2)/2 + 1 = 50$

2.5.2. The following formula can be used to compute the sum of series integers that have a common difference.

$$S = m \times n$$

Where m is the middle number and n is how many numbers in the addition.

Examples:

Compute:

(1). $1 + 2 + 3 + 4 + 5 + \ldots + 20$

$$= \frac{(a+b)n}{2} = \frac{(1+20) \times 20}{2} = 21 \times 10 = 210$$

(2). $1 + 3 + 5 + 7 + 9 + 11 + 13 + 15$

$$= \frac{(1+15) \times 8}{2} = 16 \times 4 = 64$$

(3). $37 + 38 + 39 + 40 + 41 + 42 + 43$

$$= 40 \times 7 = 280$$

(4). $38 + 39 + 40 + 41 + 42 + 43$

$$= (\frac{40 + 41}{2}) \times 6 = 81 \times 3 = 243$$

3. ADDITION AND SUBTRACTION PROBLEMS EXPANDED

Examples:

(1). What is the smallest positive value that the expression

$1 - 2 - 3 - 4 - 5 - 6 - 7 - 8$

can have when parenthesized in any way? (Multiplication and division are not allowable operations.) (Mathcounts Handbooks).

Solution: 2.

$(1 - 2) - (3 - 4) - (5 - 6) - (7 - 8) = 2.$

(2). The digital root of a number is computed by adding its digits, adding the digits of the resulting sum, and so on, until a single digit results. To find the root of 637, for example, add

$$6 + 3 + 7 = 16$$
$$1 + 6 = 7$$

and the digital root of 637 is 7. Given that n is a three-digit number whose digital root is 7 and that two of the digits are 2 and 5, what is the largest possible value of n? (Mathcounts Handbooks).

Solution: 952.
Method 1: We are given that the digit root of 637 is 7. We know that n also has 7 as its digit root.
The largest possible value of n can be obtained this way:
$$6 + 3 + 7 = 7 + 6 + 3 = 8 + 5 + 3 = 9 + 5 + 2$$
The largest possible value of n is 952.

Method 2: We know that we can get the digit root module 9.
Let the third digit be m, we can write:
$$2 + 5 + m = 7 \qquad \Rightarrow \qquad m = 0;$$
Or
$$2 + 5 + m = 16 \qquad \Rightarrow \qquad m = 9$$
The largest possible value of n is 952.

Note $2 + 5 + m = 25$ is not obtainable since m is at most 9.

(3). What is the sum of all positive odd multiple of 3 that are less than 100? (Mathcounts Handbooks).

Solution: 867.
The smallest value is 3 and the greatest value is 99:
$$3 + 9 + 15 + \ldots + 99 = \frac{(3 + 99)}{2} \times 17 = 867.$$

4. ADDITION AND SUBTRACTION RELATED TO DIGITS

Examples:

(1). Placing each of the digits 2, 4, 6, 8, and 9 in exactly one of the boxes in the addition problem shown. Find the greatest possible sum.

Solution: 1,046

We place "9" in the hundred position, then we put 8 and 6 on the ten's digit positions. Other two digits will fit in to the units digit places. The greatest possible sum is $984 + 62 = 940 + 44 + 60 + 2 = 1,000 + 46 = 1,046$.

(2). Variables have replaced some digits in the addition problem that follows. Given that each digit 1 through 9 appears exactly once in the problem, which digit should replace the letter b? (Mathcounts Handbooks).

$$\begin{array}{r} a4b \\ +\ 2c5 \\ \hline d1e \end{array}$$

Solution: $b = 3$.

We know that $c = 6$ or $c = 7$. a can only be 3 or 6. If $c = 6$, a must be 3 and we also get $d = 6$. This does not work. So $c = 7$. Since $a + 2 + 1 = d$ and $b + 5 = e$. We have the four digits (3, 6, 8, and 9) to be used. a can only be 6 and b can only be 3.

(3). In the following addition problem, each letter represents a digit. What is the value of $a + b + c + d$? (Mathcounts Handbooks).

$$\begin{array}{r} aaa \\ +\quad b \\ \hline cddc \end{array}$$

Solution: 12.

Since the 3-digit number "aaa" becomes a 4-digit number when a one-digit number is added, we know that a should be "9", d should be "0" and c should be "1". So b = 2. We have $a + b + c + d = 9 + 2 + 1 + 0 = 12$.

(4). Each of the digits 0 – 9 was used exactly once in this addition problem. Someone erased all but three of the digits. Replace the letters with the missing digits. Which digit will replace d ? (Mathcounts Handbooks).

Solution: 3.

We know right way that $e = 1$. We have 2, 3, 4, 5, 6, and 8 left. If d is any of these digits, when $d + 9$, it carries up. So we are sure $b + 7$ will carry. Then we know that $a + c = 9$. We have two cases:

Case I: a could be 5 and c could be 4. d will be 3 and $b = 8$. It works.

Case II: a could be 6 and c could be 3. No combination of these digits will work.

(5). Given that the digits 1, 2, 3, 4, 5, and 6 are placed in the boxes shown, what is the greatest possible positive difference that can be obtained? (Mathcounts competitions).

Solution: 531

Since we want to get the greatest positive difference, we want to have the three-digit number ABC as large as possible and DEF as small as possible. So we assign the letter $A = 6$, $B = 5$, $C = 4$, $D = 1$, $E = 2$, and $F = 3$. The greatest difference is then 531.

(6). In the following subtraction problem, A, B, C, and D represent distinct digits. What is the value of $A + B + C + D$?

Solution:

We start with the ones digit.

Step (1). Subtract ones. We do not have enough ones. We regroup ones and get $D = 13 - 6 = 7$.

Step (2). Subtract tens. The greatest value for B is 9. If $B = 9$, since we regrouped in step (1), we have 8 left and $8 - 2$ is less than 7. So $B = 9$ not work. We regroup tens and we get $10 + B - 1 - 2 = 7$ or $7 + B = 7$. Then $B = 0$.

Step (3). Subtract hundreds. We do not have enough hundreds. We regroup hundreds. $10 + 3 - 1 - C = 7$, or $12 - C = 7$. $C = 5$.

Step (4). It is clear that $A = 8$.

So $A + B + C + D = 8 + 0 + 5 + 7 = 20$.

EXERCISES

1. Calculate:
   (1) $75 + 26 + 25$;
   (2) $72 + 67 + 28$;
   (3) $116 + 625 + 84$;
   (4) $321 + 679 + 52$;
   (5) $536 + 541 + 464 + 459$;
   (6) $125 + 428 + 875 + 572$;
   (7) $12\,345 + 87\,655 + 234$;
   (8) $9,495 + 9,697 + 505 + 303$.

2. Calculate:
   (1) $1,000 - 463$;
   (2) $10,000 - 7,535$;
   (3) $100,000 - 98,625$;
   (4) $110,000 - 7,525$;
   (5) $11,111,111,110,000,000,000 - 1,111,111,111$;
   (6) $637,189,600,000,000 - 6,371,896$;
   (7) $6,581,299 - 75,325 - 24,675$;
   (8) $225,200 - 173 - 827$;
   (9) $225,236 - 26 - 25 - 98 - 2 - 175 - 74$;
   (10) $625 - 75 - 125 - 28 - 72$.

3. Calculate:
   (1) $87 + (15 + 13) + 185$;
   (2) $39 + 264 + 97$;
   (3) $9,996 + 2,597 + 7,407$;
   (4) $3,487 + 6,927 + 1,586$;
   (5) $7,923 - (923 - 725)$;
   (6) $3,728 - 780 + 80$;
   (7) $8,457 + (900 - 457)$;
   (8) $6,432 - (800 + 432)$.

4. Calculate:
   (1) $1,272 - 998$;
   (2) $156 - 94$;
   (3) $9,999 + 999 + 99 + 9$;
   (4) $1,998 + 998 + 98$;
   (5) $568 - 128 + 332 - 72$;
   (6) $2,000 - 1,348 - 323 + 1,663$;
   (7) $537 - (543 - 163) - 57$.

5. Find the sums:
   (1) $756 + 758 + 761 + 764 + 770$;
   (2) $990 + 992 + 994 + 996 + 998$;
   (3) $1,975 + 1,980 + 1,998 + 1,985 + 1,994$.

6.

   (1). Each letter d, n and a in the addition below represents a different digit. What is the sum $d + n + a$? (Mathcounts Handbooks).

$$\begin{array}{r} dna \\ + \quad dan \\ \hline and \end{array}$$

   (2). In the addition shown, different letters stand for different digits. If O stands for 7, what digit does W represent? (Mathcounts Handbooks).

$$\begin{array}{r} TWO \\ + \quad TWO \\ \hline FOUR \end{array}$$

   (3). Place each of the digits 0, 1, 2, 3, 4, 5, and 6 in one of the boxes shown to create a true equation .What is the sum for the addition problem? (Mathcounts Handbooks).

$$\begin{array}{r} \square\square \\ + \quad \square\square \\ \hline \square\square\square \end{array}$$

(4). The set of ordered triples $\{(A, B, C,)\}$ is the solution set for the alpha numeric

$$\begin{array}{r} AA \\ + BB \\ \hline CC \end{array}$$

Where A, B, and C are distinct natural numbers. How many distinct ordered triples are in the solution set? (Mathcounts Competitions).

(5). Each of the digits 2, 4, 5, 6, 8 and 9 is placed in exactly one of the boxes of the subtraction problem shown. What is the least possible positive difference? (Mathcounts competitions).

(6). If q, r and s each represent a different integer 0-9, what is the value of s? (Mathcounts competitions).

$$\begin{array}{r} qqqq \\ rrrr \\ + \quad ssss \\ \hline rqqqs \end{array}$$

(7). In the addition problem shown, a, b and c represent three different digits. What is the three-digit sum? (Mathcounts competitions).

$$\begin{array}{r} abc \\ + \quad acb \\ \hline cba \end{array}$$

(8). Each different letter in the addition problem represents a different digit. What is the value of H? (Mathcounts competitions).

$$\begin{array}{r} HALF \\ + \quad HALF \\ \hline WHOLE \end{array}$$

26

(9). In the addition problem shown, whole numbers less than 10 are missing from the triangles. In the problem is done correctly, what is the sum of the numbers in these boxes?

$$
\begin{array}{r}
\triangle 63 \\
7\triangle 2 \\
+ \quad 58\triangle \\
\hline
\triangle 042
\end{array}
$$

(10). What units digit a will make the addition problem correct? (Mathcounts Competitions).

$$
\begin{array}{r}
23a \\
524 \\
+ \quad 36a \\
\hline
1124
\end{array}
$$

7. The pages of a book are numbered 1 through n. When the page numbers of the book were added, one of the page was mistakenly added twice, resulting in the incorrect sum of 1986. What was the number of the page that was added twice? (1986 AIME #6).

ANSWER KEYS TO EXERCISES

1.
   (1) (75 + 25) +26 = 126.
   (2) (72 + 28) + 67= 167.
   (3) (116+84) + 625=825.
   (4) (321+679) +52= 1052.
   (5) (536 + 464) + (541+459) = 2,000.
   (6) (125+875) + (428 +572) = 2,000.
   (7) (12345 + 87655) +234 = 100,234.
   (8) (9,495 + 505) + (9,697 + 303) = 20,000.

2.
 (1) 537.

(2) 2,465.

(3) 1,375.

(4) 1,00,000 + (10,000 − 7,525) = 102,475.

(5) 11, 111, 111, 100, 000, 000, 000 + 10, 000, 000, 000 − 1, 111, 111, 111 = 11, 111, 111, 108, 888, 888, 889.

(6) 637, 189, 000, 000, 000 + 600, 000, 000 − 6, 371, 896 = 637, 189, 593, 628, 104

(7) 6, 581, 299 − (75, 325 + 24, 675) = 6, 481, 299.

(8) 225, 200 − (173 + 827) = 224, 200.

(9) 225, 236 − (26 + 25 + 98 + 2 + 175 + 74)= 225, 236 − [(26 +74) + (25+175) +(98+ 2)] =225, 236 − 400 = 224, 836.

(10) 625 − (75 + 125 + 28 + 72) =625 − [(75 + 125) + (28 + 72)] =625 − 30 = 325.

3.
(1) (87 + 13) + (15 + 185) = 300.
(2) (36 + 246) + (3 + 97) =400.
(3) (9, 996 + 4) + (2, 597 + 3) + 7, 400
= 10, 000 + 2 600 + 7 400 =10, 000 + 10 000 = 20, 000.
(4) 3,414 + 73 + 6, 927 + 1,586
= (3, 414 + 1, 586) + (73 + 6, 927) = 5, 000 + 7, 000 = 12, 000.
(5) 7, 923 − 923 + 725 = 7, 000 + 725 = 7, 725.
(6) 3, 728 − (780 − 80) = 3, 028.
(7) 8, 457 − 457 + 900 = 8, 900.

(8) $(6, 432 - 432) - 800 = 5, 200.$

4.

 (1) $1, 272 - (1, 000 - 2) = 1, 272 - 1, 000 + 2$

$= 272 + 2 \ =274.$

(2) $156 - 100 + 6 = 56 + 6 = 62.$

(3) $(9, 999 + 1) + (999 + 1) + (99 + 1) + 6 = 10, 000 +1, 000 +100 + 6 =11, 106.$

(4) $(1, 998 + 2) + (998 + 2) + 94 = 2, 000 + 1, 000 + 94 = 3, 094.$

(5) $(568 + 322) - (128 + 72) = 900 - 200 = 700.$

(6) $2, 000 - 1, 348 + (1, 663 - 323) = 2, 000 - 1, 348 + 1, 340$

$= 2, 000 - (1, 348 - 1, 340) = 2, 000 - 8 = 1, 992.$

(7) $537 - 543 + 163 - 57$

$= (537 + 163) - (543 + 57) =700 - 600 = 100.$

5. (1) $(761 - 5) + (761 - 3) + 761 + (761 + 3) + (761 + 9)$

$= 761 \times 5 - 5 - 3 + 3 + 9 = 3 \ 809.$

(2) $(994 - 4) + (994 - 2) + 994 + (994 + 2) + (994 + 4)$

$= 994 \times 5 - 4 - 2 + 2 + 4 = 4,970.$

(3) $(1, 985 - 10) + (1, 985 - 5) + (1, 985 + 13) + 1, 985 + (1, 985 + 9)$

$= 1, 985 \times 5 - 10 - 5 + 13 + 9 = 9, 932.$

6. (1). 18.	(2). 6	(3).105.	(4). 32 triples.	(5). 26.
(6).8	(7).954	(8).9.	(9).24.	(10). 5.

7. Page 33.

1. BASIC KNOWLEDGE

Definition of multiplication (repeated addition)

$$\underbrace{a+a+a+a+...+a}_{b \ terms}=a\times b \qquad\qquad a\times b=c$$

Examples:

(1). $\underbrace{3+3+3+3}_{4 \ terms}=3\times 4=12$

(2). $\underbrace{5+5+5+5+...+5}_{10 \ terms}=5\times 10=50$

Definition of division

$$a \div b = c \qquad\qquad \text{or} \qquad\qquad \frac{a}{b}=c \qquad\qquad b \neq 0$$

a is the dividend, b is the divisor, and c is the quotient.

Properties

Commutative Property:
The order in which numbers are multiplied does not change the product.

$$a \times b = b \times a.$$

$3 \times 2 = 6$ $2 \times 3 = 6$

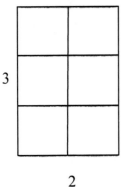

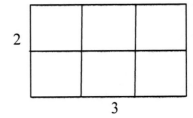

Associative Property:

The way in which factors are grouped does not change the product.

$$a \times (b \times c) = a \times b \times c$$

30

Examples:

(1) Calculate:

        (a). $4 \times (5 \times 9) = (4 \times 5) \times 9 = 20 \times 9 = 180$

        (b). $2 \times 7 \times 5 = (2 \times 5) \times 7 = 10 \times 7 = 70$

        (c). $2 \times 6 \times 5 = 2 \times (6 \times 5) = 2 \times 30 = 60$

(2). What is the product: $25 \times (12 \times 8)$?

        Solution: $25 \times (12 \times 8) = (25 \times 8) \times 12 = 200 \times 12 = 2400$.

Identity Property:

    The product of a factor and one is the factor.

    $5 \times 1 = 5$. $a \times 1 = a$.

Multiplicative Property of Zero:

    The product of a factor and zero is zero.

    $2 \times 0 = 0$. $a \times 0 = 0$.

Distributive Property:

$a(b + c) = ab + ac. \quad (a - b) \times c = a \times c - b \times c. \quad a \times (b - c) = a \times b - a \times c$

Examples:

(1). Calculate:

        (a). $3 \times (4 + 3) = 3 \times 4 + 3 \times 3 = 12 + 9 = 21$

        (b). $(25 - 5) \times 4 = 25 \times 4 - 5 \times 4 = 100 - 20 = 80$

        (c). $4 \times (25 - 5) = 4 \times 25 - 4 \times 5 = 100 - 20 = 80$

(2). Calculate $234 \cdot 997 - 233 \cdot 997$.

Solution: $234 \cdot 997 - 233 \cdot 997 = (234 - 233) \cdot 997 = 997$.

Some calculation skills

(1). $(a + b + c) \div d = a \div d + b \div d + c \div d$
$(12 + 48 + 63) \div 3 = 12 \div 3 + 48 \div 3 + 63 \div 3 = 4 + 16 + 21 = 20 + 21 = 41$

(2). $a \div (b \times c) = a \div b \div c$
$36 \div (2 \times 3) = 36 \div 2 \div 3 = 18 \div 3 = 6$

(3). $(a \times b) \div c = (a \div c) \times b$
$(48 \times 5) \div 3 = (48 \div 3) \times 5 = 16 \times 5 = 80$

(4). $a \div (b \div c) = a \div b \times c$
$48 \div (6 \div 2) = 48 \div 6 \times 2 = 8 \times 2 = 16$

(5). $(a - b) \div c = a \div c - b \div c$
$(48 - 16) \div 8 = 48 \div 8 - 16 \div 8 = 6 - 2 = 4$

(6). Difference of two squares: $a^2 - b^2 = (a + b)(a - b)$

Examples:
(1). Calculate: $50^2 - 40^2$
Solution: $50^2 - 40^2 = (50 + 40)(50 - 40) = 90 \times 10 = 900$

(2). Calculate: $25^2 - 23 \times 27$.
Solution: $25^2 - (25 - 2)(25 + 2) = 25^2 - (25^2 - 4) = 4$

(3). Calculate: $(80)(80) - (77)(83)$.
Solution: $(80)(80) - (80 - 3)(80 + 3) = (80)(80) - (80)(80) + 9 = 9$.

(4). Calculate: $29 \times 31 + 19 \times 21$.
Solution: $29 \times 31 + 19 \times 21 = (30 - 1)(30 + 1) + (20 - 1)(20 + 1)$
$= (30)(30) - 1 + (20)(20) - 1 = 1300 - 2 = 1298$.

(5). Find the value of $51^2 - 49^2 + 101^2 - 99^2$

Solution: $51^2 - 49^2 + 101^2 - 99^2 = (51 - 49)(51 + 49) + (101 - 99)(101 + 99) = 100 \times 2 + 200 \times 2 = 600.$

Multiplication table

	1	2	3	4	5	6	7	8	9
1	1	2	3	4	5	6	7	8	9
2	2	4	6	8	10	12	14	16	18
3	3	6	9	12	15	18	21	24	27
4	4	8	12	16	20	24	28	32	36
5	5	10	15	20	25	30	35	40	45
6	6	12	18	24	30	36	42	48	54
7	7	14	21	28	35	42	49	56	63
8	8	16	24	32	40	48	56	64	72
9	9	18	27	36	45	54	63	72	81

2. FAST WAYS OF MULTIPLICATION

2.1. Multiplying two 2-digit numbers with the same tens digit and the sum of their units digits is 10.

Theoretic basis:

$\overline{ab} \times \overline{ac}$ with $b + c = 10$

$(10a + b)(10a + c) = 100a^2 + 10ab + 10ac + bc = 100a^2 + 10a(b + c) + bc$
$= 100a^2 + 100a + bc = 100 \times a \times (a + 1) + bc$

Fast way: Multiply the tens digit a by $(a + 1)$ and write down the product. Follow this product by the product of the two last digits (bc).

Examples:

(1). Calculate: 27×23.
$27 \times 23 = (20 + 7)(20 + 3) = 100 \times 2 \times (2 + 1) + 7 \times 3$
$= 600 + 21 = 621$

Fast way:

2		2 + 1		7 × 3
↓		↓		↓
2	×	3 = 6		21 ⇒ 621

(2). Calculate 45^2.

$45^2 = (40 + 5)(40 + 5) = 100 \times 4 \times (4 + 1) + 5 \times 5 = 2000 + 25 = 2{,}025.$

Fast way:

4		4+1		5×5
↓		↓		↓
4	×	5 = 20		25 ⇒ 2025

2.2. Multiplying two 2-digit numbers with the same units digit and the sum of the tens digits is 10.

Theoretic basis:

$$\overline{ac} \times \overline{bc} \qquad\qquad a + b = 10$$

$$(10a + c)(10b + c) = 100ab + 10bc + 10ac + c^2 = 100ab + 10c(a + b) + c^2$$
$$= 100(ab + c) + c^2$$

Fast way: Multiply together two tens digits, then add the units digit to the product. Write down the product. Follow this product by the product of the two units digits.

Examples:

(1). Calculate:

(a). 23 × 83
$23 \times 83 = (20 + 3)(80 + 3) = 100 \times (2 \times 8 + 3) + 3 \times 3 = 1{,}900 + 9 = 1{,}909$

Fast way:

2 × 8		3		3 × 3 = 09
↓		↓		↓
16	+	3 = 19		09 ⇒ 1,909

(b). 48×68

$48 \times 68 = (40 + 8)(60 + 8) = 100 \times (4 \times 6 + 8) + 8 \times 8$

$= 3,200 + 64$

Fast way:

4×6	8	8×8
$\downarrow$	$\downarrow$	$\downarrow$
24	$+$ $8 = 32$	64 $\Rightarrow$ 3,264

2.3. Multiplying two 2-digit numbers a and b. The sum of the two digits of a is 10 and the two digits of b are the same.

$\overline{ab} \times \overline{cc}$ 　　　　　$a + b = 10$

Theoretic basis:

$$(10a + b)(10c + c) = 100ac + 10bc + 10ac + bc = 100ac + 10c(a + b) + bc$$
$$= 100ac + 100c + bc = 100(a + 1)c + bc$$

Fast way: Multiply c, the tens digit of A by $(a + 1)$ and write down the product. Follow this product by the product of the two last digits (bc).

Examples:

Calculate:

(1). 28×33 　　　　(2). 77×64 　　　　(3). 73×88 　　　　(4). 66×91

Solutions:

(1). $28 \times 33 = (20 + 8)(30 + 3) = 100 (2 + 1) \times 3 + 8 \times 3 = 924.$
(2). $77 \times 64 = (70 + 7)(60 + 4) = 100 (6 + 1) \times 7 + 7 \times 4 = 4928.$
(3). $73 \times 88 = (70 + 3)(80 + 8) = 100 (7 + 1) \times 8 + 8 \times 3 = 6424.$
(4). $66 \times 91 = (60 + 6)(90 + 1) = 100 (9 + 1) \times 6 + 6 \times 1 = 6006.$

2. 4. Multiply a two-digits number by 51 and a three-digit number by 501.

Theoretic basis:

The product $A \times B = 10^{n+1} \times \dfrac{B}{2}$.

Fast way: Divided the number B by 2. Write down the result. Follow the result by the number B.

Note when B is odd, the left-most digit of B needs to be line up with the decimal part of $B/2$.

Examples:

(1). $51 \times 64 = ?$

Solution: $51 \times 64 = 10^2 \times 64 /2 + 64 = 10^2 \times 32 + 64 = 3,200 + 64 = 3,264$

Fast way:

64	64
↓	↓
32	64 $\Rightarrow$ 3, 264

(2). $501 \times 326 = ?$

Solution: $501 \times 326 = 10^3 \times 326/2 + 326 = 10^3 \times 163 + 326 = 163,000 + 326 = 163,326$

Fast way:

326	326
↓	↓
163	326 $\Rightarrow$ 163, 326

2. 5. Two numbers are all close to 100

Theoretic basis:

$$(100 \pm b)(100 \pm c) = 10,000 \pm 100b + 100c + bc$$
$$= 100(100 \pm b \pm c) \pm bc$$

Fast way: Add the units digit of B to A. Write down the result. Follow the result by the product of the units digits of A and B.

Examples:

(1). Calculate: $106 \times 108 =$?

$$106 \times 108 = (100 + 6)(100 + 8) = 100 \times 100 + 100 \times 6 + 100 \times 8 + 6 \times 8$$
$$= 100 \times (100 + 6 + 8) + 6 \times 8$$
$$= 100 \times 114 + 6 \times 8 = 11,400 + 48 = 11,448$$

Fast way:

$106 + 8$ 6×8

$\downarrow$ $\downarrow$

114   48 $\rightarrow$ 11,448

(2). Calculate: $97 \times 99 = $?

$$97 \times 99 = (100 - 3)(100 - 1) = 100 \times (100 - 3 - 1) + 3 \times 1$$
$$= 100 \times 96 + 3 = 9603$$

Fast way:

$97 - 1$ 3×1

$\downarrow$ $\downarrow$

96   03 $\rightarrow$ 9603

2.6. Multiply a two or three-digit number by 11 or 111.
2.6.1. Multiply a two or three-digit number by 11.

Theoretic basis:

$$\overline{ab} \times 11 = (10a + b) \times 11 = 110a + 11b = 100a + 10(a + b) + b$$

$$\overline{abc} \times 11 = (100a + 10b + c) \times 11 = 1100a + 110b + 11c = 1000a + 100(a + b) + 10(b + c) + c$$

Fast way: (1) Write down the units digit. (2) Write down the sum of the two digits to the left of the digit wrote in (1). Write down the tens digit plus the carry from step (2) if there is any.

Examples:
Calculate:

$13 \times 11 = 143$ $63 \times 11 = 693$ $36 \times 11 = 396$

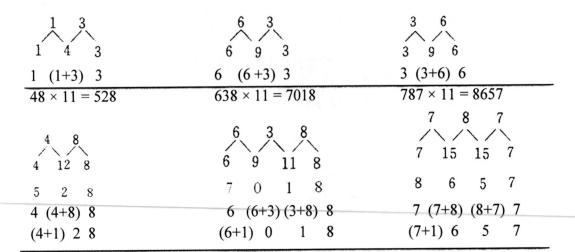

$48 \times 11 = 528$ $638 \times 11 = 7018$ $787 \times 11 = 8657$

2.6.2. Multiply a two or three-digit number by 111.

Theoretic basis:

$$\overline{ab} \times 111 = (10a + b) \times 111 = 1110a + 111b = 1000a + 100a + 10a + 100b + 10b + b$$
$$= 1000a + 100(a + b) + 10(a + b) + b$$

$$\overline{abc} \times 111 = (100a + 10b + c) \times 111 = 11100a + 1110b + 111c$$
$$= 10000a + 1000a + 1000b + 100a + 100b + 100c + 10(b + c) + c$$
$$= 10000a + 1000(a + b) + 100(a + b + c) + 10(b + c) + c$$

Fast way: (1) Write down the units digit. (2) Write down the sum of the two digits to the left of the digit wrote down in (1). (3). Repeat step (2) one more time but add the carry from step (2) if there is any. (4). Write down the tens digit plus the carry from step (2) if there is any.

$48 \times 111 = 5328$ $234 \times 111 = 25974$

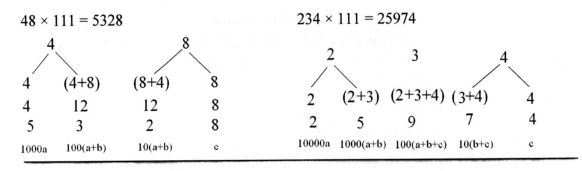

2.7. Multiplying two 2-digit numbers with "1" as the tens digit.

Fast way: (1) Get the sum of A and the units digit of B. Write down the sum, (2) get the product of the two units digits, and (3)add them together in such a way that the tens digit of the product is line up with the units digit of the sum.

$17 \times 12 = 204$ $13 \times 12 = 156$

```
┌─────────────────┐    ┌─────────────────┐
│  17 + 2 = 19    │    │   13 + 2 = 15   │
│                 │    │                 │
│  7 × 2 = 14     │    │   3 × 2 = 6     │
│                 │    │                 │
│       19        │    │         15      │
│     + 14        │    │       + 06      │
│     ─────       │    │       ─────     │
│      204        │    │        156      │
└─────────────────┘    └─────────────────┘
```

2. 8. Multiplying two 2-digit numbers with "1" as the units digit.

Fast way: (1) Find the product of the tens digits of two numbers, (2) Write down the product, (3) find the sum of the number of tens in the attendant and the second number. (4) Follow the product by the sum.

Examples:

(1). $51 \times 31 = 1581$
     Step 1: $5 \times 3 = 15$
     Step 2: $50 + 31 = 81$
     Step 3: 1581.

(2). $41 \times 21 = 861$
     Step 1: $4 \times 2 = 8$
     Step 2: $40 + 21 = 61$
     Step: 861.

3. MULTIPLICATION AND DIVISION EXPANDED

Examples:

(1). In the multiplication shown, each letter represents a different digit. What digit does the letter *C* represent? (Mathcounts Handbooks).

$$
\begin{array}{r}
A\,B\,C\,D\,E \\
\times \qquad\qquad E \\
\hline
E\,D\,A\,D\,E
\end{array}
$$

Solution: 4.

E could possibly be 1, 5, or 6. However, the value 1 for E does not work because if $E = 1$, there is no value for A since $E \times A = 1$. So we try $E = 5$. A certainly is 1 since the product is also a 5-digit integer. The multiplication can be written as follows:

$$
\begin{array}{r}
1\,B\,C\,D\,5 \\
\times \qquad\qquad 5 \\
\hline
5\,D\,1\,D\,5
\end{array}
$$

D is possibly 7 or 2. If $D = 7$, we have:

$$
\begin{array}{r}
1\,B\,C\,7\,5 \\
\times \qquad\qquad 5 \\
\hline
5\,7\ \,1\,7\,5
\end{array}
$$

$57175 \div 5 = 11435$ which does not work since $ABCDE$ are five different digits.

So $D = 2$.

$$
\begin{array}{r}
1\,B\,C\,2\,5 \\
\times \qquad\qquad 5 \\
\hline
5\,2\,1\,2\ \,5
\end{array}
$$

$52125 \div 5 = 10425 \quad \Rightarrow \quad C = 4.$

$E = 6$ will lead no solution.

(2). In the division problem, the letters A, B, C, D, and E represent five different digits. Find the digit represented by C. (Mathcounts Handbooks).

$$
\begin{array}{r}
1B \\
A\,)\overline{C7} \\
\underline{A\ \ } \\
37 \\
\underline{D5} \\
E
\end{array}
$$

Solution: 8.

40

We know that $D = 3$. And $A \times B = 35$. So A is possibly 5 or 7. We see that $A = 7$ does not work since this will force C to be larger than 9. So $A = 5$ and $C = 8$.

(3). Your school system decides to cut class periods from 55 minutes to 45 minutes. If the school year is 180 days and you take math one period each day, how many hours of math class would you lose in six years of school? (Mathcounts Handbooks).

Solution: 180 hours.

You lose $55 - 45 = 10$ minutes each school day and $10 \times 180 = 1800$ minutes $= 1800 \div 60 = 30$ hours each school year and $30 \times 6 = 180$ hours in six years.

(4). A TV mini-series was scheduled for 2 hours a night for seven consecutive nights. For each hour scheduled, the series showed for all but 10 minutes which was devoted to commercials. How many minutes of commercials were shown during the mini-series? (Mathcounts Handbooks).

Solution: 140 minutes.

Each hour there is 10 minutes of commercials. Each two-hour period will have $2 \times 10 = 20$ minutes of commercials. Seven nights will have $7 \times 20 = 140$ minutes of commercials.

(5). David and seven of his friends are to split \$112 equally. How many dollars should each person receive? (Mathcounts Handbooks).

Solutions: \$14.

There are a total of $7 + 1 = 8$ kids to split the \$112. The answer will be $112 \div 8 = 14$.

(6). In a class experiment, Mr. Jones gave 41 beans to each of his 39 students. How many beans did he need to conduct the experiment? (Mathcounts Handbooks).

Solution: 1599.

Since each student will get 41 beans, 39 students will get $41 \times 39 = 1599$ beans.

EXERCISES:

Problem 1. A school has an enrollment of 500 students. Each student takes 6 classes per day. Each class has 25 students and each teacher teaches 5 classes per day. How many teachers does the school have? (Mathcounts Competitions).

Problem 2. What is the sum of the digits a and b in the following multiplication problem?

$$
\begin{array}{r}
b\,3\,a\,1 \\
\times \qquad b\,4 \\
\hline
9\,4\,0\,4 \\
+\ 4\,7\,0\,b\,0 \\
\hline
a\,6\,4\,b\,4
\end{array}
$$

Problem 3. Evaluate $234 \cdot 997 - 233 \cdot 997$.

Problem 4. Compute: $(29)^2 - 58(9) + 9^2$.

Problem 5. Find the value of $51^2 - 49^2 + 101^2 - 99^2$.

Problem 6. Find: $103 \times 97 + 9$.

Problem 7. In the multiplication problem shown, A and C represent distinct non-zero digits. What is the value of $A + C$?

$$
\begin{array}{r}
CC \\
\times \quad C \\
\hline
A9C
\end{array}
$$

Problem 8. The alphanumeric code shown represents the standard base-ten multiplication of two three-digit numbers. Each of the letters $A, B, C, D, E,$ and F represents a different digit chosen from the set $\{1, 2, 3, 4, 5, 6\}$. (Mathcounts Competitions).

```
        E C F
    ×   D A B
      F C 8 B
      9 E A
  F F D D
  _____
  F E B F E B
```

Find the value which is *B* less than the product *FEBFEB* divided by 1001.

Problem 9. The digits 0, 2, 4, 6, and 8 are to be place one in each box, in the multiplication problem shown, so that the product is as large as possible. What is the product?

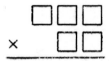

Problem 10. What is the largest possible product obtained by placing the digits 5, 6, 7, 8, and 9 in the boxes shown?

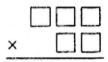

Problem 11. In the following multiplication problem, the * represents the same digit in each number: (73*)(*3) = 389**. What digit does the * represent? (Mathcounts Competitions).

Problem 12. The product of two numbers has been accidentally erased by a student. All that remains is shown here. The student only remembers that the product was larger than 4000. Name the larger factor. (Mathcounts Competitions).

```
            _ 8
    ×       _ _
    _____
        3 _ _
      _ 1 2
    _____

      _ _ _ _
```

Problem 13. In the equation shown, each letter represents a different digit. If A is not zero, what is the largest possible value of D?

$$
\begin{array}{r}
A\,B\,C \\
\times \quad\quad C \\
\hline
D\,B\,C
\end{array}
$$

Problem 14. Select four different digits from the set $\{1, 2, 3, 4\}$ and place one in each box. What is the largest possible product that can be obtained?

$$\square\square \times \square\square$$

Problem 15. Find the value of $A + B$ in this multiplication table. (Mathcounts Handbooks).

$\times$	?	?	?
?	B	12	20
?		21	
?	18	27	A

Problem 16. The product $4 \cdot 2178$ equals 8712, which has the same digits in reverse order as the original factor 2178. What four-digit number, when multiplied by 9, has its digits reversed?

Problem 17. Each asterisk in the diagram indicates a missing digit in the division. What is the value of the two-digit divisor? (Mathcounts Handbooks)

$$
\begin{array}{r}
8** \\
\,)\overline{***} \\
\underline{**} \\
*** \\
\underline{***} \\
** \\
\underline{**}
\end{array}
$$

Problem 18. If each * represents a digit, and none of the digits in the divisor appear again in the problem, what is the value of the quotient? (Mathcounts Handbooks).

```
            **
      _____
135 ) ****
      ***
       ***
       ***
```

Problem 19. Express $57600 \div 800$ in simplest form.

Problem 20. A girl wants to buy a new bicycle which costs $87. She has already saved $15 and then gets a job which pays a net amount of $4 per hour. How many hours must she work to earn the money she still needs for the bicycle?

Problem 21. Find the answer, in simplest form, when you multiply 586 by 96 and divide the product by 192?

Problem 22. Evaluate: $(9999) \times (8)$.

Problem 23. Find the product of 3,475,000 and 33,397,000.

Problem 24. Evaluate: 999999×999999.

Problem 25. David's uncle loaned him $900 with no interest. David paid all of the money in equal monthly payments over 3 years. How much were the monthly payments? (Mathcounts Competitions).

Problem 26. How many 32-passenger buses will be needed to take 200 students on a field trip?

Problem 27. What is the product of the numbers 1, 2, 3, 4, 5, 6, 7, 8, 9 and 0?

ANSWER KEYS

Problem 1. 24	**Problem 2.** 7	**Problem 3.** 997
Problem 4. 400	**Problem 5.** 600	**Problem 6.** 10000
Problem 7. 9	**Problem 8.** 120	**Problem 9.** 52480
Problem 10. 84000	**Problem 11.** 5	**Problem 12.** 95
Problem 13. 8	**Problem 14.** 1312	**Problem 15.** 53
Problem 16. 1089	**Problem 17.** 12	**Problem 18.** 22
Problem 19. 72	**Problem 20.** 18 hours	**Problem 21.** 293

Problem 22. 79992   **Problem 23.** 116,054,575,000,000

Problem 24. 999998000001 **Problem 25.** $25   **Problem 26.** 7 buses

Problem 27. 0

1. BASIC KNOWLEDGE

Even and odd integers

Even integer:

An integer with the last digit of 0, 2, 4, 6, or 8. General form: $2n$ or $2n + 2$, where n is any integer.

Examples: Even integers: 10, 12, 14, 16, and 18.

Odd integers:

An integer with the last digit of 1, 3, 5, 7, or 9. General form: $2n + 1$ or $2n - 1$.

Examples: Odd integers: 11, 13, 15, 17, and 19.

Parity:

An even number has even parity and an odd number has odd parity.

Properties:

even + even = even.	12 + 14 = 26.
even + odd = odd.	12 + 13 = 25
odd + odd = even.	13 + 13 = 26
odd × odd = odd.	15 × 15 = 225
odd ÷ odd = odd.	1001 ÷ 11 = 91
odd × even = even.	11 × 12 = 132
odd ≠ even.	1 ≠ 2

The sum of any even integer and 1 is odd: 4 + 1 = 5
The sum of two consecutive integers is odd: $n + (n + 1) = 2n + 1$; 12 + 13 = 25
The product of two consecutive integers is even: $n(n + 1)$; 12 × 13 = 156
Any two consecutive integers have opposite parity: 12 is even and 13 odd.
$a + b$ and $a - b$ have the same parity: 15 − 5 = 10 even; 15 + 5 = 20 even.

If the product of n positive integers is even, at least one of these n positive integers is even.

If the product of *n* positive integers is odd, all of these *n* positive integers are odd.

If the number of odd integers is even, then the sum of them is even.

If the number of odd integers is odd, then the sum of them is odd.

2. EXAMPLES

Example 1: Add any 30 consecutive positive integers together. Is the sum even or odd?

Solution: Odd.

There are 15 even and 15 odd positive integers among these 30 positive integers. The sum of 15 even positive integers is even. The sum of 15 odd integers is odd. The final answer is: even + odd = odd.

Try it yourself:

Add any 2012 consecutive positive integers together. Is the sum even or odd?

Answer: Even.

Example 2: 300 is the sum of 15 consecutive even positive integers. What is the greatest even positive integer among them?

Solution: 34.

The middle number in these 15 integers is the average of them, which is 300/15 = 20. Because the integers increase by 2, the greatest even number will be 7 × 2 = 14 more than the middle number. The answer is 20 + 14 = 34.

Try it yourself:

2000 is the sum of 25 consecutive even positive integers. What is the greatest even positive integer among them?

Answer: 104.

Example 3: The sequence 1, 1, 2, 3, 5, 8, 13, 21, … is formed like this: any term is the sum of the two terms before it, starting from the third term. How many are even numbers of the first 63 terms of the sequence?

Solution: 21.

The numbers are listed as: odd, odd, even; odd, odd, even;… There is one even number in every three consecutive terms. $63/3 = 21$, so there are 21 sets of three terms. Since each set has one even number, there are 21 even numbers.

Try it yourself:

The sequence 1, 1, 2, 3, 5, 8, 13, 21, … is formed like this: any term is the sum of the two terms before it, starting from the third term. How many of the first 2012 terms are even?

Answer: 670.

Example 4: All the positive even integers greater than 0 are arranged in five columns (*A, B, C, D,* and *E*) as shown. Continuing the pattern, in what column will the integer 50 be?

A	B	C	D	E
	2	4	6	8
16	14	12	10	
	18	20	22	24
32	30	28	26	
....

Solution: *B.*

Method 1: Every row has 4 even integers. 50 is the $50/2 = 25^{th}$ even integer. $25 = 4 \times 6 + 1$. So 50 is the first term in the 7th row. The first term in an odd numbered row is in the column B, so 50 is in column *B*.

Method 2: We see a pattern for every 8 integers in the table. 50 is the 25th integer and $25 \equiv 1$ mod 8. This means that 50 is in the same column as the first number in the first row. The answer is *B*.

Try it yourself:

All the positive even integers greater than 0 are arranged in five columns (*A, B, C, D,* and *E*) as shown. Continuing the pattern, in what column will the integer 2012 be?

A	B	C	D	E
	2	4	6	8
16	14	12	10	
	18	20	22	24
32	30	28	26	

....

Answer: *C.*

Example 5: The sum of all multiples of 3 from 20 to 100 is *S*. Is *S* even or odd?

Solution: Even.

Method 1: All the multiples of 3 can be written out as 21, 24, 27, 30, …, 93, 96, and 99. The odd numbers are 21, 27, 33, 39, 45, …, 93, and 99, and the number of odd terms is $(99-21) \div 6 + 1 = 14$. The sum of these 14 odd integers is even.

Method 2: There are $\left\lfloor \dfrac{100}{3} \right\rfloor = 33$ multiples of 3 from 1 to 100. 16 of them are even and 17 of them are odd. There are $\left\lfloor \dfrac{20}{3} \right\rfloor = 6$ multiples of 3 from 1 to 20. Three of them (3, 9, and 15) are odd. So there are 17 − 3 = 14 odd numbers that are multiples of 3 and the sum of them is even.

Try it yourself:

The sum of all multiples of 3 from 30 to 100 is S. Is S even or odd?

Answer: There are $(99 - 33)/6 + 1 = 12$ odd multiples of 3. The sum should be even.

Example 6. An operation consists of two steps: (1) write three positive integers in the blackboard, and (2) erase one of them and replace with the sum or difference of other two. Continue the operation until you get the following three numbers: 64, 78, and 119. Is it possible that the original three numbers are 1, 3, and 5?

Solution: Not possible.

If the original numbers were 1, 3, and 5, the resulting numbers after one operation will be one even number and two odd numbers. This parity will not change with any further operations. Therefore the final results could not be 64, 78, and 119 (one odd number and two even numbers).

Try it yourself:

Write three positive integers in the blackboard. Erase one of them and replace with the sum of other two numbers minus 1. Continue the process until you get the following three numbers: 117, 2001, and 2012. Is it possible that the original three numbers be 2, 2, and 2?

Answer:

No. The parity of the three numbers after one operation will be even, even, and odd.

Example 7: There are nine rooms in a big house as shown in the figure below. Each room is connected to other rooms. Alex tries to enter each room once starting from the top left corner room and come back. Is he able to do that?

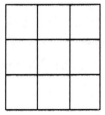

Solution: No.

Method 1: We number each room as follows.

1	2	3
4	5	6
7	8	9

Alex moves from room to room in the following way:

odd (first room) $\Rightarrow$ even $\Rightarrow$ odd $\Rightarrow$ even $\Rightarrow$ odd $\Rightarrow$ even $\Rightarrow$ odd $\Rightarrow$ even $\Rightarrow$ odd

At this time, he has visited all 9 rooms. His next step is to move to a room with even number, but room 1 is labeled odd, so he can't enter room 1.

Method 2: We color each room as shown below. Alex first enters the room colored black. He must enter a room colored white the next step, and then he enters another room colored black, and so on. He needs to move nine times in order to visit 9 rooms. In the nth move, if n is odd, he enters a room colored black, and when n is even, he enters a room colored white. After he has visited each room once and he is ready to move one more time to get back where he starts, $n = 10$, he should enter a room colored white, not black, so he is not able to get back to the top left corner room.

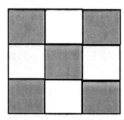

Try it yourself:

There are 16 rooms in a big house as shown in the figure. Each room is connected to other rooms. Alex tries to visit each room once starting from the top left corner room and ending at the bottom right corner room. Is he able to do that?

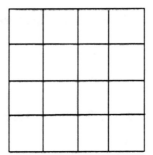

Answer: No.

Example 8:

Five lamps are arranged in a row as shown in the figure below. Each lamp has its own switch. All five lamps A, B, C, D, and E are now off. Ben starts to turn each switch from A to E and he repeats the pattern (always from A to E in order) until he turns the switches 126 times. Which lamps are on in the end?

          A   B   C   D   E

Solution: B, C, D and E.

If a lamp is switched an even number of times, it does not change its on or off state.

If a lamp is switched an odd number of times, it changes from on to off or from off to on depending on the original on-off position.

$126 = 5 \times 25 + 1$.

All lamps are switched 25 times except A, which is switched 26 times.

So lamp A is still off and all others are on.

Try it yourself:

Five lamps are arranged in a row as shown in the figure below. Each lamp has its own switch. All five lamps A, B, C, D, and E are now off. Ben starts to turn each switch from A to E and he repeats the pattern (always from A to E in order) until he turns the switches 2012 times. Which lamps are on finally?

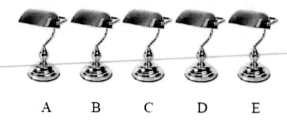

A   B   C   D   E

Answer: $2012 = 5 \times 402 + 2$. *A* and *B* are on. Others are off.

Example 9: There are 7 coins on a table with all heads up. If you turn over four coins each time, are you able to make all the coins tails up?

Solution: No.

Each coin is assigned the value 0 if the head is up and 1 if the tail is up. At the beginning, each coin is facing down so the sum of seven values is 0, which is an even number.

If it is possible to turn all the coins tail up, the sum of the seven values is 7, which is an odd number.

 Every time four coins are turned over, the parity of each assigned number changes its parity (from 1 to 0 or from 0 to 1). The parity of the sum of these seven numbers changed an even number of times (4 in this case), which is no change at all.

Since even $\neq$ odd, it is not possible to make all the coins tails up.

Try it yourself:

There are 10 coins on the table with all heads up. If you turn over six coins each time, are you able to make all the coins tails up?

Answer: Yes.

Example 10: Can you completely cover an 8 × 8 chessboard by 15 "T" shaped and one "田" shaped paper board?

Solution: No.
We color the chessboard with black and white colors:

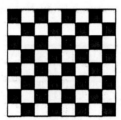

There are 32 black and 32 white small squares. If 15 "T" shaped paper and one "田" shaped paper can cover completely the chessboard, they should be able to cover each white square.

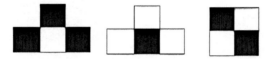

However, one "T" shaped paper can only cover one or three white squares. 1 and 3 are both odd numbers, so the number of white squares that 15 "T" shaped paper covers is an odd number. One "田" shaped paper can cover two white squares, so the total number of white squares 15 "T" shaped and one "田" shaped papers can cover is odd. Since odd ≠ even, it is not possible to cover completely an 8 × 8 chessboard by 15 "T" shaped and one "田" shaped paper board.

Try it yourself:

Can you cover completely an 8 × 8 chessboard by seven 2×2 squares and nine 4×1 rectangles?

Answer: No.

EXERCISES

Problem 1. The sequence 1, 1, 2, 4, 7, 13, 24, ... is formed like this: any term is the sum of the three terms before it starting from the fourth term. Is the 100th term even or odd in the sequence?

Problem 2. There are 49 rooms in a big house as shown in the figure. Each room is connected to other rooms. Alex tries to enter each room once starting from the top left corner room (numbered with 1) then comes back to that room. Is he able to do that?

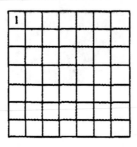

Problem 3. If n is an odd number, then which statement(s) in the following list must be false? (Mathcounts Competitions).

a) $n + n + n$ is not divisible by three

b) $3(n + 1)$ is divisible by six

c) $2n + 1$ is odd

d) $(1 + n)(n + 1)$ is divisible by four

e) $(n - 1)(n + 1)$ is odd.

Problem 4. Find the difference between the sum of all positive even numbers and the sum of all positive odd numbers from 0 through 1000. (Mathcounts Competitions).

Problem 5. An electrical panel has 100 switches in a row, all in the "OFF" position. Every second switch is turned to the "ON" position, and then every third switch is changed from whatever position it is in to the other position. How many switches are now in the "ON" position? (Mathcounts handbooks).

Problem 6. How many of 21 integers must be odd if their product is odd? (Mathcounts handbooks)

Problem 7. On a chessboard, a knight starts from square $a1$, and returns there after making several moves. Show that the knight makes an even number of moves. (Mathematics circles).

Problem 8. Mary and her friends stand in a circle. It turns out that both neighbors of each child are of the same gender. If there are seven boys in the circle, how many girls are there?

Problem 9. Can a 5×5 square checkboard be covered by 1×2 dominoes?

Problem 10. Alex bought a notebook containing 96 pages, and numbered them from 1 through 192. Bob tore out 25 pages of Alex's notebook, and added the 50 numbers he found on the pages. Could Bob have gotten 2012 as the sum?

Problem 11. The product of 18 integers is equal to 1. Show that their sum cannot be zero.

Problem 12. The numbers 1 through 10 are written in a row. Can the signs "+" and " – " be placed between them, so that the value of the resulting expression is 0? Note that negative numbers can also be odd or even.

Problem 13. The numbers 1, 2, 3, . . . , 1984, 1985 are written on a blackboard. We decide to erase from the blackboard any two numbers, and replace them with their positive difference. After this is done several times, a single number remains on the blackboard. Can this number equal 0?

Problem 14. Three natural numbers a, b, and c satisfy the following conditions:
        (1) The sum of a and b is odd
        (2) The sum of a and c is even
        (3) The product of a and c is odd
Which of the following is true?
        (A) b must be even
        (B) b must be odd
        (C) b may be either even or odd

Problem 15. The sum of four consecutive odd integers is 112. What is the greatest of the four integers? (2004 Mathcounts Handbook).

Problem 16. The odd positive integers, 1, 3, 5, 7,..., are arranged in five columns continuing with the pattern shown on the right. Counting from the left, the column in which 1985 appears is: (A) first, (B) second, (C) third, (D) fourth, (E) fifth (1985 AMC).

	1	3	5	7
15	13	11	9	
	17	19	21	23
31	29	27	25	
	33	35	37	39
47	45	43	41	
	49	51	53	55

Problem 17. The counting numbers are arrange in four columns as shown at the right. Under which column letter will 2012 appear?

A	B	C	D
1	2	3	4
8	7	6	5
9	10	11	12
...	14	13	

Problem 18. Suppose all the counting numbers are arranged in columns as shown at the right. Under what column-letter will 2012 appear?

A	B	C	D	E	F	G
1	2	3	4	5	6	7
8	9	10	11	12	13	14
15	16	17	18	19	_	_

Problem 19. How many integers among 1, 2, 3, ..., 98 can be expressed as the difference of two square numbers? (1998 China Middle School Math Competition).

Problem 20. The sum of a positive integer and 100 is a square number. The sum of the positive integer and 168 is also a square number. Find the positive integer. (2001 China Middle School Math Competition).

ANSWER KEYS

Problem 1. Solution: Even.

Problem 2. Solution: No.

We color each room with black and white as shown below. If Alex is in a room colored back, then he must enter the room colored white in his next step. He needs to move 50 times in order to be back to the room he started with. With each nth move, if n is odd, he is in a room colored white, and if n is even, he is in a room colored black. When $n = 49$, he should be in a room colored white. Since the room he begins in is colored white, he will not be able end up in that room when $n = 50$.

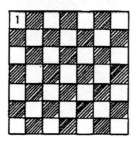

Problem 3. Answer: a and e

Problem 4. Answer: 500

Problem 5. Answer: 51

Problem 6. Answer: 21

Problem 7. A knight always moves from a square of one color to square of the opposite color. Thus the colors of the squares occupied by the knight alternate between white and black. To get back to a square of the same color as he started on (in particular, the same square), he must make evenly many moves.

Problem 8. Answer: seven. If any of Mary's friends are standing next to children of their own gender, then it is clear that all the children are of the same gender. This means that the boys and girls must alternate, so that there are as many girls as boys.

Problem 9. Answer: No There are 25 squares on the board. Since each domino covers two squares, the dominoes can only cover an even number of squares.

Problem 10. Answer: No. The sum of the pair of numbers on each page is odd, and the sum of 25 odd numbers will also be odd. The number 2012 is even.

Problem 11. Answer: Clearly, each integer is either +1 or –1, and there are an even number of   –1's (since their product is positive). If their sum were zero, there would have to be nine –1's and nine +1's, which is a contradiction.

Problem 12. Answer: No. The sum of the numbers from 1 through 10 is 55, which is odd. Changing the sign of each number will not change the parity of the sum. The sum must thus remain odd.

Problem 13. Answer: No. It is not hard to see that the given operation does not change the parity of the sum of the numbers on the blackboard. Since this parity is initially odd, the sum can never be 0.

Problem 14. Answer: A.

Problem 15. Answer: 31.

Problem 16. Solution: B.

Method 1: Every row has 4 odd integers. 1985 is the 993rd odd integer. $993 = 4 \times 248 + 1$. So 1985 is the first term in 249th rows. The first number in an odd numbered row is in the column B. So 1985 is in column B.

Method 2: We see the pattern for every 8 integers in the table. 1985 is the 993rd integers and $993 \equiv 1$ mod 8. We know that 1985 is in the same column as the first number in the first row. The answer is B.

Problem 17. Solution:

Method 1: We know that there are 2 even integers in every row. 2012 is the 1006th even integer. $1006 = 2 \times 503 = 2 \times 502 + 2$. This means that 2012 will be in the column where the 2nd even integer located (even integer 4 in column D, in this case).

Method 2: We see the pattern in every 8 numbers. $2012 \equiv 4$ mod 8. So 2012 is in the column where the 4th number located (even integer 4 in column D, in this case).

Problem 18. Solution: C.

Method 1: We know that there are 7 even integers every two row. 2012 is the 1006th even integer. $1006 = 7 \times 143 + 5$. This means that 2012 will be in the column where the fifth even integer (10, in this case) located.

Method 2: We see the pattern in every 7 numbers. $2012 \equiv 3 \mod 7$. So 2012 is in the column where the third number located (column C in this case).

Problem 19. Solution: 73.

Let x be any number from 1 to 98. m and n be two integers with $m > n$.
$$x = m^2 - n^2 = (m-n)(m+n)$$
We know that $m - n$ and $m + n$ have the same parity. If $m + n$ is even, $(m-n)(m+n)$ is a multiple of 4. If $m + n$ is odd, $(m-n)(m+n)$ is odd and x is odd.

So x is any number that is either a multiple of 4 or odd. There are 49 odd numbers and 24 numbers that are multiples of 4. The answer is $49 + 24 = 73$.

Problem 20. Solution: 156.
Let the positive integer be n.
$$n + 168 = a^2 \quad n + 100 = b^2$$
$$a^2 - b^2 = (a+b)(a-b) = 68 = 2^2 \times 17$$
We know that $a + b$ and $a - b$ are the same parity, so:
$$(a+b) = 34 \text{ and } a - b = 2 \quad \Rightarrow \quad a = 18 \text{ and } n = 156.$$

BASIC KNOWLEDGE

1. TERMS:

Fraction: A part of a whole or a quotient of two numbers, expressed as $\frac{a}{b}$. a and b are whole numbers. $b \neq 0$. $\frac{a}{b}$ is the same as $a \div b$.

> Example: Three of five cupcakes were eaten at dinner. The portion of the cupcakes which were eaten can be written as a fraction: $\frac{3}{5}$.
>
> The 5 denotes the total number of parts and is called the denominator. The 3 represents the number of parts and is called the numerator.

Proper fraction: A fraction in which the numerator is less than the denominator: $\frac{3}{5}$. Such a fraction has a value less than 1.

Improper fraction: A fraction in which the numerator is greater than or equal to the denominator: $\frac{5}{3}$. It has a value greater than or equal to 1.

Mixed number: A mixed number contains both a whole number part and a fraction part and can be written as an improper fraction: $2\frac{1}{3} = \frac{2 \times 3 + 1}{3} = \frac{7}{3}$.

Equivalent fraction (Cancellation Law): Two fractions are equal if they represent the same portion of a whole.

$$\frac{1}{2} \qquad = \qquad \frac{2}{4} \qquad = \qquad \frac{6}{12}$$

Examples: $\frac{38}{57} = \frac{2 \times 19}{3 \times 19} = \frac{2}{3}$; $\frac{38}{57} = \frac{38 \div 19}{57 \div 19} = \frac{2}{3}$

Fundamental Law of Fractions:

For any fraction $\dfrac{a}{b}$ and any number $c \neq 0$, $\dfrac{a}{b} = \dfrac{a \times c}{b \times c}$.

(The value of a fraction does not change if its numerator and denominator are multiplied by the same nonzero number).

Examples: $\dfrac{2}{3} = \dfrac{2 \times 5}{3 \times 5} = \dfrac{10}{15}$.

Lowest (reduced; simplest) term: A fraction in which the numerator and the denominator have no common terms except 1. The lowest terms are obtained by taking all the common factors out of the numerator and the denominator.

$\dfrac{10}{15}$ is not a fraction in the lowest term but $\dfrac{2}{3}$ is. ($\dfrac{10}{15} = \dfrac{2 \times \cancel{5}}{3 \times \cancel{5}} = \dfrac{2}{3}$).

2. ADDITON AND SUBTRACTION:

When working with fractions, only the numerators in fractions are added or subtracted.

(1). Two fractions having the same denominators:

We just add or subtract the numerators.

$$\frac{a}{b} + \frac{c}{b} = \frac{a+c}{b} \qquad \Rightarrow \qquad \frac{3}{5} + \frac{1}{5} = \frac{3+1}{5} = \frac{4}{5}$$

$$\frac{a}{b} - \frac{c}{b} = \frac{a-c}{b} \qquad \Rightarrow \qquad \frac{3}{5} - \frac{1}{5} = \frac{3-1}{5} = \frac{2}{5}$$

(2). Two fractions having the different denominators:

We convert them to the same denominators first, and then add the numerators.

$$\frac{a}{b} + \frac{c}{d} = \frac{a \times d}{b \times d} + \frac{c \times b}{b \times d} = \frac{a \times d + c \times b}{b \times d} \Rightarrow \frac{1}{2} + \frac{2}{5} = \frac{1 \times 5}{2 \times 5} + \frac{2 \times 2}{5 \times 2} = \frac{5+4}{10} = \frac{9}{10}$$

$$\frac{a}{b} - \frac{c}{d} = \frac{a \times d}{b \times d} - \frac{c \times b}{b \times d} = \frac{a \times d - c \times b}{b \times d} \Rightarrow \frac{1}{2} - \frac{2}{5} = \frac{1 \times 5}{2 \times 5} - \frac{2 \times 2}{5 \times 2} = \frac{5-4}{10} = \frac{1}{10}$$

3. MULTIPLICATION OF FRACTIONS

The numerator of the product is obtained by multiplying together the numerators. The denominator of the product is obtained by multiplying together the denominators.

$$\frac{a}{b} \times \frac{c}{d} = \frac{a \times c}{b \times d} \qquad \Rightarrow \qquad \frac{2}{5} \times \frac{3}{7} = \frac{2 \times 3}{5 \times 7} = \frac{6}{35}$$

$$\frac{8}{9} \times 5 = \frac{8}{9} \times \frac{5}{1} = \frac{8 \times 5}{9 \times 1} = \frac{40}{9} = 4\frac{4}{9}$$

$$5\frac{1}{3} \times 4\frac{1}{2} = \frac{16}{3} \times \frac{9}{2} = \frac{16 \times 9}{3 \times 2} = \frac{8 \times 3}{1 \times 1} = \frac{24}{1} = 24$$

4. DIVISION OF FRACTIONS

To divide by a fraction, we simply multiply by its reciprocal.

$$\frac{a}{b} \div \frac{c}{d} = \frac{a}{b} \times \frac{d}{c} = \frac{ad}{bc} \qquad \Rightarrow \qquad \frac{2}{5} \div \frac{3}{7} = \frac{2}{5} \times \frac{7}{3} = \frac{2 \times 7}{5 \times 3} = \frac{14}{15}$$

The reciprocal of a number is obtained by switching the numerator and the denominator.

For example, the reciprocal of $\frac{2}{3}$ is $\frac{3}{2}$, and the reciprocal of 2 (note that 2 can be written

as $\frac{2}{1}$) is $\frac{1}{2}$.

$$\frac{\dfrac{a}{b}}{\dfrac{c}{d}} = \frac{ad}{bc}$$

5. COMPARING FRACTIONS

(1). Same Denominator:

The fraction with a larger numerator is larger.

64

$$\frac{3}{5} > \frac{1}{5}$$

(2). Same Numerator:

The fraction with a larger denominator is smaller.

$$\frac{3}{7} < \frac{3}{5}$$

(3). Both the numerator and denominator are not the same

$3 \times 11 = 33$ $4 \times 8 = 32$

$$\frac{3}{8} \quad \underset{}{\overset{}{\times}} \quad \frac{4}{11} \qquad \Rightarrow \qquad 33 > 32 \qquad \Rightarrow \qquad \frac{3}{8} > \frac{4}{11}$$

(4). Useful formulas:

If $m < n$, k is a positive integer:

$$\frac{m}{n} < \frac{m+k}{n+k} \qquad\qquad \Rightarrow \qquad \frac{3}{5} < \frac{3+2}{5+2} = \frac{5}{7}$$

If $m < n$, k is a positive integer and $k < m$:

$$\frac{m}{n} > \frac{m-k}{n-k} \qquad\qquad \Rightarrow \qquad \frac{3}{5} > \frac{3-2}{5-2} = \frac{1}{3}$$

If $m > n$, k is a positive integer:

$$\frac{m}{n} > \frac{m+k}{n+k} \qquad\qquad \Rightarrow \qquad \frac{7}{5} > \frac{7+2}{5+2} = \frac{9}{7}$$

If $m > n$, k is a positive integer and $k < m$:

$$\frac{m}{n} < \frac{m-k}{n-k} \qquad\qquad \Rightarrow \qquad \frac{7}{5} < \frac{7-2}{5-2} = \frac{5}{3}$$

Examples:

(1). Which fraction is larger, $\dfrac{666665}{666667}$ or $\dfrac{777776}{777778}$?

Solution:

Method 1:

$$\frac{777776}{777778} = \frac{666665 + 111111}{666667 + 111111}$$

We know that if $m < n$, k is a positive integer: $\dfrac{m}{n} < \dfrac{m+k}{n+k}$ $\Rightarrow$ $\dfrac{666665}{666667} < \dfrac{777776}{777778}$

Method 2:

$$\frac{666665}{666667} = 1 - \frac{2}{666667}; \qquad \frac{777776}{777778} = 1 - \frac{2}{777778}$$

Since $\dfrac{2}{666667} > \dfrac{2}{777778}$ $\Rightarrow$ $1 - \dfrac{2}{666667} < 1 - \dfrac{2}{777778} \Rightarrow \dfrac{666665}{666667} < \dfrac{777776}{777778}$

(2). Which fraction is larger, $\dfrac{53^{2000}}{53^{1999}}$ or $\dfrac{53^{2000} - 2000}{53^{1999} - 2000}$?

Solution:

Method 1:

If $m > n$, k is a positive integer and $k < n$: $\dfrac{m}{n} < \dfrac{m-k}{n-k}$ $\Rightarrow$ $\dfrac{53^{2000}}{53^{1999}} < \dfrac{53^{2000} - 2000}{53^{1999} - 2000}$

Method 2: We can use the cross multiplication:

$$\frac{53^{2000}}{53^{1999}} \diagdown\!\!\!\!? \frac{(53^{2000} - 2000)}{(53^{1999} - 2000)}$$

$53^{2000}(53^{1999} - 2000) = 53^{3999} - 53^{2000} \times 2000$;

66

$$53^{1999}(53^{2000} - 2000) = 53^{3999} - 53^{1999} \times 2000.$$

Since $53^{1999} \times 2000 < 53^{2000} \times 2000$

So: $53^{3999} - 53^{2000} \times 2000 < 53^{3999} - 53^{1999} \times 2000 \quad \Rightarrow \quad \dfrac{53^{2000}}{53^{1999}} < \dfrac{53^{2000} - 2000}{53^{1999} - 2000}$

(3). If $S = \dfrac{1}{\dfrac{1}{1980} + \dfrac{1}{1981} + \dots + \dfrac{1}{1997}}$, what is the integer part of S?

Solution:

We estimate the value of the denominator first:

$$\frac{1}{1980} + \frac{1}{1981} + \dots + \frac{1}{1997} < \frac{1}{1980} + \frac{1}{1980} + \dots + \frac{1}{1980} = \frac{18}{1980}$$

$$\frac{1}{1980} + \frac{1}{1981} + \dots + \frac{1}{1997} > \frac{1}{1997} + \frac{1}{1997} + \dots + \frac{1}{1997} = \frac{18}{1997}$$

So $\dfrac{1980}{18} < S < \dfrac{1997}{18} \qquad \Rightarrow \qquad 110 < S < 110\dfrac{17}{18}$

The integer part of S is 110.

(4). Determine the fraction $\dfrac{p}{q}$, where p and q are positive integers and $q < 100$, that is closest to but less than $\dfrac{3}{7}$.

Solution: $\dfrac{p}{q} = \dfrac{41}{96}$.

We set $\dfrac{p}{q} < \dfrac{3}{7}$, then we have $7p < 3q$, or $7p \le 3q - 1 \Rightarrow p \le \dfrac{3q - 1}{7}$.

Since p is a positive integer, we want $3q - 1$ divisible by 7. Starting from 99, we test that when $q = 96$, $3q - 1$ is divisible by 7. And we get $p = 41$. So the solution is $\dfrac{p}{q} = \dfrac{41}{96}$.

6. SUM OF A SERIES OF FRACTIONS

(1). Useful formulas:

$$\frac{1}{n(n+1)} = \frac{1}{n} - \frac{1}{n+1} \qquad \Rightarrow \qquad \frac{1}{3(3+1)} = \frac{1}{3} - \frac{1}{3+1} = \frac{1}{3} - \frac{1}{4}$$

$$\frac{1}{n} = \frac{1}{2n} + \frac{1}{2n} \qquad \Rightarrow \qquad \frac{1}{3} = \frac{1}{2 \times 3} + \frac{1}{2 \times 3} = \frac{1}{6} + \frac{1}{6}$$

$$\frac{1}{n(n+k)} = \frac{1}{k}\left(\frac{1}{n} - \frac{1}{n+k}\right) \qquad \Rightarrow \qquad \frac{1}{3(3+2)} = \frac{1}{2}\left(\frac{1}{3} - \frac{1}{5}\right)$$

$$\frac{1}{mn} = \frac{1}{n-m}\left(\frac{1}{m} - \frac{1}{n}\right) \qquad \Rightarrow \qquad \frac{1}{3 \times 5} = \frac{1}{5-3}\left(\frac{1}{3} - \frac{1}{5}\right) = \frac{1}{2}\left(\frac{1}{3} - \frac{1}{5}\right)$$

$$\frac{1}{(n-1)(n+1)} = \frac{1}{2}\left(\frac{1}{n-1} - \frac{1}{n+1}\right) \qquad \Rightarrow \qquad \frac{1}{(3-1)(3+1)} = \frac{1}{2}\left(\frac{1}{3-1} - \frac{1}{3+1}\right) = \frac{1}{2}\left(\frac{1}{2} - \frac{1}{4}\right)$$

$$\frac{1}{n(n+1)(n+2)} = \frac{1}{2}\left[\frac{1}{n(n+1)} - \frac{1}{(n+1)(n+2)}\right]$$

$$\frac{1}{2 \times 3 \times 4} + \frac{2}{3 \times 4 \times 5} + \cdots + \frac{n}{(n+1)(n+2)(n+3)} = \frac{n(n+1)}{4(n+2)(n+3)}$$

$$\frac{1}{3 \times 4 \times 5} + \frac{2}{4 \times 5 \times 6} + \cdots + \frac{n}{(n+2)(n+3)(n+4)} = \frac{n(n+1)}{6(n+3)(n+4)}$$

Examples:

(1). Find the sum: $\dfrac{1}{1 \times 2} + \dfrac{1}{2 \times 3} + \cdots + \dfrac{1}{49 \times 50}$.

(2). Find the sum: $\dfrac{1}{1\times 3}+\dfrac{1}{3\times 5}+\cdots+\dfrac{1}{11\times 13}$.

(3). Calculate: $\dfrac{1}{2\times 4}+\dfrac{1}{4\times 6}+\cdots+\dfrac{1}{98\times 100}$.

(4). Calculate: $\dfrac{3}{1\times 4}+\dfrac{3}{4\times 7}+\dfrac{3}{7\times 10}+\cdots+\dfrac{3}{19\times 22}$.

Solutions:

(1). $\dfrac{1}{1\times 2}+\dfrac{1}{2\times 3}+\cdots+\dfrac{1}{49\times 50}=\dfrac{1}{1}-\dfrac{1}{2}+\dfrac{1}{2}-\dfrac{1}{3}+\dfrac{1}{3}-\dfrac{1}{4}+\cdots-\dfrac{1}{50}=1-\dfrac{1}{50}=\dfrac{49}{50}$

(2). $\dfrac{1}{1\times 3}+\dfrac{1}{3\times 5}+\cdots+\dfrac{1}{11\times 13}=\dfrac{1}{2}(\dfrac{1}{1}-\dfrac{1}{3}+\dfrac{1}{3}-\dfrac{1}{5}+\dfrac{1}{5}-\ldots+\dfrac{1}{11}-\dfrac{1}{13})=\dfrac{1}{2}\times(1-\dfrac{1}{13})=\dfrac{6}{13}$

(3). $\dfrac{1}{2\times 4}+\dfrac{1}{4\times 6}+\cdots+\dfrac{1}{98\times 100}$

$=\dfrac{1}{2}(\dfrac{1}{2}-\dfrac{1}{4}+\dfrac{1}{4}-\dfrac{1}{6}+\dfrac{1}{6}-\ldots+\dfrac{1}{98}-\dfrac{1}{100})=\dfrac{1}{2}\times(\dfrac{1}{2}-\dfrac{1}{100})=\dfrac{1}{2}(\dfrac{50}{100}-\dfrac{1}{100})=\dfrac{49}{200}$

(4). $\dfrac{3}{1\times 4}+\dfrac{3}{4\times 7}+\dfrac{3}{7\times 10}+\cdots+\dfrac{3}{19\times 22}$

$=\dfrac{1}{1}-\dfrac{1}{4}+\dfrac{1}{4}-\dfrac{1}{7}+\dfrac{1}{7}\ldots-\dfrac{1}{19}+\dfrac{1}{19}-\dfrac{1}{22}=1-\dfrac{1}{22}=\dfrac{21}{22}$

7. CONTINUED FRACTIONS

The simple continued fraction representation of a number is given by:

$$a_0 + \cfrac{1}{a_1 + \cfrac{1}{a_2 + \cfrac{1}{a_3 + \cfrac{1}{a_4 + \dots}}}}$$

where a_0 is an integer, any other a_i members are positive integers, and n is a non-negative integer.

Examples:

(1). Simplify: $\cfrac{1}{8 + \cfrac{1}{8 + \cfrac{1}{8}}}$

Solution:

$$\cfrac{1}{8 + \cfrac{1}{8 + \cfrac{1}{8}}} = \cfrac{1}{8 + \cfrac{1}{\cfrac{65}{8}}} = \cfrac{1}{8 + \cfrac{8}{65}} = \cfrac{1}{\cfrac{528}{65}} = \cfrac{65}{528}.$$

(2). Express as a simplified mixed number: $3 + \cfrac{2}{3 + \cfrac{2}{3 + \cfrac{2}{3}}}$

Solution:

$$3 + \cfrac{2}{3 + \cfrac{2}{3 + \cfrac{2}{3}}} = 3 + \cfrac{2}{3 + \cfrac{2}{\cfrac{11}{3}}} = 3 + \cfrac{2}{3 + \cfrac{6}{11}} = 3 + \cfrac{2}{\cfrac{39}{11}} = 3\frac{22}{39}$$

(3). Simplify: $1 + \cfrac{1}{1 + \cfrac{1}{1 + 1}}$. Express your answer as a common fraction.

Solution:

$$1 + \cfrac{1}{1+\cfrac{1}{1+1}} = 1 + \cfrac{1}{1+\cfrac{1}{2}} = 1 + \cfrac{1}{\frac{3}{2}} = 1 + \frac{2}{3} = \frac{5}{3}$$

(4). Simplify: $\cfrac{1}{2+\cfrac{1}{2+\frac{1}{2}}}$. Express your answer as a common fraction.

Solution:

$$\cfrac{1}{2+\cfrac{1}{2+\frac{1}{2}}} = \cfrac{1}{2+\cfrac{1}{\frac{5}{2}}} = \cfrac{1}{2+\frac{2}{5}} = \cfrac{1}{\frac{12}{5}} = \frac{5}{12}$$

Another way to simplify a continued fraction:

Simplify: $\cfrac{1}{2+\cfrac{1}{2+\frac{1}{2}}}$.

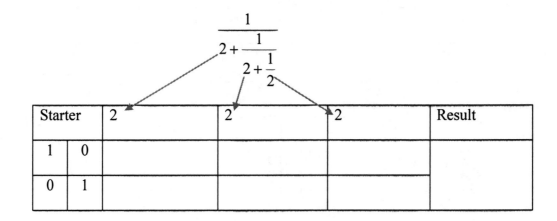

Starter		2	2	2	Result
1	0				
0	1				

71

Starter		2	2	2	Result
1	0	$1 + 0 \times 2 = 1$			
0	1				

Starter		2	2	2	Result
1	0	1			
0	1	$0 + 1 \times 2 = 2$			

Starter		2	2	2	Result
1	**0**	1	$0 + 1 \times 2 = 2$		
0	1	2			

Starter		2	2	2	Result
1	0	1	2		
0	**1**	2	$1 + 2 \times 2 = 5$		

Starter		2	2	2	Result
1	0	**1**	2	$1 + 2 \times 2 = 5$	
0	1	2	5		

Starter		2	2	2	Result
1	0	1	2	5	$\dfrac{5}{12}$
0	1	**2**	5	$2 + 5 \times 2 = 12$	

Starter		2	2	2	Result
1	0	1	2	5	$\dfrac{5}{12}$
0	1	2	5	12	

EXERCISES

Problem 1. Simplify: $\dfrac{1}{1+\dfrac{1}{2}}$

Problem 2. Express as a common fraction in lowest terms: $\dfrac{\dfrac{2}{6}}{7}$

Problem 3. Express in simplest form: $\dfrac{4}{5}$ of 75

Problem 4. Express in simplest form: $\dfrac{7}{10}$ of 40

Problem 5. Simplify: $\dfrac{5\dfrac{1}{2}-\dfrac{7}{16}}{3}$. Express your answer as a mixed number.

Problem 6. Find the reciprocal of $\dfrac{5+\dfrac{1}{5}}{5-\dfrac{1}{5}}$ and express your answer as a common fraction.

Problem 7. Give the common fraction equivalent to

$$\dfrac{\dfrac{6}{10}\times\dfrac{24}{18}\times\dfrac{3}{36}\times\dfrac{48}{24}\times 3\dfrac{3}{4}}{\dfrac{4\dfrac{1}{3}}{2\dfrac{3}{5}}}$$

Problem 8. The Stars played 12 games and won $\dfrac{3}{4}$ of them. How many games did they lose?

Problem 9. Write the product as a common fraction: $\dfrac{1}{3}\cdot\dfrac{6}{10}\cdot\dfrac{15}{21}\cdot\dfrac{28}{36}\cdot\dfrac{45}{55}$.

Problem 10. Express as a mixed number: $25\dfrac{22}{32}-7\dfrac{7}{16}$.

Problem 11. Express as a mixed number: $1\frac{2}{7} \div 1\frac{6}{7} \div \frac{2}{13} \div 9$.

Problem 12. Express as a mixed number: $2\frac{1}{2} \times 3\frac{7}{10}$.

Problem 13. Express as a common fraction: $2\frac{7}{10} \div 10\frac{4}{5}$.

Problem 14. Express as a mixed number: $6\frac{1}{5} - 2\frac{2}{3}$.

Problem 15. Divide 2/3 of 48 by the product of 1/8 and 16.

Problem 16. Express as a mixed number: $\dfrac{\frac{1}{2} + (\frac{3}{4} \div \frac{1}{2})}{(\frac{1}{6} + \frac{2}{3}) \div \frac{3}{5}}$

Problem 17. Express as a mixed number: $14 - 7\frac{3}{7}$.

Problem 18. Express as a common fraction: $\dfrac{\frac{2}{5} \times \frac{5}{6}}{\frac{2}{9} \times 4\frac{1}{2}}$.

Problem 19. Express in simplest form: $2\frac{1}{2} \times \frac{2}{5} \times 3\frac{1}{3} \times \frac{3}{10}$.

Problem 20. Express as a common fraction: $\dfrac{1}{3 + \dfrac{\frac{1}{2}}{\frac{2}{3}}}$.

Problem 21. Express as a common fraction: $\frac{8}{3} + \frac{7}{9} - \frac{2}{18}$.

Problem 22. What is the result when you divide 60 by $\frac{1}{2}$ and add 20 to the quotient?

Problem 23. Express as a common fraction: $(1 - \frac{1}{3})(1 - \frac{1}{4})(1 - \frac{1}{5})(1 - \frac{1}{6})$

Problem 24. What is the product of $\dfrac{2}{3}$ and 18 divided by the product of $\dfrac{3}{4}$ and 24? Express your answer as a common fraction.

Problem 25. The hockey team lost $\dfrac{5}{8}$ of the 40 games they played. How many games did the team win?

Problem 26. Express as a common fraction: $(\dfrac{1}{2}+\dfrac{1}{3})(\dfrac{1}{2}-\dfrac{1}{3})$.

Problem 27. Choose the letter which corresponds to the largest number.

a) $\dfrac{1}{1+\dfrac{2}{\dfrac{1}{2}}}$

b) $\dfrac{1}{3+\dfrac{1}{1+2}}$

c) $\dfrac{1}{5+\dfrac{1}{1+\dfrac{1}{2}}}$

Problem 28. Simplify as a common fraction: $\dfrac{3}{4-\dfrac{5}{6-\dfrac{7}{8}}}$.

Problem 29. Simplify as a common fraction: $\dfrac{1}{1+\dfrac{1}{1+\dfrac{2}{3}}}$.

Problem 30. Simplify as a common fraction: $\dfrac{1}{2+\dfrac{3}{4+\dfrac{5}{6}}}$.

Problem 31. What is the sum of the reciprocals of 8, 9, 10, 11, and 12? Write your answer as a fraction.

Problem 32. Find the sum of the reciprocals of the first five positive powers of 3. Express your answer as a common fraction.

Problem 33. Find the units digit in the value of A:

$$\frac{1}{7} \cdot \frac{1}{7} \cdot \frac{1}{7} \cdot \frac{1}{7} = 7 \cdot 7 \cdot \frac{1}{A}$$

Problem 34. Simplify: $\cfrac{1}{1+\cfrac{1}{1+\cfrac{1}{1+\cfrac{1}{2}}}}$

Problem 35. Express as a common fraction: $2 + \cfrac{1}{1-\cfrac{1}{3+\cfrac{1}{1-\cfrac{1}{2}}}}$.

Problem 36. Compute: $(\frac{3}{5} \cdot \frac{5}{6}) \div \frac{5}{8}$.

Problem 37. Evaluate and express as a common fraction:

$$\cfrac{\cfrac{1}{2}-\cfrac{1}{3}}{\cfrac{1}{8}} .$$

Problem 38. If $1 - \cfrac{1}{7+\cfrac{1}{7+\cfrac{1}{7}}} = \cfrac{1}{a+\cfrac{1}{b+\cfrac{1}{c+\cfrac{1}{d}}}}$, what is the product of a, b, c, and d?

Problem 39. Find the value of x if $\cfrac{1}{1+\cfrac{1}{2+\cfrac{1}{3+\cfrac{1}{4+\cfrac{1}{x}}}}} = \cfrac{67}{96}$.

Problem 40. Find the product of the 9 factors $(1-\frac{1}{2})(1-\frac{1}{3})(1-\frac{1}{4})...(1-\frac{1}{10})$

A) $\dfrac{1}{10}$ B) $\dfrac{1}{9}$ C) $\dfrac{1}{2}$ D) $\dfrac{10}{11}$ E) $\dfrac{11}{2}$

Problem 41. (1985 AMC8 #10) The fraction halfway between $\dfrac{1}{5}$ and $\dfrac{1}{3}$ (on the number line) is

A) $\dfrac{1}{4}$ B) $\dfrac{2}{15}$ C) $\dfrac{4}{15}$ D) $\dfrac{53}{200}$ E) $\dfrac{8}{15}$

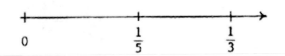

Problem 42. Calculate the value of $\dfrac{2}{1-\dfrac{2}{3}}$.

A) -3 B) $-\dfrac{4}{3}$ C) $\dfrac{2}{3}$ D) 2 E) 6

Problem 43. The range of the sum of $2\dfrac{1}{7}+3\dfrac{1}{2}+5\dfrac{1}{19}$ is

A) 12 and $12\dfrac{1}{2}$ B) $10\dfrac{1}{2}$ and 11 C) $11\dfrac{1}{2}$ and 12 D) 11 and $11\dfrac{1}{2}$

E) 10 and $10\dfrac{1}{2}$.

Problem 44. Which value is the largest of the following fractions?

A) $\dfrac{100}{201}$ B) $\dfrac{17}{35}$ C) $\dfrac{4}{9}$ D) $\dfrac{3}{7}$ E) $\dfrac{151}{301}$

Problem 45. What is the reciprocal of $(\frac{1}{2}+\frac{1}{3})$?

A) $\frac{5}{2}$ B)   5   C) $\frac{6}{5}$ D) $\frac{1}{6}$ E) $\frac{2}{5}$.

Problem 46. Find the value of $(2\times3\times4)(\frac{1}{2}+\frac{1}{3}+\frac{1}{4})$.

A)   3   B)   24   C)   9   D)   1   E)   26

Problem 47. Find the value of $\dfrac{1-\frac{1}{3}}{1-\frac{1}{2}}$

A) $\frac{3}{2}$ B) $\frac{3}{4}$ C) $\frac{2}{3}$ D) $\frac{1}{3}\frac{3}{2}$ E) $\frac{4}{3}$

Problem 48. Which of the following is not equal to $\frac{5}{4}$?

A) $1\frac{3}{12}$ B) $1\frac{10}{40}$ C) $\frac{10}{8}$ D) $1\frac{1}{5}$ E) $1\frac{1}{4}$

ANSWER KEYS:

Problem 1. $\dfrac{2}{3}$ **Problem 2.** 7/3   **Problem 3.** 60

Problem 4. 28   **Problem 5.** $1\dfrac{11}{16}$.   **Problem 6.** 13/12

Problem 7. 3/10   **Problem 8.** 3   **Problem 9.** 1/11

Problem 10. $18\dfrac{1}{4}$ **Problem 11.** ½   **Problem 12.** 9 ¼

Problem 13. ¼   **Problem 14.** $3\dfrac{8}{15}$ **Problem 15.** 16

Problem 16. $1\dfrac{11}{25}$ **Problem 17.** $6\dfrac{4}{7}$ **Problem 18.** 1/3

Problem 19. 1   **Problem 20.** 2/9.   **Problem 21.** 10/3

Problem 22. 140.   **Problem 23.** 1/3.   **Problem 24.** 2/3.

Problem 25. 15.   **Problem 26.** 5/36   **Problem 27.** b

Problem 28. 123/124   **Problem 29.** 5/8.   **Problem 30.** 29/76

Problem 31. 2021/3960   **Problem 32.** 121/243   **Problem 33.** 9

Problem 34. 5/8   **Problem 35.** 13/4   **Problem 36.** 4/5.

Problem 37. 4/3   **Problem 38.** 294.   **Problem 39.** 2.

Problem 40. A   **Problem 41.** C   **Problem 42.** E

Problem 43. B   **Problem 44.** E   **Problem 45.** C

Problem 46. E   **Problem 47.** E   **Problem 48.** D.

BASIC KNOWLEDGE

1. Decimal representation:

A decimal is used to represent a portion of whole. It contains three parts: an integer (which indicates the number of wholes), a decimal point (which separates the integer on the left from the decimal on the right), and a decimal number (which represents a number between 0 and 1).

The decimal 3.14159 is read "three and fourteen thousand one hundred fifty – nine hundred-thousandths". The dot is the decimal point and is read as "and".

3	.	1	4	1	5	9
Units	And	Tenths	Hundredths	Thousandths	Ten-thousandths	Hundred-thousandths

Whole numbers can also be written with one or more zeros after the decimal point:
$3 = 3.0 = 3.00 = 3.000$

The number line representations of decimals:

0.5   0.05

Examples: How would you write "six and nine hundredths" as a decimal? Answer: 6.09.
How would you write "three and nine tenths" as a decimal? Answer: 3.9.
How would you write "five hundredths" as a decimal?   Answer: 0.05.

2. Changing Decimals to Fractions

Move the decimal points to the right such that the numerator becomes an integer. Do the same thing for the denominator.

$$0.27 = \frac{0.27}{1.00} = \frac{02.7}{10.0} = \frac{027}{100} = \frac{27}{100}$$

$$0.36 = \frac{0.36}{1.00} = \frac{03.6}{10.0} = \frac{036}{100} = \frac{36}{100} = \frac{4 \times 9}{4 \times 25} = \frac{9}{25}$$

3. Decimal addition and subtraction

Adding and subtracting decimal numbers is the same as adding whole numbers. The key point is to line up the decimal points.

Examples: Compute:

(1) $3.1415926 + 2.7182818 =$

$$
\begin{array}{r}
3.1415926 \\
+ \quad 2.7182818 \\
\hline
5.8598744
\end{array}
$$

(2) $3.1415926 - 2.7182818 =$

$$
\begin{array}{r}
3.1415926 \\
- \quad 2.7182818 \\
\hline
0.4233108
\end{array}
$$

(3) $3.57 + 7.76 - 4.33 =$

$3.57 + (7.76 - 4.33) = 3.57 + 3.43 = 7.$

(4) $7.65 + 9.38 + 4.35 =$

$7.65 + 9.38 + 4.35 = (7.65 + 4.35) + 9.38 = 12 + 9.38 = 21.38.$

(5) $15.83 + 9.76 + 4.17 =$

$(15.83 + 4.17) + 9.76 = 20 + 9.76 = 29.76$

(6) $3.98 + 4.67 - 1.98 =$

$(3.98 - 1.98) + 4.67 = 2 + 4.67 = 6.67.$

(7) $53.75 - 24.98 - 23.75 =$

$(53.75 - 23.75) - 24.98 = 30 - 24.98 = 5.02.$

(8) 32.98 + 12.29 =

$\quad$ (33 – 0.02) + 12.29 = (33 + 12.29) – 0.02 = 45.29 – 0.02 = 45.27.

(9) 24.86 – 9.97 =

$\quad$ 24.86 – 10 + 0.03 = 14.86 + 0.03 = 14.89.

(10) 72.19 + 6.48 + 27.81 – 1.38 – 5.48 – 0.62 =

$\quad$ (72.19 + 27.81) +(6.48 – 5.48) – (1.38 + 0.62) = 100 + 1 – 2 = 99.

4. Decimal multiplication and division

Multiplication of Two Decimals:

(1) Change both decimals to integers by moving the decimal point to the right.

(2) Count n, the total number of times the decimal point is moved.

(3) Multiply two integers and get the product.

(4) Put a decimal point on the right of the units digit of the product.

(5) Move the decimal point n times to the left.

Note that we don't have to line up the decimal points to multiply.

Examples:

(1) 3.6 × 4.5 =

3.6 $\quad\Rightarrow\quad$ 36 $\qquad$ (we move the decimal point to the right one time)

4.5 $\quad\Rightarrow\quad$ 45 $\qquad$ (we move the decimal point to the right one time)

$\qquad\qquad\qquad\qquad$ One time + one time = two times.

36 × 45 = 1620.

1620. $\qquad\Rightarrow\qquad$ 16.20 (we move the decimal point to the left two times)

(2) 3.14 × 1.1 =

3.14 $\quad\Rightarrow\quad$ 314 $\qquad$ (we move the decimal point to the right two times)

1.1 $\quad\Rightarrow\quad$ 11 $\qquad$ (we move the decimal point to the right one time)

$\qquad\qquad\qquad\qquad$ Two times + one time = three times.

314 × 11 = 3454.

3454 $\qquad\Rightarrow\qquad$ 3.454 (we move the decimal point to the left three times)

Division of Two decimals:

(1) Change the divisor from decimal to integer by moving the decimal point to the right.

(2) Count n, the total number of times to move the decimal point of the divisor to the end of the number.

(3) Move the decimal point of the dividend n times to the right.

(4) Perform the division and move the decimal point up to the quotient.

Examples: Compute:

(1) $3.14 \div 0.2 =$

$$0.2\overline{)3.14} \quad\Rightarrow\quad 2\overline{)31.4} \quad\Rightarrow\quad \begin{array}{r} 15.7 \\ 2\overline{)31.4} \\ \underline{2} \\ 11 \\ \underline{10} \\ 14 \\ \underline{14} \\ 0 \end{array}$$

$3.14 \div 0.2 = 15.7.$

(2) $5.6 \times 16.5 \div 0.7 \div 1.1 =$

$(5.6 \div 0.7) \times (16.5 \div 1.1) = (56 \div 7) \times (165 \div 11) = 8 \times 15 = 120.$

(3) $1.25 \times 67.875 + 125 \times 6.7875 + 1250 \times 0.053375 =$

$1.25 \times 67.875 + 1.25 \times 678.75 + 1.25 \times 53.375 = 1.25 \times (67.875 + 678.75 + 53.375) = 1.25 \times 800 = 1000.$

(4) $19 \times 3.1 =$

$19 \times (3 + 0.1) = 19 \times 3 + 19 \times 0.1 = 57 + 1.9 = 58.9.$

(5) $0.4 \times 0.2 \times 8 \times 0.25 \times 0.5 =$

$(0.2 \times 0.5) \times (0.4 \times 0.25) \times 8 = 0.1 \times 0.1 \times 8 = 0.08.$

(6) $0.2 \times 0.11 \times 0.4 \times 0.5 =$
$(0.2 \times 0.5) \times (0.11 \times 0.4) = 0.1 \times 0.044 = 0.0044.$

(7) $0.24 \times 9.6 \times 0.25 \times 0.125 =$
$(0.24 \times 0.25) \times (9.6 \times 0.125) = 0.06 \times 1.2 = 0.072.$

(8) $8.99 \times 6 =$
$(9 - 0.01) \times 6 = 9 \times 6 - 0.01 \times 6 = 54 - 0.06 = 53.94.$

(9) $0.32 \div (0.08 \div 0.25) =$
$(0.32 \div 0.08) \times 0.25 = (32 \div 8) \times 0.25 = 4 \times 0.25 = 1.$

(10) $0.12 \times 0.5 \times 8 \div 0.04 =$
$(0.12 \div 0.04) \times (0.5 \times 8) = (12 \div 4) \times 4 = 12.$

5. Decimals and fractions:

Decimal	Fraction	Common fraction
4.3	$4 + \dfrac{3}{10}$	$4\dfrac{3}{10}$ or $\dfrac{43}{10}$
0.01	$0 + \dfrac{0}{10} + \dfrac{1}{100}$	$\dfrac{1}{100}$
3.0103	$3 + \dfrac{0}{10} + \dfrac{1}{100} + \dfrac{0}{1000} + \dfrac{3}{10000}$	$3\dfrac{103}{10000}$ or $\dfrac{30103}{10000}$

6. Terminating Decimals and Repeating Decimals

Any rational number can be expressed as either a terminating decimal or a repeating decimal.

A decimal such as 0.25, which stops, is called a terminating decimal.

A rational number a/b in lowest terms results in a repeating decimal if a prime other than 2 or 5 is a factor of the denominator.

$$\frac{1}{3} = 0.33333.... = 0.\overline{3}.$$

$$\frac{1}{7} = 0.142857142857.... = 0.\overline{142857}.$$

$$\frac{1}{13} = 0.076923076923.... = 0.\overline{076923}.$$

A rational number a/b in lowest terms results in a terminating decimal if the only prime factor of the denominator is 2 or 5 (or both).

$$\frac{1}{2} = 0.5, \qquad\qquad \frac{1}{5} = 0.2, \qquad\qquad \frac{1}{10} = 0.1.$$

Example: How many positive integers less than 100 have reciprocals with terminating decimal representations?

Solution: 14.

The reciprocals of numbers can be a terminating decimal:

2	4	8	16	32	64
5	25				
10	20	40	80		
50					
1					

Repeating block

(1). If the denominator has only 2 and 5 as its factors, this fraction can become a terminating decimal. The length of the decimal part equals the greater power of 2 or 5. Example:

$$\frac{1}{5} = 0.2 \qquad \frac{1}{25} = 0.04 \qquad \frac{1}{125} = 0.008 \qquad \frac{1}{625} = 0.0016$$

Length of the decimal part   1   2   3   4

(2). If the denominator has only factors other than 2 and 5, then this fraction can become repeating decimal. The length of the repeating block (period) is the smallest number of nines needed for the number containing 9's to be divisible by the denominator.

Examples:

For $\frac{1}{11}$, the repeating block is 2 since $\frac{99}{11} = 9$.　　　　　$(\frac{1}{11} = 0.\overline{09})$

For $\frac{1}{37}$, the repeating block is 3 since $\frac{999}{37} = 27$.　　　　$(\frac{1}{37} = 0.\overline{027})$.

For $\frac{1}{101}$, the repeating block is 4 since $\frac{9999}{101} = 99$.　　　$(\frac{1}{101} = 0.\overline{0099})$.

For $\frac{1}{7}$, the repeating block is 6 since $\frac{999999}{7} = 142857$.　　$(\frac{1}{7} = 0.\overline{142857})$.

For $\frac{1}{13}$, the repeating block is 6 since $\frac{999999}{13} = 76923$.　　$(\frac{1}{13} = 0.\overline{076923})$.

(3) If the denominator has 2 or 5 as factors and other prime factors, this fraction can become a mixed repeating decimal. The non-repeating block length is the greater power of 2 or 5. The repeating block length (the repeating period) is the smallest number of nines needed to be divisible by the denominator.

(4). Given $1/n$, n is a positive integer, the repeating block is r and $r \le n - 1$.

For $\frac{1}{7}$, $n = 7$ and $r \le n - 1 = 6$. In fact $\frac{1}{7} = 0.\overline{142857}$.

(5). $10^r \equiv 1 \pmod{p}$. r is the smallest positive integer.

Repeating Block of 1/p (for primes p)											
p	block	p	block	p	block	p	block	p	block	p	block
2	–	3	1	5	–	7	6	11	2	13	6
17	16	19	18	23	22	29	28	31	15	37	3

41	5	43	21	47	46	53	13	59	13	61	13
67	33	71	35	73	8	79	13	83	41	89	44
97	96	101	4	103	34	107	53	109	108	113	112

6. Operation with Repeating Decimals

Examples:

(1) Convert the repeating decimal $0.\overline{1}$ to a fraction.

Solution: Let $x = 0.\overline{1} = 0.111111\ldots$ (1)

Multiply both sides by 10: $10x = 1.11111\ldots$ (2)

(2) – (1): $9x = 1$ $\Rightarrow$ $x = 1/9$

(2) Convert the repeating decimal $0.\overline{25}$ to a fraction.

Solution: We set $x = 0.\overline{25} = 0.25252525\ldots$ and multiply both sides by 100:

$100x = 25.25252525\ldots$

Next we subtract:

$$100x = 25.25252525\ldots$$
$$-\quad x = \quad .25252525\ldots$$

$99x = 25.00000$

Next we divide both sides by 99 to get: $x = 25/99$

(3) The fraction of any single digit repeating decimal is the digit over 9. $\Rightarrow$ $0.\overline{5} = \dfrac{5}{9}$

(4) The fraction of any 2-digit repeating decimal is the digits over 99. $\Rightarrow$ $0.\overline{55} = \dfrac{55}{99}$

(5) $0.\overline{3123} = \dfrac{3123}{9999} = \dfrac{347}{1111}$.

(6) $0.17\overline{857142} = 0.\underbrace{17}_{2\,\text{digits}}\underbrace{\overline{857142}}_{6\,\text{digits}} = \dfrac{17857142 - 17}{\underbrace{999999}_{6\ 9's}\underbrace{00}_{2\ 0's}}$

(7) Express $0.72\overline{45}$ as a common fraction.

Solution:

Method 1: $0.72\overline{45} = \dfrac{7245 - 72}{9900} = \dfrac{7173}{9900} = \dfrac{797}{1100}$

Method 2: Let $x = 0.72\overline{45}$ (1)

$100x = 72.\overline{45}$ (2)

$10000x = 7245.\overline{45}$ (3)

(3) − (2): $9900x = 7173$ (4)

$x = \dfrac{7173}{9900} = \dfrac{797}{1100}$.

(8) Calculate: $3.\overline{14} + 0.\overline{32}$.

Solution:

Since $\begin{array}{r} 3.14 \\ + 0.32 \\ \hline 3.46 \end{array}$, so : $3.\overline{14} + 0.\overline{32} = 3.\overline{46}$

(9) Calculate: $2.\overline{48} + 2.\overline{83}$

Solution:

89

Since $\dfrac{\begin{array}{r}2.48\\+2.83\\\hline 5.31\end{array}}{}$, and the sum of the first repeating digits (4 in $2.\overline{48}$ and 8 in $2.\overline{83}$)

in the addends carries 1, so the last digit of the resulting number needs to be increased by $1: 2.\overline{48}+2.\overline{83}=5.\overline{32}$

(10) Calculate: $1.\overline{436}-0.\overline{312}$

Solution: Since $\dfrac{\begin{array}{r}1.436\\-0.312\\\hline 1.124\end{array}}{}$, so $1.\overline{436}-0.\overline{312}=1.\overline{124}$

(11) Calculate: $3.\overline{215}-1.\overline{307}$

Solution: Since $\dfrac{\begin{array}{r}3.215\\-1.307\\\hline 1.908\end{array}}{}$, and the first repeating digit (2 in $3.\overline{215}$) in the top

number is smaller than the corresponding digit (3 in $1.\overline{307}$) in the bottom number, so the last digit of the resulting number needs to be decreased by 1:
$3.\overline{215}-1.\overline{307}=1.\overline{907}$

(12) Calculate: $1.\overline{36}+2.\overline{375}$

Solution:

Since the first addend has 2 repeating digits and the second addend has 3 repeating digits, the sum should have $2 \times 3 = 6$ repeating digits (the least common multiple of 2 and 3).

$$\begin{array}{r}1.363636\\+2.375375\\\hline 3.739011\end{array}$$

So $1.\overline{36}+2.\overline{375}=1.\overline{363636}+2.\overline{375375}=3.\overline{739011}$.

(13) Calculate: $0.3\overline{42} + 2.\overline{35}$

Solution:

$2.\overline{35} = 2.3535353..... = 2.3\overline{53}$ and $\begin{array}{r} 0.342 \\ + 2.353 \\ \hline 2.695 \end{array}$, so $0.3\overline{42} + 2.\overline{35} = 0.3\overline{42} + 2.3\overline{53} = 2.6\overline{95}$.

(14) Calculate: $2.25 - 1.3\overline{6}$

Solution:

Method 1: $2.25 - 1.3\overline{6} = 2.25\overline{0} - 1.3\overline{6} = 2.25\overline{0} - 1.36\overline{6} == 0.88\overline{3}$

Method 2: $2.25 - 1.3\overline{6} = \dfrac{225}{100} - \dfrac{136 - 13}{90} = \dfrac{2025 - 1230}{900} = \dfrac{795}{900}$.

We see that both expressions are the same:

$0.88\overline{3} = \dfrac{883 - 88}{900} = \dfrac{795}{900}$.

(15) Calculate: $0.\overline{142857} \times 3.\overline{5}$

Solution:

$0.\overline{142857} \times 3.\overline{5} = \dfrac{142857}{999999} \times 3\dfrac{5}{9} = \dfrac{1}{7} \times 3\dfrac{5}{9} = \dfrac{1}{7} \times \dfrac{32}{9} = \dfrac{32}{63}$.

(16) Calculate: $0.\overline{27} \div 3.\overline{2}$

Solution:

$0.\overline{27} \div 3.\overline{2} = \dfrac{27}{99} \div 3\dfrac{2}{9} = \dfrac{27}{99} \div \dfrac{29}{9} = \dfrac{27}{99} \times \dfrac{9}{29} = \dfrac{27}{319}$

EXERCISES

Problem 1. Add: 3.28 + 17.5 + 39

Problem 2. Subtract: 275.4 − 187.93

Problem 3. Find the product: 1 · 2 · 3 · (0.2) · (0.5) · (4 · 5)

Problem 4. Multiply: 4.08 × 0.98

Problem 5. Divide: 12.98 ÷ 2.36

Problem 6. Divide: 0.007 ÷ 0.35

Problem 7. Simplify: (7 − 0.25)(6 + 1.2)

Problem 8. Simplify: 0.25(8.125 + 24.375)

Problem 9. Simplify: (12.7 − 7.45)

Problem 10. What is the product of 3.85 and 0.5?

Problem 11. Express the product 2.1 × 1.01 as a decimal number.

Problem 12. Find the sum of 18.1, 7.56 and 0.97. Express your answer as a decimal.

Problem 13. Divide 9.62 by 3.7 and express your answer as a decimal.

Problem 14. Find the product of 3.9 and 4.7 and express your answer as a decimal.

Problem 15. Express the difference 36 − 4.781 as a decimal.

Problem 16. Subtract 241.346 from 3568 and express your answer as a decimal.

Problem 17. Express in simplest form:

$$\frac{10(0.2) + 8(0.15) - 6(0.5)}{8(0.125)}$$

Problem 18. Find the sum $4.16 + 36.5 + 216$ and express your answer as a decimal.

Problem 19. Express as a decimal: 1001×3.63

Problem 20. Express as a decimal: $170.2 \div 46$

Problem 21. Express the product as a decimal: $(60.5)(0.25)(4.4)$

Problem 22. Express the quotient as a decimal: $9.648 \div 2.4$

Problem 23. Find $347 \div 25$. Express your answer as a decimal.

Problem 24. Express as a decimal: $4.48962 \div 0.02$

Problem 25. Express as a decimal: $3.86 + 38.6 + 386.$

Problem 26. Express as a decimal: $17952 \div 10560.$

Problem 27. Express as a decimal: $0.0004 \div 25.$

Problem 28. Express as a decimal: $150.8 - 14.75$

Problem 29. Express as a decimal rounded to the nearest thousandth: $1948 \div 39$

Problem 30. Write as a decimal: $800 - 0.005.$

Problem 31. Express the product as a decimal: $(0.125)(4.8)(0.025)(1.6)$

Problem 32. Express as a decimal: $0.1125 \times 600.$

Problem 33. Express as a decimal to the nearest tenth: $1713.249 \div 817$

Problem 34. Express as a decimal to the nearest thousandth: $9132.123 \div 9123$

Problem 35. Express in simplest form: $24(0.708\overline{3}) - 6(0.8\overline{3})$.

Problem 36. Express in simplest form: $18.\overline{18} + 81.\overline{81}$.

Problem 37. Express as a decimal: $(3.8)(120) - 38.75$.

Problem 38. Simplify: $\dfrac{(0.3)(0.056)}{1.2 - 0.08}$.

Problem 39. Express as a common fraction: $\dfrac{3\frac{1}{0.\overline{2}}}{0.75}$

Problem 40. Simplify: $(0.25 - 0.24\overline{9}) + (0.75 - 0.74\overline{9})$

Problem 41. A sheet of paper is 0.0075cm thick. How many centimeters high is a stack of 500 sheets?

Problem 42. Express the reciprocal of 0.0625 in decimal form.

Problem 43. Compute: $378.63 - 5.72 - 78.63 - 4.28$

Problem 44. Compute: $176.2 + 348.3 + 42.47 + 252.5 + 382.23$

Problem 45. Compute: $(6.4 \times 7.5 \times 8.1) \div (3.2 \times 2.5 \times 2.7)$

Problem 46. Compute: $15.37 \times 7.88 - 9.37 \times 7.37 + 1.537 \times 21.2 - 93.7 \times 0.263$

Problem 47. Compute: $1.25 \times 17.6 + 36 \div 0.8 + 2.64 \times 12.5$

ANSWER KEYS

Problem 1. 59.78	**Problem** 2. 87.47	**Problem** 3. 12
Problem 4. 3.9984	**Problem** 5. 5.5	**Problem** 6. 0.02
Problem 7. 48.6	**Problem** 8. 8.125	**Problem** 9. 5.25
Problem 10. 1.925	**Problem** 11. 2.121	**Problem** 12. 26.63
Problem 13. 2.6	**Problem** 14. 18.33	**Problem** 15. 31.219
Problem 16. 3326.654	**Problem** 17. 0.2	**Problem** 18. 256.66
Problem 19. 3633.63	**Problem** 20. 3.7	**Problem** 21. 66.55
Problem 22. 4.02	**Problem** 23. 13.88	**Problem** 24. 224.481
Problem 25. 428.46	**Problem** 26. 1.7	**Problem** 27. 0.000016
Problem 28. 136.05	**Problem** 29. 49.949	**Problem** 30. 799.995
Problem 31. 0.024	**Problem** 32. 67.5	**Problem** 33. 2.1
Problem 34. 1.001	**Problem** 35. 12	**Problem** 36. 100
Problem 37. 417.25	**Problem** 38. 0.015	**Problem** 39. 99/10
Problem 40. 0	**Problem** 41. 3.75	**Problem** 42. 16.0
Problem 43. 290	**Problem** 44. 1201.7	**Problem** 45. 18
Problem 46. 60	**Problem** 47. 100	

BASIC KNOWLEDGE

Terms

A percent is a ratio that compares a number to 100. It also means hundredths, or per hundred. The symbol for percent is %.

Note: The word "percent" consists of two parts: per and cent. Per means "divide by" and *cent* means "hundred."

Percent is a special form of decimals and a more special form of fractions. For example, $50\% = \dfrac{50}{100} = 0.5$.

All the operation rules of decimals and fractions will apply to percent.

Percent of change: A number is changed from the value of a to the value of b,

if $b > a$, the percent of change (increase) is $\dfrac{b-a}{a} \times 100\%$.

if $b < a$, the percent of change (decrease) is $\dfrac{a-b}{a} \times 100\%$.

Percent of a number

Examples:

(1) Find 50% of 300.
Solution: 150.
$$\frac{50}{100} \times 300 = 50 \times 3 = 150$$

(2) Find: $\dfrac{1}{3}\%$ of 600
Solution: 2.
$$\frac{1}{3}\% \times 600 = \frac{1}{300} \times 600 = 1 \times 2 = 2$$

96

(3) Find $33\frac{1}{3}$% of 900.

Solution: 300.

$$33\frac{1}{3}\% \times 900 = \frac{100}{300} \times 900 = 300$$

(4) Find 2.5% of 2500.
Solution: 62.5.

$$2.5\% \times 2500 = \frac{2.5}{100} \times 2500 = 62.5$$

(5). Simplify: 20% · (100 + 200 + 300 + 400).

Solution: 200.

$$\frac{20}{100} \times 1000 = 200$$

(6). Of the 24 members of a class, 25% are seniors. How many members are not seniors? (Mathcounts Handbooks).

Solution: 18.

$$24 - \frac{25}{100} \times 24 = 24 - 6 = 18.$$

Basic types of percent problems:

		What number is c % of b?
$\dfrac{x}{b} = \dfrac{c}{100} \quad \Rightarrow \quad x = \dfrac{c}{100}b$		What number is c % of b?
$\dfrac{a}{b} = \dfrac{x}{100} \quad \Rightarrow \quad a = \dfrac{x}{100}b$		a is what % of b?
$\dfrac{a}{x} = \dfrac{c}{100} \quad \Rightarrow \quad a = \dfrac{c}{100}x$		a is c % of what number?

Translation of words to math symbols

Word form	Math symbol	Meaning
what number	x	unknown symbol
is	$=$	equals
of	$\times$	multiplication

Examples:

(1) What number is 25% of 3500?

Solution: 875.

Let x be the number: $x = \dfrac{25}{100} \times 3500 = 875$.

(2) Erica has saved $63 toward the purchase of a $300 camera. What percent of the total price has she saved?

Solution: 21%.

This question is the same as to ask: 63 is what percent of 300?

Method 1: $\dfrac{63}{300} = \dfrac{3 \times 21}{3 \times 100} = \dfrac{21}{100} = 21\%$.

Method 2: 63 is x percent of 300: $63 = \dfrac{x}{100} \times 300 \qquad \Rightarrow \quad x = \dfrac{63}{3} = 21$

(3) 25% of what number is 30?

Solution: 120.

$\dfrac{25}{100} \times x = 30 \qquad \Rightarrow \quad x = 120$.

(4) 3 is 0.4% of what number?

Solution: 750.

$$3 = \frac{0.4}{100} \times x \qquad \Rightarrow \quad x = 750.$$

(5). 12 is what percent of 20?

Solution: 60.

$$12 = x\% \times 20 \qquad \Rightarrow \qquad x = 60.$$

(6). What number is 25% of 1696?

Solution: 424.

$$x = 25\% \times 1696 \qquad \Rightarrow \qquad x = \frac{1}{4} \times 1696 = 424.$$

(7). Write $12\frac{1}{2}\%$ of 24 in simplest form.

Solution: 3.

$$\frac{25}{200} \times 24 = \frac{1}{8} \times 24 = 3.$$

Percent Increase and Decrease

(1). A student has an average of 85% on 3 one-hour exams. If each counts the same and the final counts twice as much as a one-hour exam, what percent must the student make on the final to have an overall average of 90% for the course?

Solution: 97.5%.

Method 1: If the overall average is 90, the total points will be $5 \times 90 = 450$ (three 85's and two for the final since the final counts twice). $450 - 85 \times 3 = 195$. The final score is $195 / 2 = 97.5$ or 97.5%.

Method 2: Let x be the final percent.

$$\frac{0.85 \times 3 + 2x}{5} = 0.9 \qquad \Rightarrow \qquad x = 0.975 = 97.5\%$$

(2). A softball team won seven of its first dozen games. How many of the remaining 20 games does the team have to win to have a season record of winning 75% of its games?

Solution: 17 games.

Method 1: The total games for the season is $12 + 20 = 32$. The total number of games the team won is $\dfrac{75}{100} \times 32 = 24$. So there are $24 - 7 = 17$ games the team needs to win.

Method 2: Let x be the number of games the team has to win of the remaining 20 games.

$$\dfrac{7 + x}{12 + 20} = \dfrac{75}{100} \qquad \Rightarrow \qquad x = 17.$$

(3). In a certain school $37\dfrac{1}{2}\%$ of the students were on the honor roll. Of the students on the honor roll $8\dfrac{1}{3}\%$ had a straight A average. If 58 students had a straight A average, how many students were enrolled in the school?

Solution: 1856(students)

Let x be the number of students enrolled in the school.

$$37\dfrac{1}{2}\% \times x \times 8\dfrac{1}{3}\% = 58 \qquad \Rightarrow \qquad x = 1856.$$

Discounts

(1). A worker was taken off the job for the first 40 working days of the year with no pay. If the worker's pay for 200 working days is $22,000, what percent raise must the worker get in order to receive $22,000 over the next 160 working days?

Solution: 25 %.

The number of dollars he earned each day over 160 days is $\dfrac{22000}{160} = 137.5$.

The number of dollars he earned each day over 200 days is $\dfrac{22000}{200} = 110$.

The percent raise the worker must get in order to receive $22,000 over the next 160 working is $\dfrac{137.5 - 110}{110} = 0.25 = 25\%$.

(2). The price of a skateboard is reduced 20% for the spring sale. It is then marked up 20%. What fraction represents the new price compared to the original? (Mathcounts Handbook).

Solution: 24/25.

Let the original price be 1. After the price is reduced 20%, it becomes $(\frac{100}{100} - \frac{20}{100})$. The fraction representing the new price after a marked up of 20% compared to the original is:

$(\frac{100}{100} - \frac{20}{100})(\frac{100}{100} + \frac{20}{100}) = \frac{24}{25}$.

(3). After a recent diet, a dieter weighed in at 135 lbs. This represented a weight loss of 10% on the pre-diet weight of the dieter. How many pounds did the dieter weigh prior to the diet?

Solution: 150 lbs.

The number of pounds the dieter weighted before is $\frac{135}{0.9} = 150$.

Discounts on Discounts

(1). Given that 1% of 1% of a number is 5, what is the number?

Solution: 50000.
Let the number be x.
$1\% \times 1\% \times x = 5$ $\Rightarrow$ $x = 50000$.

(2). Successive discounts of 20%, 10%, and 50% would be equivalent to a single discount of t%. What is the value of t ?

Solution: 64%.
Let x be the original price. The final sale price is $0.8 \times 0.9 \times 0.5x = 0.36x$.
The single discount value will be $1 - 0.36 = 0.64 = 64\%$.

(3). Over the past 4-year period the price of sugar reflected the following consecutive changes: 25% increase the 1st year, 25% increase the 2nd year, 20% decrease the 3rd year and a 10% decrease the 4th year. What is the ratio of the price of sugar today to that of 4 years ago? Express your answer in the form $a:b$ where a and b are relatively prime positive integers.

Solution: 9:8.

Let x be the original price 4 years ago. The final price is $1.25 \times 1.25 \times 0.8 \times 0.9 = 1.125x$.

$$\frac{a}{b} = \frac{1.125x}{x} = 9:8$$

(4). The value of a machine declines 10% of its current value for each year of use. If the original cost of the machine was $5,000, after a minimum of how many full years will its value be less than 50% of it's original value?

Solution: 7 yrs.

$50000 \times 0.9 \times 0.9 \times \ldots \times 0.9 = 23914.845$ for 7 0.9's.

(5). In 1990 the population of a city was 150,000. If the population increases 5% each year in 1991 and 1992, decreases 4% in 1993, and increases 10% in 1994, what will the population be at the end of 1994? (Mathcounts Handbook).

Solution: 174,636.

$150,000 \times 1.05 \times 1.05 \times 0.96 \times 1.1 = 174636$.

(6). On Monday, Euler's Bakery discounted the price of pies 20%. On Tuesday, it discounted the pies an additional 70%. What is the combined percent discount? (Mathcounts Handbook).

Solution: 76.

Method 1: The equivalent one single discount is $1 - 0.8 \times 0.3 = 1 - 0.24 = 0.76 = 76\%$.

Method 2: $d = d_1 + d_2 - d_1 \times d_2 = \frac{20}{100} + \frac{70}{100} - \frac{20}{100} \times \frac{70}{100} = \frac{76}{100}$

(7). Successive discounts of 10% and 20% are equivalent to a single discount of:

(A) 30% (B) 15% (C) 72% (D) 28% (E) none of these

(1950 AMC).

Solution: D.

Method 1: Let p be the original price. Then a discount of 10% gives a new price $p - 0.1p$ = $0.9p$. Following this by a discount of 20%, we have

$$0.9p - 0.2 \times (0.9p) = 0.72p.$$

Thus the net discount is $p - 0.72p = 0.28p$ or 28%;

Method 2: Net discount = $d = d_1 + d_2 - d_1 \times d_2 = \dfrac{10}{100} + \dfrac{20}{100} - \dfrac{2}{100} = 28\%$

Simple Interest

(1). If $1200 is deposited in a savings account at 7.5% interest per year, what is the simple interest in dollars earned in two years?

Solution: $180.

The interest earns in a year is $1200 \times 0.075 = 90$. The interest will be $90 \times 2 = 180$ in two years.

(2). If $1500 was borrowed at an annual interest rate of 12%, how much, in dollars, was the simple interest paid for 8 months?

Solution: $120.

The interest paid for 12 months is $1500 \times 0.12 = 180$.
For 8 months it will be $\dfrac{180}{12} \times 8 = 120$.

(3). If $5000 is invested at 9% simple interest for one year, how much in dollars would have to be invested at 7.5% simple interest to earn an equal amount for one year?

Solution: $6000.

The interest eared at 9% is $5000 \times 0.09 = 450$.

The money needed to get this amount of interest at 7.5% will be $\dfrac{450}{0.075} = 6000$.

Profit and Loss

(1). A house was sold for $73,780. If the selling price represented 8.5% profit over the purchase price, what was the purchase price in dollars of the house?

Solution: $68,000

Let x be the purchase price.
$x \times 1.085 = 73780$ $\Rightarrow$ $x = 68000$

(2). A house was sold for $64,900. If the selling price represented a 25% profit over the purchase price, what was the purchase price in dollars of the house?

Solution: $51,920.
Let x be the purchase price.
$x \times 1.25 = 64900$ $\Rightarrow$ $x = 51920$

(3). Fran bought a pair of roller blades for $100 and sold them to Toni for a 10% profit. Toni then sold the roller blades back to Fran for 10% loss. Fran then sold the roller blades to Gary for $100. What percent profit did Fran earn on the original $100?

Solution: 11 percent.

	Fran Paid	Fran got
	100	110 (100×1.1)
	99 ($110 \times 90\%$)	100
Total	199	210

The difference is $210 - 199 = 11$.

The percent profit Fran earned on the original $100 is then $11/100 = 11\%$.

(4). A house was sold for $230,000. If the selling price represents a 15% profit over the purchase price, how many dollars were in the purchase price of the house?

Solution:

Let x be the purchase price.
$x \times 1.15 = 230,000$ $\Rightarrow$ $x = 200,000$

104

(5). Mr. A owns a home worth $10,000. He sells it to Mr. B at a 10% profit based on the worth of the house. Mr. B sells the house back to Mr. A at a 10% loss. Then:

(A) A comes out even   (B) A makes $1100 on the deal
(C) A makes $1000 on the deal   (D) A loses $900 on the deal
(E) A loses $1000 on the deal
(1951 AMC).

Solution: $S_1 = 10,000 + 1000 = 11,000$, $S_2 = 11,000 - 1100 = 9900$,

$S_1 - S_2 = 1100$. $\therefore$ (B) is the correct choice.

Diluting Solutions

(1) Thirty ounces of vinegar with a strength of 30% was mixed with 50 ounces of a 20% vinegar solution. What was the percentage of the resulting solution?

Solution: 23.75%.
We introduce the "C-V-S" method. C is the concentration or the strength of the solution. V is the volume of the solution. S is the substance of the solution.
Note: $C \times V = S$, $V_A + V_B = V_D$, and $S_A + S_B = S_D$. There is no relationship for C_A, C_B, and C_D.

Name	C	$\times$	V	$=$	S
A	0.3	$\times$	30	$=$	$0.3 \times 30 = 9$
			+		+
B	0.2	$\times$	50	$=$	$0.2 \times 50 = 10$
			$\parallel$		$\parallel$
Mixture	x	$\times$	80	$=$	$80\,x$

$9 + 10 = 80x$ $\Rightarrow x = 0.2375 = 23.75\%$.

(2) How many liters of a 20% alcohol solution must be added to 90 liters of a 50% alcohol solution to form a 45% solution?

Solution: 18 liters.

Name	C	V	S
A	0.2	x	$0.2 \times x$
B	0.5	90	45
Mixture	0.45	$90 + x$	$0.45(90 + x)$

$$0.45(90 + x) = 0.2 \, x + 45 \qquad \Rightarrow \qquad x = 18 \text{ liters.}$$

(3) How many ounces of pure acid (100%) should be added to 120 fluid ounces of a 20% acid solution to obtain a 40% acid solution?

Solution: 40 liters.

Name	C	V	S
A	1	x	x
B	0.2	120	24
Mixture	0.4	$120 + x$	$0.4(120 + x)$

$$x + 24 = 0.4(120 + x) \Rightarrow \qquad x = 40 \text{ liters.}$$

(4) Forty ounces of a punch containing 40% pomegranate juice was added to 60 ounces of a similar punch containing 10% juice. Find the percent of pomegranate juice in the resulting punch.

Solution: 22%.

Name	C	V	S
A	0.4	40	16
B	0.1	60	6
Mixture	x	100	$100x$

$$16 + 6 = 100x \qquad \Rightarrow \qquad x = 0.22 = 22\%.$$

(5) A chemist needs a 15% alcohol solution and has only a 60% solution. How much water should be added to obtain 10 liters of the weaker solution?

Solution: 7.5 liters.

Name	C	V	S
A	0	x	0
B	0.6	y	$0.6y$
Mixture	0.15	10	1.5

$$0.6y = 1.5 \qquad \Rightarrow \qquad y = 2.5.$$
$$x + y = 10. \qquad \Rightarrow \qquad x = 7.5.$$

(6). One bottle contains 1000 grams of 15% alcohol solution. Alcohol solution A of 100 grams and alcohol solution B of 400 grams were added to the bottle to form a 14% alcohol solution. The percentage of alcohol solution A is twice as much as the percentage of alcohol solution B. What was the percentage of the solution A?

Solution: 20%.

Name	C	V	S
A	$2x$	100	$200\,x$
B	x	400	$400\,x$
D	0.15	1000	150
Mixture	0.14	1500	210

$$200x + 400x + 150 = 210 \quad \Rightarrow \quad x = 0.1 = 10\%. \quad \Rightarrow \quad 2x = 20\%.$$

(7). A 36% alcohol solution is added x grams pure water to make a 30% alcohol solution. When y grams pure water was added again to the solution, a 24% alcohol solution was obtained. Find ratio of y to x.

Solution: 1.5.

	Name	C	V	S
Step 1	A	0.36	m	$0.36m$
	B	0	x	0
	Mixture	0.3	$x + m$	$0.3(x + m)$
Step 2	D	0.3	$x + m$	$0.3(x + m)$
	E	0	y	0
	Mixture	0.24	$x + m + y$	$0.24(x + m + y)$

$0.36m = 0.3(x + m) \quad \Rightarrow \quad m = 5x$

$0.3(x + m) = 0.24(x + m + y) \quad \Rightarrow \quad 0.3(x + 5x) = 0.24(x + 5x + y)$

$1.8x = 1.44x + 0.24y \quad \Rightarrow \quad y/x = 1.5.$

(8). 100 kg of a fruit contained 90% water one week ago. How many kg of the fruit containing 80% water are there now?
Solution: 50.

Name	C	V	S
A	0.1	100	10
B	0.2	x	$0.2\,x$

The substance does not change before or after the evaporating: $10 = 0.2x \quad \Rightarrow x = 50.$

EXERCISES

Problem 1. Express in simplest form: 20% of (5 + 10 + 15 + 20 + 25)

Problem 2. What number is $66\frac{2}{3}\%$ of 495?

Problem 3. What percent of 3 is 6?

Problem 4. Find $6\frac{5}{12}\%$ of $720. Express your answer as a decimal number of dollars.

Problem 5. Write 23% of 200 in simplest form.

Problem 6. Find $2\frac{1}{2}\%$ of 120.

Problem 7. What is a value of 10 increased by 120%?

Problem 8. Express in simplest form:

$$1\frac{1}{4}\% \text{ of } 400 + 1\frac{1}{4}\% \text{ of } 320 + 1\frac{1}{4}\% \text{ of } 240$$

Problem 9. Write $16\frac{2}{3}\%$ of 72 in simplest form.

Problem 10. What number is 12 ½ % of 37920?

Problem 11. Twenty-eight is 28 4/7 % of what number?

Problem 12. Twenty-four is the result when a certain number is increased by $33\frac{1}{3}\%$. What is the original number?

Problem 13. If the number 36 is increased by 150%, what is the value of the result?

Problem 14. Three hundred is what fractional part of 360?

Problem 15. Find 10% of 20% of 40% of 250.

Problem 16. Find $3\frac{1}{3}$% of 600.

Problem 17. Express $16\frac{3}{4}$% of 4 as a decimal.

Problem 18. If 750 students attended a concert and seating was available for 39, by what percent, to the nearest percent, did attendance exceed available seats?

Problem 19. What percent of 10 is $\frac{1}{2}$?

Problem 20. What is 25% of 50% of 270? Express your answer as a decimal.

Problem 21. Travis paid $11,700 for a new car. This is 2.5% less than George paid for an identical car. How much, in dollars, did George pay for his car?

Problem 22. What is 8 2/3 % of 600?

Problem 23. What is 40% of 50% of 60% of 150?

Problem 24. What is 50% of 40% of 30?

Problem 25. What is $\frac{1}{4}$% of 180?

Problem 26. In legislative elections, held every two years, 80% of the incumbents are reelected. Based on this assumption, how many of the 250 legislators elected in 1990 will be reelected in 1996? (Assume all 250 are up for reelection every two years.)

Problem 27. What is (1/8)% of 320?

Problem 28. In 1896, the winning pole vault in the Olympics measured 10 feet, 10 inches. In 1988, the winning vault was 19 feet, 9.25 inches. By what percent, to the nearest tenth, did the winning distance increase in that time?

Problem 29. What is the value of the expression below which is not equivalent to the other four? Express your answer as a decimal to the nearest tenth.

15% of 60;   60% of 15;   6% of 150;   0.15% of 600;   150% of 6

Problem 30. A multivitamin contains 162 milligrams of calcium which represents 16.2% of the recommended daily allowance for an adult. How many milligrams of calcium are in the recommended daily allowance for an adult?

Problem 31. According to an ancient belief, when a friend visits a sick person, $\frac{1}{60}$ of his or her illness is taken away. How many friends need to visit to take away at least 99% of a person's illness?

Problem 32. Mecklenburg, in Culver County, has population 2570. The population of Culver County is 64,250. What percent of the county population lives in Mecklenburg?

Problem 33. Genia has 50% more money than Arizona, and Jamal has 25% more money than Arizona. What percent more money does Genia have than Jamal?

Problem 34. A human baby's body has 350 bones. As the baby grows to adulthood, some bones grow together. An adult's body only has 206 bones. To the nearest whole number, find the percent decrease in the number of bones.

Problem 35. Of the 1.5 million people of voting age in Smithville, 76% are registered voters. Of those registered, 42% voted in the most recent election. The winning candidate for mayor received 53% of those votes. How many votes did the mayor receive?

Problem 36. In 1999, there were 150 IMAX theaters, 28 of which had 3-D capabilities. What percent had 3-D capabilities? Express your answer to the nearest whole number.

ANSWER KEYS

Problem 1. 15	**Problem** 2. 330	**Problem** 3. 200%
Problem 4. $46.20	**Problem** 5. 46	**Problem** 6. 3
Problem 7. 22	**Problem** 8. 12	**Problem** 9. 12
Problem 10. 4740	**Problem** 11. 98	**Problem** 12. 18
Problem 13. 90	**Problem** 14. 5/6	**Problem** 15. 2
Problem 16. 20	**Problem** 17. 0.67	**Problem** 18. 1823%
Problem 19. 5%	**Problem** 20. 33.75	**Problem** 21. $12000
Problem 22. 52	**Problem** 23. 18	**Problem** 24. 6
Problem 25. 0.45 or 9/20	**Problem** 26. 128	**Problem** 27. 0.4
Problem 28. 82.5%	**Problem** 29. 0.9	**Problem** 30. 1000
Problem 31. 275	**Problem** 32. 4	**Problem** 33. 20
Problem 34. 41	**Problem** 35. 253,764	**Problem** 36. 19

1. BASIC KNOWLEDGE

Pigeonhole Principle:

If you have five apples and four boxes, no matter how you put the apples into these boxes, you will see that at least one box contains at least two apples.

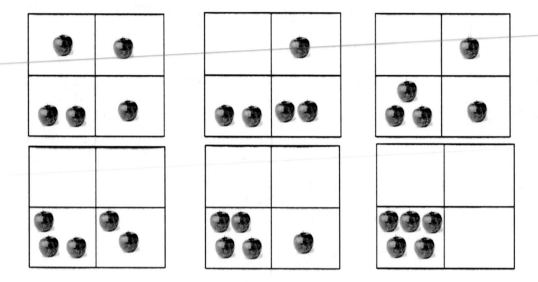

If you have five apples and six boxes, no matter how you put the apples into these boxes, you will see that at least one box has no apple in it.

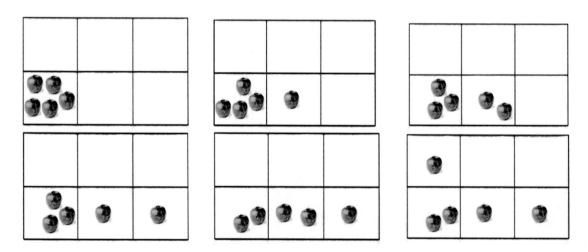

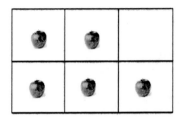

Pigeonhole Principle I: If $n + 1$ balls are put into n boxes, then at least one box contains two balls.

Pigeonhole Principle II: If $n - 1$ balls are put into n boxes, then at least one box contains no balls.

Generalized Pigeonhole Principle: If n balls are put into k boxes, then there exists a box containing at least $\left\lceil \dfrac{n}{k} \right\rceil$ balls.

The ceiling of x is written as $\lceil x \rceil$, it is the smallest integer greater than or equal to x. The floor of x is written $\lfloor x \rfloor$. It is the largest integer that is less than or equal to x. For instance $\lceil \pi \rceil = 4$ and $\lfloor \pi \rfloor = 3$.

Other equivalent expressions:

(*a*) If $m = nq$ $(m \geq 1)$ balls are put into n boxes, then at least one box contains q balls.

(*b*) If $m = nq + r$ $(m \geq 1, 0 < r < n)$ balls are put into n boxes, then at least one box contains $q + 1$ balls.

(*c*) If $mn + 1$ balls are put into n boxes, then one box must contains at least $m + 1$ balls.

(*d*) If $mn - 1$ balls are put into n boxes, then one box must contains at most $m - 1$ balls.

2. SOME SKILLS TO CONSTRUCT BALLS AND BOXES

Birthdays

Example 1: 366 students were graduated in 2001 from Phillips High School. Prove at least two students have the same birthday.

Solution:
365 birthdays are boxes and students are balls. According to Pigeonhole Principle I: at least one day is the birthday for 2 students.

Example 2: There are 97 people in a room. Prove at least nine people were born in the same month.

Solution:
Method 1: Twelve months are boxes and 97 people are balls. By the rule (c) If $mn + 1$ balls are put into n boxes, then one box must contains at least $m + 1$ balls.
$97 = 8 \times 12 + 1$
So at least $8 + 1 = 9$ people were born in the same month.

Method 2: By Generalized Pigeonhole Principle: If n balls are put into k boxes, then there exists a box containing at least $\left\lceil \dfrac{n}{k} \right\rceil$ balls.

$$\left\lceil \frac{n}{k} \right\rceil = \left\lceil \frac{97}{12} \right\rceil = \left\lceil 8.08\overline{3} \right\rceil = 9 \text{ people.}$$

Ball selections

Example 3: A bowl contains 10 red balls and 10 blue balls. A woman selects balls at random without looking at them. How many balls must she select to be sure to have at least three balls of the same color?

Solution: 5 balls.
Let the boxes be the colors red and blue.

By the rule (c) If $mn + 1$ balls are put into n boxes, then one box must contains at least $m + 1$ balls.

We know that $n = 2$ and $m + 1 = 3$ $\Rightarrow$ $m = 2$ $\Rightarrow$ $mn + 1 = 5$.

Note: If 4 balls are picked then we could have 2 red and 2 blue.

Example 4: A bowl contains 5 red balls and 5 blue balls. A woman selects balls at random without looking at them. How many balls must she select to be sure to have at least two blue balls?

Solution: 7.

If 6 balls are picked we could have 5 red and 1 blue. So we must pick up one more ball to have at least 3 blue.

Playing cards

Example 5: At least how many cards must be selected from a standard deck to be certain that these cards are from three suites?

Solution: $13 \times 2 + 1 = 27$ (cards).

Note: Standard 52 - playing card deck: 13 of each suit clubs (♣), diamonds (♦), hearts (♥) and spades (♠).

Example 6: At least how many cards must be selected from a standard deck to be certain that 4 cards have the same numbers?

Solution: 40.

There are 13 different numbers in each suite and there are 4 suites. At least $13 \times 3 + 1 = 40$ cards should be selected.

Draw socks

Example 7: A drawer contains 10 pairs of socks. Each pair is either black or white. What is the minimum number of socks that must be drawn at random from the drawer to ensure that 3 pair of socks of the same color is selected?

Solution: 11 socks.

Considering the worst case, we draw 5 socks of each color. We need to draw one more sock to meet the requirement. So the answer is $2 \times 5 + 1 = 11$.

Example 8: A drawer contains 60 pairs of socks. Each pair is one of four colors. What is the minimum number of socks that must be drawn at random from the drawer to ensure that a pair of socks of the same color is selected?

Solution: 5 socks.

Method 1: Considering the worst case, we would draw four socks, one from each color and we would not have a pair yet. If we draw one more sock, that one will pair with one of the four socks we had drawn before.

Method 2: We have m colors and we want to find N, the minimum number of socks that must be drawn at random from the drawer to ensure that n pairs of socks of the same color are selected: $N = 2n + m - 1$

So $N = 2n + m - 1 = 2 \times 1 + 4 - 1 = 5$.

Sum of integers

Example 9: How many numbers must be selected from 15 numbers 1, 2, 3, ..., 15 to ensure that there must have two numbers with the sum of 16?

Solution:

We construct 8 boxes the following way: {1, 15}, {2, 14}, {3, 13}, {4, 12}, {5, 11}, {6, 10}, {7, 9}, and {8}.

We first take out 8 numbers and one from each box. When we take the 9th number, we must take a number that is the first 7 boxes. Then we know that we have taken two numbers from the same box, and their sum must be 16.

Example 10: Randomly take out 7 different numbers from the following ten numbers: 1, 2, 3, 4, 5, 6, 7, 8, 9, and 10. Prove there must be two numbers such that the sum of the two numbers is 10.

Solution:

We have 7 balls (7 numbers) and we need to put them into 6 boxes. We construct the boxes (groups) such that the sum of the two numbers in the group is 10.

We divided these 10 numbers into the following groups: $\{1, 9\}$, $\{2, 8\}$, $\{3, 7\}$, $\{4, 6\}$. Two numbers 5 and 10 are two groups: $\{5\}$ and $\{10\}$.

We first take out 6 numbers and one from each group. When we take the seventh number, we must take a number that is the first 4 groups. Then we know that we have taken two numbers from the same box, and their sum must be 10.

Example 11: Randomly take out 13 different numbers from the following twenty numbers: 1, 4, 7, 10,…, 58. Prove there must be two pairs such that the sum of the two numbers in each pair is 62.

Solution:

Divide these 20 numbers into the following 11 groups (11 boxes): $\{4, 58\}$, $\{7, 55\}$, $\{10, 52\}$, … $\{28, 34\}$, $\{1\}$, and $\{31\}$.

Each of the first 9 boxes contains a pair of numbers with the sum of 62. Each of the last two groups contains one number. If we take out 13 different numbers from them, at least 11 of them are from the first 9 boxes. The worst case is that we take 9 numbers from 9 boxes, with each number from one box. Since $11 = 9 + 2$, other two numbers must pair two numbers from these 9 boxes. So we are sure that there are at least two pairs and each pair is from the same box and the sum is 62.

Example 12: Randomly divide 1, 2, 3,…, 20 into four groups. Each group contains 5 numbers. Prove that there must be one group in which the sum of five numbers is greater than 52.

Solution:

Four groups are four boxes. The sum of all numbers is: $1 + 2 + 3 +…+ 20 = 210$. There are 210 balls. $210 = 52 \times 4 + 2$.

By the rule (c): If $mn + 1$ balls are put into n boxes, then one box must contain at least $m + 1$ balls.

We know that there must be one group in which the sum of five numbers is greater than 52.

Multiple of integers

Example 13: Given any five positive integers, there must be 2 of them having a difference that is a multiple of 4.

Solution:
When a positive integer is divided by 4, the remainder can be 0, 1, 2, or 3. These 4 remainders are 4 boxes. 5 positive integers are 5 balls. When 5 balls are put into 4 boxes, at least two balls will be in the same box, which means that these two numbers will have the same remainder when divided by 4. Their difference is zero when divided by 4, that is, the difference is a multiple of 4.

Example 14: Randomly take out 5 numbers from the following 8 numbers: 1, 2, 3, 4, 5, 6, 7, and 8. Prove there must be two numbers such that one is a multiple of another.

Solution:
Divide these 8 numbers into the following 4 groups (4 boxes): Box A: {1, 2, 4, 8}; Box B:{3, 6}; Box C: {5}; and Box D: {7}.

Now we take out 5 numbers using the worst case scenario. We take one number from Box C. We take another number from Box D. We have three more numbers to take.

Case I: If we take all three numbers from Box A, we know there must be two numbers such that one is a multiple of another (for example, we take 2, 4, and 8).
Case II: If we take two numbers from Box A and one number from Box B, or we take two numbers from Box B and one number from Box A, we are also sure that there must be two numbers such that one is a multiple of another.

Geometry

Example 15: Choose 5 points on an equilateral triangle with side length 2. Show that there are two points whose distance apart is less than or equal to 1.

Solution:
Connect the midpoints of each side to form four smaller
triangles. The five points are the balls, the four equilateral
triangles of side length 1 are the boxes.

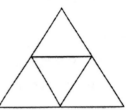

When you put five points into these triangles, at least two points
will be in the same triangle and their distance is smaller or equal to 1.

Example 16: Choose 13 points on a square with side length 1. Show that there must have

four points to from a quadrilateral whose area is less than or equal to $\frac{1}{4}$.

Solution:
We divide the square into four regions (four boxes) as shown below.
$13 = 3 \times 4 + 1$.

By the rule (c): If $mn + 1$ balls are put into n boxes, then one box must contains at least
$m + 1$ balls.

There must have four points on or inside a small square. The quadrilateral formed by

these four points will have an area less than or equal to $\frac{1}{4}$.

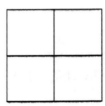

Note: We can also construct the boxes as follows:

 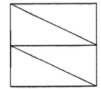

EXERCISES

Problem 1. A bag contains beads of two colors: black and white. What is the smallest number of beads which must be drawn from the bag, without looking, so that among these beads there are two of the same color? (Math Circles)

Problem 2. Given twelve integers, show that two of them can be chosen whose difference is divisible by 11. (Math Circles)

Problem 3. Twenty-five crates of apples are delivered to a store. The apples are of three different sorts. And all the apples in each crate are of the same sort. Show that among these crates there are at least nine containing the same sort of apple. (Math Circles)

Problem 4. Given 8 different natural numbers, none greater than 15, show that at least three pairs of them have the same positive difference (the pairs need not be disjoint as sets.) (Math Circles)

Problem 5. Show that in any group of five people, there are two who have an identical number of friends within the group. (Math Circles)

Problem 6. Five young workers received as wages 1500 rubles altogether. Each of them wants to buy a cassette player costing 320 rubles. Prove that at least one of them must wait for the next paycheck to make his purchase. (Math Circles)

Problem 7. Prove that of any 52 integers, two can always be found such that the difference of their squares is divisible by 100. (Math Circles)

Problem 8. The digits $1, 2, \ldots, 9$ are divided into three groups. Prove that the product of the numbers in one of the groups must exceed 71. (Math Circles)

Problem 9. Given 11 different natural numbers, none greater than 20. Prove that two of these can be chosen, one of which divides the other. (Math Circles)

Problem 10. A drawer in a darkened room contains 100 red socks, 80 green socks, 60 blue socks, and 40 black socks. A youngster selects socks one at a time from the drawer but was unable to see the color of the socks drawn. What is the smallest number of socks that must be selected to guarantee that the selection contains at least 10 pairs? (A pair of socks is two socks of the same color. No sock may be counted in more than one pair). (AMC)

(A) 21 (B) 23 (C) 24 (D) 30 (E) 50

Problem 11. A drawer contains a dozen each of red, blue, green, and white socks, all unmatched. Joan takes socks out at random in the dark. How many socks must Joan take out to be sure she has two pairs of white socks? (AMC)

(A) 38 (B) 39 (C) 40 (D) 41 (E) 42

Problem 12. Assume every student enrolled in a university comes from one of the fifty states in the U.S. Find the smallest number of students that must be enrolled in the university to guarantee that there are at least 100 students from the same state. (AMC)

(A) 5000 (B) 4950 (C) 4951 (D) 4999 (E) 5001

Problem 13. How many cards must be selected from a standard deck to be certain that three cards from the same suit are drawn?

SOLUTIONS:

Problem 1. Solution. We can draw three beads from the bag. If there were no more than one bead of each color among these, then there would be no more then two beads altogether. This is obvious, and contradicts the fact that we have chosen three beads. On the other hand, it is clear that choosing two beads is not enough. Here the beads play the role of pigeons,and the colors (black and white) play the role of pigeon holes. (Math Circles).

Problem 2. Solution: The pigeon holes are the remainders when divided by 11. The pigeons are the numbers. If two numbers have the same remainder when divided by 11, their difference must be divisible by 11. (Math Circles).

Problem 3. Solution: We are putting 25 "pigeons" (crates) into 3 "pigeon holes" (sorts of apples). Since $25 = 3 \cdot 8 + 1$, we can use the General Pigeon Hole Principle for $N = 3$, $k = 8$. We find that some "pigeon hole" must contain at least 9 crates. In analyzing this solution, it is instructive to restate it without any form of the Pigeon Hole Principle, using only a trivial counting argument (of the sort with which we proved the Pigeon Hole Principle). (Math Circles).

Problem 4. Solution: In solving this problem, we encounter a seemingly insuperable obstacle. There are 14 possible differences between the 8 given numbers (the values of the differences being 1 through 14). These are the 14 pigeon holes. But what are our pigeons? They must be the differences between pairs of the given numbers. However, there are 28 pairs, and we can fit them in our 14 pigeon holes in such a way that there are exactly two "pigeons" in each hole (and therefore no hole containing three). Here we must use an additional consideration. We cannot put more than one pigeon in the pigeon hole numbered 14, since the number 14 can be written as a difference of two natural numbers less than 15 in only one way: $14 = 15 - 1$. This means that the remaining 13 pigeon holes contain at least 27 pigeons, and the General Pigeon Hole Principle gives us our result. (Math Circles).

Problem 5. Solution: There are five possible numbers of acquaintances for any person: 0, 1, 2, 3, or 4. So it would seem that each could have a different number of friends. However, if any person has four acquaintances, then no person may have zero acquaintances. Hence two people must have the same number of acquaintaneds. (Math Circles).

Problem 6. Solution. The sum S of their earnings is 1500 rubles, so the above principle guarantees that at least one worker earned no more that $1500/5 = 300$ rubles. Such a worker must wait for his cassette player. (Math Circles).

Problem 7. Solution: When divided by 100, a perfect square can give only 51 remainders, since the numbers x^2 and $(100 - x)^2$ give the same remainder. Hence of 52 integers, the squares of two must must have the same remainder when divided by 100. These two squares differ by a multiple of 100. (Math Circles).

Problem 8. Solution: The product of the numbers in all the groups is $9! = 362880$. If the product of each group were no greater than 71, the product of all the numbers could only by $71^3 = 357911$. It should be noted here that this method of proof is, in a way, more general than the simple Pigeon Hole Principle. (Math Circles).

Problem 9. Solution: We can divide the numbers from 1 through 20 into ten disjoint sets, such that if a pair of numbers is selected from the same set, one of the pair divides the other: $\{11\}, \{13\}, \{15\}, \{17\}, \{19\}, \{1, 2, 4, 8, 16\}, \{3, 6, 12\}, \{5, 10, 20\}, \{7, 14\}, \{9, 18\}$. Then, of any eleven numbes not greater than 20, two of them must fit in one of these pigeon holes, and one fo these two divides the other. (Math Circles).

Problem 10. Solution: (B) For any selection, at most one sock of each color will be left unpaired, and this happens if and only if an odd number of socks of that color is selected. Thus, 24 socks suffice: at most 4 will be unpaired, leaving at least 20 in pairs. However, 23 will do! Since 23 is not the sum of four odd numbers, at most 3 socks of the 23 will be unpaired. On the other hand, 22 will not do: if the numbers of red, green, blue, and black socks are 5,5,5,7, then four are unpaired, leaving 9 pairs. Thus, 23 is the minimum.

Problem 11. (C) Suppose Joan picked a dozen each of the other colors before picking a white sock. Then she has picked $(12)(3) = 36$ socks from the drawer. The remaining socks are white, so to pick two pairs of socks requires four more draws. So the total number of socks Joan needs to remove to be sure she has two pairs of white socks is 40.

Problem 12. (C) Let x be the number of students and let the boxes be the 50 states. By the generalized Pigeon Principle, we need to find the smallest x so that $\left\lceil \dfrac{x}{50} \right\rceil = 100$. Now since $\left\lceil \dfrac{4950}{50} \right\rceil = 99$ and $\left\lceil \dfrac{4951}{50} \right\rceil = 100$, the answer is 4951.

Problem 13. 9 (cards).

BASIC KNOWLEDGE

General converting methods

Fractions, decimals, and percents are different names for the same number.

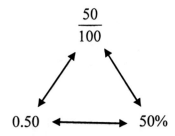

(a) To express a decimal as a percent, you just need to move the decimal point two times to the right.

(b) To express a fraction as a percent, first express the fraction as a decimal, then follow the step (a).

(c) To express a percent ($r\%$) as a fraction in simplest form, express the percent in the form $\dfrac{r}{100}$ and simplify.

(d) To express a percent ($r\%$) as a decimal, ignore "%" sign and treat r as an integer, then move the decimal point two times to the left.

Examples:

(1) Numbers with the denominator 10:

$0.5 = 0.50 = 50\%$ $\qquad$ $4.7 = 4.70 = 470\%$ $\qquad$ $25.8 = 25.80 = 2580\%$

(2) Integer to percent:

$4 = 4.00 = 400\%$ $\qquad$ $10 = 10.00 = 1000\%$ $\qquad$ $47 = 47.00 = 4700\%$

(3) Numbers with the denominators 1000, 10000,...:

$0.314 = 31.4\%$ $15.046 = 1504.6\%$ $0.4765 = 47.65\%$

$3.076481 = 3.076 = 307.6\%$

(4) Fraction to percent

$\dfrac{3}{5} = 0.6 = 60\%$ $1\dfrac{3}{4} = 1.75 = 175\%$ $\dfrac{9}{20} = 0.45 = 45\%$

$\dfrac{3}{40} = 0.075 = 7.5\%$ $\dfrac{5}{6} = 0.8\overline{3} \approx 0.83 = 83\%$ $\dfrac{5}{11} = 0.\overline{45} \approx 0.455 = 45.5\%$

$\dfrac{6}{7} = 0.\overline{857142} \approx 0.8571 = 85.71\%$

(5) Percent to fraction

$25\% = \dfrac{25}{100} = \dfrac{1}{4}$ (need to simplify) $75\% = \dfrac{75}{100} = \dfrac{3}{4}$ (need to simplify)

(6) Percents to decimals

$39\% = 0.39$ (only need to move the decimal point two times to the left)

$236.4\% = 2.364$ (only need to move the decimal point two times to the left)

Basic conversion numbers (need to memorize)

$1\% = 0.01 = \dfrac{1}{100}$ $12.5\% = 0.125 = \dfrac{1}{8}$ $75\% = 0.75 = \dfrac{3}{4}$

$2\% = 0.02 = \dfrac{1}{50}$ $15\% = 0.15 = \dfrac{3}{20}$ $100\% = 1$

$4\% = 0.04 = \dfrac{1}{25}$ $20\% = 0.2 = \dfrac{1}{5}$ $125\% = 1.25 = 1\dfrac{1}{4}$

$5\% = 0.05 = \dfrac{1}{20}$ $25\% = 0.25 = \dfrac{1}{4}$ $150\% = 1.5 = 1\dfrac{1}{2}$

$10\% = 0.1 = \dfrac{1}{10}$ $50\% = 0.5 = \dfrac{1}{2}$ $175\% = 1.75 = 1\dfrac{3}{4}$

$200\% = 2$

Examples: Calculate:

(1) 2.4×0.5
$= (2.4 \div 2) \times (0.5 \times 2) = 1.2 \times 1 = 1.2$

(2) 21.2×25
$= (21.2 \div 4) \times (25 \times 4) = 5.3 \times 100 = 530$

(3) 7.2×125
$= (7.2 \div 8) \times (125 \times 8) = 0.9 \times 1000 = 900$

(4) $13.6 \div 5$
$= (13.6 \times 2) \div (5 \times 2) = 27.2 \div 10 = 2.72$

(5) $14.4 \div 25$
$= (14.4 \times 4) \div (25 \times 4) = 57.6 \div 100 = 0.576$

(6) $3.5 \div 125$
$= (3.5 \times 8) \div (125 \times 8) = 28 \div 1000 = 0.028$

Decimals can be converted to fractions with the denominator 8.

$$0.125 = \frac{1}{8} \qquad 0.25 = \frac{2}{8} \qquad 0.375 = \frac{3}{8} \qquad 0.5 = \frac{4}{8}$$

$$0.625 = \frac{5}{8} \qquad 0.75 = \frac{6}{8} \qquad 0.875 = \frac{7}{8}$$

Examples: Compute

(**1**) 8×0.125 (**2**) 8×0.25 (**3**) 8×0.375 (**4**) 8×0.5

(**5**) 8×0.625 (**6**) 8×0.75 (**7**) 8×0.875

(**8**) $1 \div 0.125$ (9) $2 \div 0.25$ (10) $3 \div 0.375$ (11) $4 \div 0.5$

(12) $5 \div 0.625$ (13) $6 \div 0.75$ (14) $7 \div 0.875$

Decimals can be converted to fractions with the denominator 16.

$0.0625 = \dfrac{1}{16}$

$0.125 = \dfrac{2}{16}$

$0.1875 = \dfrac{3}{16}$

$0.25 = \dfrac{4}{16}$

$0.3125 = \dfrac{5}{16}$

$0.375 = \dfrac{6}{16}$

$0.4375 = \dfrac{7}{16}$

$0.5 = \dfrac{8}{16}$

$0.5625 = \dfrac{9}{16}$

$0.625 = \dfrac{10}{16}$

$0.6875 = \dfrac{11}{16}$

$0.75 = \dfrac{12}{16}$

$0.8125 = \dfrac{13}{16}$

$0.875 = \dfrac{14}{16}$

$0.9375 = \dfrac{15}{16}$

Examples: Compute:

(**1**) 16×0.0625

(**2**) 16×0.125

(**3**) 16×0.1875

(**4**) 16×0.25

(**5**) 16×0.3125

(**6**) 16×0.375

(**7**) 16×0.4375

(**8**) 16×0.5

(**9**) 16×0.5625

(**10**) 16×0.625

(**11**) 16×0.6875

(**12**) 16×0.75

(1**3**) 16×0.8125

(**14**) 16×0.875

(**15**) 16×0.9375

(**16**) $1 \div 0.0625$

(17) $2 \div 0.125$

(18) $3 \div 0.1875$

(19) $4 \div 0.25$

(20) $5 \div 0.3125$

(21) $6 \div 0.375$

(22) $7 \div 0.4375$

(23) $8 \div 0.5$

(24) $9 \div 0.5625$

(25) $10 \div 0.625$

(26) $11 \div 0.6875$

(27) $12 \div 0.75$

(28) $13 \div 0.8125$

(29) $14 \div 0.875$

(30) $15 \div 0.9375$

Some Fractions to Decimals Conversions:

(Rule: $\dfrac{a}{b} = m\dfrac{2a}{b}\%$, $m = b \times c$)

$\dfrac{1}{7}$	$14\dfrac{2}{7}\%$	$\dfrac{3}{7}$	$42\dfrac{6}{7}\%$
$\dfrac{2}{7}$	$28\dfrac{4}{7}\%$	$\dfrac{4}{7}$	$56\dfrac{8}{7}\%\ (57\dfrac{1}{7}\%)$
$\dfrac{5}{7}$	$70\dfrac{10}{7}\%\ (71\dfrac{3}{7}\%)$	$\dfrac{6}{7}$	$84\dfrac{12}{7}\%\ (85\dfrac{5}{7}\%)$

(Rule: $\dfrac{a}{b}=m\dfrac{a}{b}\%$, $m=11a$)

$\dfrac{1}{9}$	$11\dfrac{1}{9}\%$	$\dfrac{5}{9}$	$55\dfrac{5}{9}\%$
$\dfrac{2}{9}$	$22\dfrac{2}{9}\%$	$\dfrac{6}{9}$	$66\dfrac{6}{9}\%$
$\dfrac{3}{9}$	$33\dfrac{3}{9}\%$	$\dfrac{7}{9}$	$77\dfrac{7}{9}\%$
$\dfrac{4}{9}$	$44\dfrac{4}{9}\%$	$\dfrac{8}{9}$	$88\dfrac{8}{9}\%$

(Rule: $\dfrac{a}{b}=m\dfrac{a}{b}\%$, $m=9a$)

$\dfrac{1}{11}$	$9\dfrac{1}{11}\%$	$\dfrac{6}{11}$	$54\dfrac{6}{11}\%$
$\dfrac{2}{11}$	$18\dfrac{2}{11}\%$	$\dfrac{7}{11}$	$63\dfrac{7}{11}\%$
$\dfrac{3}{11}$	$27\dfrac{3}{11}\%$	$\dfrac{8}{11}$	$72\dfrac{8}{11}\%$
$\dfrac{4}{11}$	$36\dfrac{4}{11}\%$	$\dfrac{9}{11}$	$81\dfrac{9}{11}\%$
$\dfrac{5}{11}$	$45\dfrac{5}{11}\%$	$\dfrac{10}{11}$	$90\dfrac{10}{11}\%$

TYPICAL PROBLEMS IN MATHCOUNTS COMPETITIONS

Percents and Fractions

Example 1: Write the fraction equivalent to 80%.

Solution: $\dfrac{4}{5}$.

$$\frac{80}{100} = \frac{8}{10} = \frac{4}{5}$$

Example 2: Write the percent equivalent to $\dfrac{3}{4}$.

Solution: 75%.

Method 1: $\dfrac{3}{4} = \dfrac{3 \times 25}{4 \times 25} = \dfrac{75}{100} = 75\%$

Method 2: $\dfrac{3}{4} = 0.75 = 75\%$

Example 3: Write the percent equivalent of $\dfrac{3}{2}$.

Solution: 150%.

Method 1: $\dfrac{3}{2} = 1.5 = \dfrac{1.5}{1} = \dfrac{15}{10} = \dfrac{150}{100} = 150\%$.

Method 2: $\dfrac{3}{2} = \dfrac{3 \times 50}{2 \times 50} = \dfrac{150}{100} = 150\%$.

Example 4: Write the fraction equivalent to $62\dfrac{1}{2}\%$.

Solution: 5/8.

$$62\frac{1}{2}\% = \frac{125}{200} = \frac{5 \times 25}{8 \times 25} = \frac{5}{8}$$

Example 5: Write the percent equivalent to $\dfrac{7}{200}$.

Solution: 3.5%.

$$\frac{7}{200} = \frac{7 \div 2}{200 \div 2} = \frac{3.5}{100} = 3.5\%.$$

Fractions and Decimals

Example 1: Write the decimal equivalent of $\dfrac{7}{8}$.

Solution: 0.875.

$\dfrac{7}{8} = 7 \div 8 = 0.875.$

Example 2: Write the decimal equivalent of $\dfrac{3}{11}$.

Solution: $0.\overline{27}$.

$\dfrac{1}{11} = 0.\overline{09} \qquad \Rightarrow \qquad 3 \times \dfrac{1}{11} = 3 \times 0.\overline{09} = 0.\overline{27}$

Example 3: Write the decimal equivalent of $\dfrac{3}{16}$.

Solution: 0.1875.

$\dfrac{1}{16} = 0.0625 \quad \Rightarrow \quad 3 \times \dfrac{1}{16} = 3 \times 0.0625 = 0.1875$

Example 4: Express $1.4\overline{12}$ as a common fraction. .

Solution: $\dfrac{233}{165}$.

$1.4\overline{12} = 1 + 0.4\overline{12} = 1 + \dfrac{412 - 4}{990} = 1 + \dfrac{408}{990} = 1 + \dfrac{408 \div 6}{990 \div 6} = 1 + \dfrac{68}{165} = \dfrac{233}{165}$

Example 5: Express the product $0.\overline{63} \times 3.\overline{6}$ as a mixed fraction.

Solution: $2\dfrac{1}{3}$.

Example 6: What is the absolute value of the difference between $0.\overline{35}$ and $0.\overline{49}$? Express your answer as a common fraction.   (Mathcounts Competitions).

Solution: $\dfrac{14}{99}$.

$0.\overline{49} - 0.\overline{35} = \dfrac{49}{99} - \dfrac{35}{99} = \dfrac{14}{99}$.

Example 7: Express 0.0138 as a common fraction.

Solution: $\dfrac{69}{5000}$.

$$0.0318 = \frac{318}{10000} = \frac{69}{5000}$$

Example 8: Express $0.\overline{25} \div 0.\overline{5}$ as a common fraction.

Solution: $\dfrac{5}{11}$.

Method 1: $0.\overline{25} \div 0.\overline{5} = \dfrac{25}{99} \div \dfrac{5}{9} = \dfrac{25}{99} \times \dfrac{9}{5} = \dfrac{5}{11}$.

Method 2: $0.\overline{25} \div 0.\overline{5} = 0.\overline{25} \div 0.\overline{55} = \dfrac{0.\overline{25}}{0.\overline{55}} = \dfrac{5}{11}$.

Example 9: Express as a fraction: $0.\overline{1} + 0.\overline{001}$.

Solution: $\dfrac{112}{999}$.

Method 1: $0.\overline{1} + 0.\overline{001} = 0.\overline{111} + 0.\overline{001} = 0.\overline{112} = \dfrac{112}{999}$

Method 2: $0.\overline{1} + 0.\overline{001} = \dfrac{1}{9} + \dfrac{1}{999} = \dfrac{112}{999}$

Example 10: Express as a mixed number: $\dfrac{0.\overline{85}}{0.\overline{25}}$. (Mathcounts Competitions).

Solution: $3\dfrac{2}{5}$.

Method 1: $\dfrac{0.\overline{85}}{0.\overline{25}} = \dfrac{17}{5} = 3\dfrac{2}{5}$.

Method 2: $\dfrac{0.\overline{85}}{0.\overline{25}} = \dfrac{\dfrac{85}{99}}{\dfrac{25}{99}} = \dfrac{17}{5} = 3\dfrac{2}{5}$.

Decimals and percents

Example 1: Write the percent equivalent of 1.5.

Solution: 150%.

$$1.5 = \dfrac{1.5}{1} = \dfrac{150}{100} = 150\%$$

Example 2: Express as a decimal: 222% of $\dfrac{1}{2}$.

Solution: 1.11

Method 1: $222\% \times \dfrac{1}{2} = \dfrac{222}{100} \times \dfrac{1}{2} = \dfrac{111}{100} = 1.11$.

Method 2: $222\% \times \dfrac{1}{2} = 2.22 \times \dfrac{1}{2} = .111$.

Example 3: Subtract $0.1\overline{6} - \dfrac{4}{25}$

Solution: $\dfrac{1}{150}$.

$0.1\overline{6} - \dfrac{4}{25} = \dfrac{16-1}{90} - \dfrac{4}{25} = \dfrac{15}{90} - \dfrac{4}{25} = \dfrac{1}{6} - \dfrac{4}{25} = \dfrac{25-24}{150} = \dfrac{1}{150}$.

Example 4: Find the product $(\dfrac{3}{11})(2.\overline{4}) \times (0.\overline{6})$

Solution: $\dfrac{4}{9}$.

$$(\frac{3}{11})(2.\overline{4}) \times (0.\overline{6}) = \frac{3}{11} \times 2\frac{4}{9} \times \frac{6}{9} = \frac{3}{11} \times \frac{22}{9} \times \frac{6}{9} = \frac{4}{9}.$$

Example 5: Express 10% of 30% of 50 as decimal.

Solution: 1.5.
10% × 30% × 50 = 0.3 × 5 =1.5

Example 6: How many of the first 10 positive integers have reciprocals that are repeating decimals? (Mathcounts Competitions).

Solution: 4 integers.
1, 2, 4, 5, 8, and 10 will generate terminating decimals. 10 – 6 = 4.

Example 7: What number is 10% of 20% of 30% of 40? Express your answer as a decimal to the nearest hundredth. (Mathcounts Competitions).

Solution: 0.24.
10% × 20% × 30% × 40 = 0.1 × 0.2 × 0.3 × 40 = 0.24.

EXERCISES

Percents and Fractions

1. Write the common fraction equivalent to $8\frac{1}{3}$%.

2. Subtract 28.35 from 50 and express your answer as a mixed number.

3. To which common fraction is 0.09% equivalent?

4. Write the common fraction equivalent to $31\frac{1}{4}$%.

5. Express $42\frac{6}{7}$% as a common fraction.

6. Express $\frac{3}{8}$% as a common fraction.

7. Express $16\frac{2}{3}$% of $33\frac{1}{3}$ as a mixed number. (Mathcounts Competitions).

8. Express $12\frac{3}{4}$% as a common fraction.

9. Express $3\frac{3}{4}$% as a common fraction.

Fractions to Decimals

1. Express $\frac{13}{40}$ as a decimal percent.

2. Express as a decimal: $3\frac{2}{10} \times 4\frac{7}{10}$

3. Write the decimal equivalent of $\frac{7}{16}$.

4. What is the common fraction which is the reciprocal of 1.8?

5. Express $\dfrac{3}{41}$ as a decimal rounded to the nearest hundredth.

6. 0.125 is equivalent to what common fraction?

7. Express as a common fraction: $0.\overline{3} \times 0.\overline{6}$

8. Express the sum as a common fraction: $0.\overline{8} + 0.\overline{2}$

9. Express the ratio of $\dfrac{2}{7}$ to $1.0\overline{9}$ as a common fraction.

10. The decimal representation of a fraction ends on $0.\overline{3}$. When the decimal is changed to a common fraction and reduced to lowest terms, what is the denominator of the fraction?

11. Express $0.1\overline{73}$ as a common fraction.

12. Express the reciprocal of 2.3 as a common fraction.

13. Express as a decimal the value of $\dfrac{1}{2} + \dfrac{1}{4} + \dfrac{1}{10} + \dfrac{1}{20} + \dfrac{1}{100}$. (Mathcounts Competitions).

14. Express as a common fraction: $0.\overline{5} + 0.\overline{1} - 0.\overline{3}$.

15. What is the reciprocal of $0.\overline{63}$? Express your answer as a common fraction.

16. Express $0.4\overline{5}$ as a common fraction.

17. Express $0.1\overline{35}$ as a common fraction.

18. Express as a common fraction: $\dfrac{0.\overline{7}}{0.\overline{8}}$ (Mathcounts Competitions).

19. Simplify: $\dfrac{0.\overline{6}+0.\overline{3}}{0.\overline{9}}$ (Mathcounts Competitions).

20. Given $\dfrac{1}{13}=0.\overline{076923}$, find $\dfrac{3}{13}$.

21. Compute: $0.\overline{7}-0.\overline{4}+0.\overline{2}.$ Express your answer as a common fraction.   (Mathcounts Competitions).

22. Express the sum of $0.\overline{31}$ and $0.\overline{8}$ as a common fraction.

23. Compute: $1.\overline{1}\times0.01.$ Express your answer as a common fraction. (Mathcounts Competitions).

24. Express $0.\overline{45}+0.\overline{54}+0.5+0.4$ as a common fraction.

25. Write the fraction equivalent to $0.\overline{3}$.

26. Express $\dfrac{5}{16}$ as a decimal.

27. Write the decimal equivalent for $\dfrac{7}{8}$.

28. Write 0.76 as a common fraction.

29. Express $\dfrac{1}{30}$ as a decimal.

30. Express the reciprocal of 2.75 as a common fraction.

31. Express $0.\overline{26}$ as a common fraction.

32. Find the simplest common fraction equivalent to $0.03\overline{7}$.

33. Express the sum of $\dfrac{8}{9}$ and $\dfrac{9}{8}$ as a repeating decimal.

34. Find, in simplified fraction form, the reciprocal of 3.2. (Mathcounts Competitions).

Decimals and percents

1. Add: $0.\overline{2} + \dfrac{7}{9}$

2. Express the product $62.3 \times 2\dfrac{2}{5}$ as a decimal.

3. Write the decimal equivalent of 8%.

4. Express as a mixed number: $7\dfrac{3}{4} + 0.875 + 75.250$

5. Express 47% of 138 as a decimal correct to three significant digits.   (Mathcounts Competitions).

6. Compute 1.67% of 10 and express the answer as a decimal. (Mathcounts Competitions).

ANSWER KEYS:

Percents and Fractions

1. 1/12   2. 21 13/20   3. 9/10000   4. 5/16   5. 3/7

6. 3/800   7. $5\dfrac{5}{9}$ 8. $\dfrac{51}{400}$ 9. $\dfrac{3}{80}$

Fractions to Decimals

1. 32.5%   2. 15.04   3. 0.4375   4. 5/9

5. 0.07   6. 1/8   7. 2/9   8. 10/9

9. 20/77   10. 3   11. 86/495   12. 10/23

13. 0.91   14. $\dfrac{1}{3}$ 15. $\dfrac{11}{7}$ 16. $\dfrac{41}{90}$

17. $\dfrac{67}{495}$ 18. $\dfrac{7}{8}$ 19. 1   20. $0.\overline{230769}$

21. $\dfrac{5}{9}$ 22. $\dfrac{119}{99}$ 23. $\dfrac{1}{90}$ 24. $\dfrac{19}{10}$

25. 1/3   26. 0.3125   27. 0.875   28. 19/25

29. $0.0\overline{3}$ 30. $\dfrac{4}{11}$ 31. $\dfrac{26}{99}$ 32. $\dfrac{17}{450}$

33. $2.01\overline{38}$ 34. $\dfrac{5}{16}$

Decimals and percents

1. 1   2. 149.52   3. 0.08   4. 83 7/8

5. 64.9   6. 0.167

BASIC KNOWLEDGE

(1). RATIOS:

Ratios are used to compare two or more numbers.

For any two numbers a and b ($b \neq 0$), the ratio is written as $a : b = a \div b = \dfrac{a}{b} = a/b$.

Example 1: If 24 students in a class of 30 students were present, what percent of the students were absent?

Solution: 20%.

The number of student who were absent: $30 - 24 = 6$.

$6/30 = 0.2 = 20\%$.

Example 2: There are 16 girls in a class of 30 students. Find the ratio of girls to boys. Express your answer as a common fraction.

Solution: 8/7.

The number of boys in the class is $30 - 16 = 14$. $\Rightarrow$ $16/14 = 8/7$.

Properties of ratios:

The first term of a ratio can be any number. The second term can also be any number except zero.

If the two terms are multiplied by the same number d, the ratio does not change.

$a : b = (a \times d) : (b \times d)$

Example 4: $3 : 7 = (3 \times 5) : (7 \times 5) = 15 : 35$

If the two terms are divided by the same number c ($c \neq 0$), the ratio does not change.

$a : b = (a \div c) : (b \div c)$

Example 4: $10 : 15 = (10 \div 5) : (15 \div 5) = 2 : 3$

140

Example 5: $\dfrac{5}{6}:\dfrac{10}{13}=(\dfrac{1}{6}):(\dfrac{2}{13})=13:12$

If the total number of parts is $m = A + B$, and $A : B = a : b$, then

the fractional part of a is $\dfrac{a}{a+b}$, and

the fractional part of b is $\dfrac{b}{a+b}$.

$$A = \dfrac{a}{a+b}\times m, \text{ and } B = \dfrac{b}{a+b}\times m.$$

If the total number of parts is $m = A + B + C$, and $A : B : C = a : b : c$, then

the fractional part of a is $\dfrac{a}{a+b+c}$,

the fractional part of b is $\dfrac{b}{a+b+c}$, and

the fractional part of c is $\dfrac{c}{a+b+c}$.

$$A = \dfrac{a}{a+b+c}\times m, \quad B = \dfrac{b}{a+b+c}\times m, \text{ and } C = \dfrac{c}{a+b+c}\times m.$$

Example 6: A certain paint color is created by mixing 3 parts of blue with every 5 parts of red. How many gallons of blue paint are needed to mix 40 gallons of this color?

Solution: 15.

$$A = \dfrac{a}{a+b}\times m = \dfrac{3}{3+5}\times 40 = 15.$$

Example 7: In a group of 72 students if the ratio of boys to girls is 5: 3, how many boys are in the group?

Solution: 45.

$$A = \frac{a}{a+b} \times m = \frac{5}{5+3} \times 72 = 45.$$

Example 8: Keith bought paper for making origami figure. He bought 2 packages of orange paper, 3 packages of yellow paper, and 5 packages of blue paper. What fraction of the papers was blue?

Solution: $\frac{1}{2}$.

$$\frac{a}{a+b+c} = \frac{5}{2+3+5} = \frac{5}{10} = \frac{1}{2}$$

Example 9: Keith bought 10 packages of paper for making origami figure. The ratio of orange paper, yellow paper, and blue paper is 2 : 3 : 5. How many packages of blue paper did he buy?

Solution: 5.

$$A = \frac{a}{a+b+c} \times m = \frac{5}{2+3+5} \times 10 = 5.$$

(2) RATES:

A rate is a ratio used to compare two numbers of different units. If the second term of the ratio is 1, the rate is called a unit rate.

Example 10: Sam drove 100 miles in 2 hours. What are his rate and the unit rate?

Solution: The rate is 100 miles/2 hours and the unit rate is 50/1 or 50 miles per hour.

Example 11: Alex types 250 words in 20 minutes. How many hours will it take him to type a 7500 word paper?

Solution: 10.

The unit rate is $250 \div 20 = 12.5$ words per minute.

The time to type 7500 words is $7500 \div 12.5 = 600$ minutes $= 10$ hours.

Example 12: A car gets 27 miles per gallon. How many miles will it travel on 9 gallons of gas?

Solution: 243.

The number of miles will the car go is $27 \times 9 = 243$.

Example 13: A basketball player makes 80% of the shots he attempts in each game. In a certain game, he made 20 of his shots. How many shots did he attempt in the game?

Solution: 25.

Let x be the total number of shots he made.

$$0.8 \times x = 20. \qquad \Rightarrow \qquad x = 25.$$

Example 14: A pork roast should be cooked 50 minutes per pound. How many hours should a 6-pound roast be cooked? (Mathcounts Handbooks).

Solution: 5.

The number of hours it takes is $50 \times 6 = 300$ minutes $= 6$ hours.

(3). PROPORTIONS:

A proportion is an equation of two ratios. For example, $\dfrac{a}{b} = \dfrac{c}{d}$. We can find a if we know b, c, and d or we know b and the value of c/d.

Properties of Of Proportion:

Property 1: $\dfrac{a}{b} = \dfrac{c}{d}$ is equivalent to :

$$ad = bc, \qquad \dfrac{a}{c} = \dfrac{b}{d}, \qquad \dfrac{d}{b} = \dfrac{c}{a}, \qquad \dfrac{b}{a} = \dfrac{d}{c}.$$

Example 15: $\dfrac{8}{6} = \dfrac{4}{3} \quad \Rightarrow \quad 8 \times 3 = 4 \times 6 \qquad \dfrac{8}{4} = \dfrac{6}{3} \qquad \dfrac{3}{6} = \dfrac{4}{8} \qquad \dfrac{6}{8} = \dfrac{3}{4}$

Example 16: The ratio of width to length of a rectangular room is $\frac{4}{3}$ and the width is $8\frac{7}{10}$. What is the length?

Solution: $\frac{L}{W}=\frac{4}{3}$ $\Rightarrow$ $L=\frac{4}{3}W=\frac{4}{3}\times 8\frac{7}{10}=\frac{4}{3}\times\frac{87}{10}=\frac{58}{5}$

Property 2: If $\frac{a}{b}=\frac{c}{d}$, then $\frac{a+b}{b}=\frac{c+d}{d}$ and $\frac{a-b}{b}=\frac{c-d}{d}$

Example 17: $\frac{21}{7}=\frac{30}{10}$ $\Rightarrow$ $\frac{21+7}{7}=\frac{30+10}{10}$ $(=4)$ and $\frac{21-7}{7}=\frac{30-10}{10}$ $(=2)$.

Property 3: If $\frac{a}{b}=\frac{c}{d}$, then $\frac{a+b}{a-b}=\frac{c+d}{c-d}$.

Example 18: $\frac{21}{7}=\frac{30}{10}$ $\Rightarrow$ $\frac{21+7}{21-7}=\frac{30+10}{30-10}$ $(\frac{28}{14}=\frac{40}{20}=2)$.

Property 4: If $\frac{a_1}{b_1}=\frac{a_2}{b_2}=\frac{a_3}{b_3}=...=\frac{a_n}{b_n}$

Then $\frac{a_1+a_2+a_3+...+a_n}{b_1+b_2+b_3+...+b_n}=\frac{a_1}{b_1}$

Example 19: Find x if $\frac{2x-y}{5}=\frac{x+y}{10}=\frac{3}{5}$.

Solution: 3.

$\frac{2x-y}{5}=\frac{x+y}{10}=\frac{(2x-y)+(x+y)}{15}=\frac{3x}{15}=\frac{3}{5}$ $\Rightarrow$ $x=3$.

Example 20: If $\frac{y}{x-z}=\frac{x+y}{z}=\frac{x}{y}$ for three positive numbers x, y, and z, all different, then what is the value of $\frac{x}{y}$? (1992 AMC).

Solution: 2.

$$\frac{x}{y}=\frac{y}{x-z}=\frac{x+y}{z} \quad\Rightarrow\quad \frac{x}{y}=\frac{x+y+(x+y)}{y+(x-z)-z}=\frac{2x+2y}{x+y}=\frac{2(x+y)}{x+y}=2.$$

Proof of properties (2) and (3)

Since $\dfrac{a}{b}=\dfrac{c}{d}$, we have $\dfrac{a}{b}+1=\dfrac{c}{d}+1 \quad\Rightarrow\quad \dfrac{a}{a}+\dfrac{b}{b}=\dfrac{c}{d}+\dfrac{d}{d} \quad\Rightarrow$

$$\frac{a+b}{b}=\frac{c+d}{d} \qquad\qquad (1)$$

We also have $\dfrac{a}{b}-1=\dfrac{c}{d}-1 \quad\Rightarrow\quad \dfrac{a}{b}-\dfrac{b}{b}=\dfrac{c}{d}-\dfrac{d}{d} \quad\Rightarrow$

$$\frac{a-b}{b}=\frac{c-d}{d} \qquad\qquad (2)$$

$(1) \div (2)$, $\dfrac{a+b}{a-b}=\dfrac{c+d}{c-d}$ (note $a \neq b$ and $c \neq d$). $\qquad\qquad (3)$

Proof of Property 4: If $\dfrac{a}{b}=\dfrac{c}{d}$, then $\dfrac{a}{b}=\dfrac{c}{d}=\dfrac{a+c}{b+d}$.

We know that $\dfrac{a}{b}=\dfrac{c}{d} \Rightarrow ad=bc \qquad\qquad (1)$

Add "ab" to both sides of (1): $ab+ad=ab+bc \Rightarrow a(b+d)=b(a+c)$

$$\Rightarrow \frac{a}{b}=\frac{a+c}{b+d}.$$

We know that $\dfrac{a}{b}=\dfrac{c}{d}$. So $\dfrac{a}{b}=\dfrac{c}{d}=\dfrac{a+c}{b+d}$.

(4). CONTINUED RATIO

The ratio of three or more quantities is called the continued ratio. For example, $a{:}b{:}c$ is a combinations of three separated ratios $\Rightarrow$ $a{:}b$, $a{:}c$, and $b{:}c$.

(1) If $a : b : c = 2 : 3 : 4$, then $a : b = 2 : 3$, $b : c = 3 : 4$, and $c : a = 4 : 2$.

(2) If $a : b = 2 : 3$, $b : c = 3 : 4$, and $c : a = 4 : 2$, then

$$a : b : c = 2 : 3 : 4,$$

$$a : b = 2 : 3$$

$$b : c = 3 : 4$$

$$a : b : c = 2 : 3 : 4$$

(3) If $a : b = 2 : 3$, and $b : c = 5 : 4$ (note $3 \neq 5$), then $a : b : c = (2 \times 5) : (3 \times 5) : (3 \times 4) = 10 : 15 : 12$.

$$a : b = 2 : 3$$

$$b : c = 5 : 4$$

$$a : b : c = 10 : 15 : 12$$

Example 21: Three numbers a, b, and c in the ratios of $a : b = 3 : 4$ and $b : c = 5 : 6$ have a sum of 118. What are the values of a, b, and c?

Solution: $a = 30$, $b = 40$, and $c = 48$.

Method 1:
$a : b = 3 : 4 = 15 : 20$ and $b : c = 5 : 6 = 20 : 24$. By the property 2 of the continued ratio, we get: $a : b : c = 15 : 20 : 24$.

We also know that $a + b + c = 118$, so $a = \dfrac{15}{15 + 20 + 24} \times 118 = 30$,

Similarly, $b = 40$, and $c = 48$.
Method 2:
$a : b = 3 : 4$ and $b : c = 5 : 6$.
By the property 3 of the continued ratio, we get: $a : b : c = 15 : 20 : 24$.

so $a = \dfrac{15}{15 + 20 + 24} \times 118 = 30$, and $b = 40$, and $c = 48$.

Example 22: Machine A can fill 1 box of nails in 6 minutes. Machine B can fill 1 box of nails in 9 minutes. They started to work at the same time and they stopped also at the same time. Total they filled 100 boxes. How many were filled by machine A?

Solution: 60.

146

Method 1: Machine A would fill 3 boxes of nails in 18 minutes. Machine B would fill 2 boxes of nails in 18 minutes. So the ratio of their work is 3 : 2.

The number of boxes filled by machine A is: $\dfrac{3}{3+2} \times 100 = 60$.

Method 2: Since the ratio of their work is 3 : 2, let the number of boxes filled by machines A be $3x$, and the number of boxes filled by machines B be $2x$.

$3x + 2x = 100 \qquad \Rightarrow \qquad x = 20 \qquad \Rightarrow \qquad 3x = 60$.

Example 23: Alex paid \$945 to transport his animals by ferry. The costs are \$3, \$2 and \$1 for each cats, dog, and squirrel, respectively. The ratios of cats to dogs is 2 : 9, and dog to squirrel 3 : 7. How many cats were there?

Solution: 42.

The ratio of the number of animals can be obtained as follows:

$c : d = 2 : 9$ and $d : s = 3 : 7 \qquad \Rightarrow \qquad c : d : s = 6 : 27 : 63 = 2 : 9 : 21$.

Then the ratio of the cost is then: $(3 \times 2) : (2 \times 9) : (1 \times 21) = 2 : 6 : 7$.

So the cost for cats is calculated as follows:

$$\frac{2}{2+6+7} \times 945 = 126$$

The number of cats is $126 \div 3 = 42$.

Method 2:

$$3c + 2d + s = 945 \qquad\qquad\qquad (1)$$

$$\frac{c}{d} = \frac{2}{9} \qquad \Rightarrow \qquad d = \frac{9c}{2} \qquad\qquad (2)$$

$$\frac{d}{s} = \frac{3}{7} \qquad \Rightarrow \qquad s = \frac{7d}{3} = \frac{7}{3} \times \frac{9c}{2} = \frac{21c}{2} \qquad (3)$$

Substituting (2) and (3) into (1):

$$3c + 2 \times \frac{9c}{2} + \frac{21c}{2} = 945 \qquad \Rightarrow \qquad \frac{45c}{2} = 945 \qquad \Rightarrow \qquad c = 42.$$

EXERCISES

Problem 1. If a salesperson earns a commission of $60 for selling a $2000 article, what is the rate of commission?

Problem 2. If a realtor earns a 6% commission for selling a $70,000 home, what is the amount of the commission?

Problem 3. To keep her hair shiny, Rapunzel brushed her hair at the rate of 3 strokes every 2 seconds. How many times did she stroke her hair in an hour?

Problem 4. Jenny makes 5 out of every 6 foul shots she attempts. If she missed 36 foul shots in her career, how many did she make in her career?

Problem 5. A typist makes 5 errors for every 100 characters he types. How many errors does he make in 2 pages of typing if each page contains 25 lines with 70 characters per line?

Problem 6. A recipe for cookies calls for $\frac{1}{2}$ cup of peanut butter for every $1\frac{1}{4}$ cups of flour. How many cups of peanut butter are needed in a batch which uses 5 cups of flour?

Problem 7. If you make $20.00 for the first three hours of work, how many dollars would your total pay be if you worked a total of seven hours at the same rate? Round your answer to the nearest dollar.

Problem 8. A punch recipe calls for 21 cups of ginger ale and serves 15 people. How many cups of ginger ale would it take to make enough punch for 100 people?

Problem 9. F, U, and N lie on line l so that $\dfrac{FU}{UN} = \dfrac{2}{3}$. If $FN = 75$, find the number of units in the length of $\overline{UN}$.

Problem 10. Mushrooms are on sale for $0.98 for a half-pound. What is the cost (in dollars) of 10 pounds of mushrooms?

Problem 11. A certain map uses a scale of 1 cm on the map representing 150 km. The map distance between Pittsburgh and Mytown is 45 mm. How many kilometers from Pittsburgh is Mytown?

Problem 12. If it takes 5 gallons of paint to paint a 2000 ft² wall, how many gallons are needed to paint a similar 22,000 ft² wall?

Problem 13. The capacity of a tank sprayer is 320 gallons. If twenty gallons of water is mixed with 1.2 gallons of herbicide for each acre to be sprayed, to the nearest acre, how many acres can be sprayed if the tank is 75% full when the spraying begins?

Problem 14. A secretary types 54 words per minute. How many words can she type in 90 seconds?

Problem 15. If 60 pear pickers can pick 6000 pears in one minute, find the number of dozens of pears that 7 pear pickers can pick in one hour.

Problem 16. There are 3 more English teachers than math teachers at Harter Junior High. If the ratio of English to math teachers is 6:5, how many math teachers are there?

Problem 17. $\overline{AB}$ is a meter stick divided into centimeters, with point A at 0 and point B at 100. At which centimeter mark should point C be located so that the ratio of AC to CB is 21:4?

Problem 18. When a water tank is $\frac{1}{3}$ full, it contains 4000 gallons. How many gallons does it contain when it is $\frac{3}{4}$ full?

Problem 19. If 120 is divided into 3 parts which are proportional to 1, $\frac{1}{2}$, and $\frac{1}{6}$, what is the middle part?

Problem 20. A machine shop produces five hundred parts per hour in an eight-hour day with 0.5% of the parts defective. How many non-defective parts are produced in 7 days?

Problem 21. Find two numbers in the ratio of 2 to 5 that have a sum of 119.

Problem 22. In a factory, a machine can fill 180 jars in 15 minutes. How many jars can be filled in 50 minutes?

Problem 23. An elevator can hold the weight of 8 adults or 12 children. How many children could ride on the elevator with 6 adults?

Problem 24. If a stamp machine can make 360 stamps in 3 minutes, how many stamps can it make in eight hours?

Problem 25. A machine can fill 160 boxes of nails in 8 minutes. Each box contains 100 nails. How many boxes can be filled in one hour?

Problem 26. If 6 computer programmers can write 8 computer programs in 3 days, how many programmers will be required to write a series of 20 similar programs in 15 days?

Problem 27. How many rolls of paper will it take to wrap a box with dimensions half the dimensions of a box that requires two rolls of wrapping paper to wrap it? Express your answer as a common fraction.

Problem 28. Of a group of boys and girls at Central Middle School's after-school party, 15 girls left early to play in a volleyball game. The ratio of boys to girls then remaining was 2 to 1. Later, 45 boys left for a football game. The ratio of girls to boys was then 5 to 1. How many students attended the party?

ANSWER KEYS

Problem 1. 3%   **Problem 2.** $4200   **Problem 3.** 5400

Problem 4. 180   **Problem 5.** 175   **Problem 6.** 2

Problem 7. 47   **Problem 8.** 140   **Problem 9.** 45

Problem 10. $19.60   **Problem 11.** 675   **Problem 12.** 55 gal

Problem 13. 11   **Problem 14.** 81   **Problem 15.** 3500

Problem 16. 15   **Problem 17.** 84 cm   **Problem 18.** 9000

Problem 19. 36   **Problem 20.** 27860   **Problem 21.** 34 and 85

Problem 22. 600   **Problem 23.** 3   **Problem 24.** 57600

Problem 25. 1200   **Problem 26.** 3   **Problem 27.** 1/2

Problem 28. 90

1. BASIC KNOWLEDGE

ABBREVIATIONS:

Perimeter = P Area = A or S Length = l Width = w

Height = h Circumference = C Radius = r

Side lengths of a polygon = $a, b, c, \dots$

BASIC FORMULAS OF PERIMETERS AND AREAS

Triangle:

Perimeter of a triangle: $P = a + b + c$

Area of a triangle: $A = \dfrac{1}{2}bh_b$ h_b is the height on the side b.

For an equilateral triangle (three sides have the same length, a), the area $A = \dfrac{1}{4}a^2\sqrt{3}$.

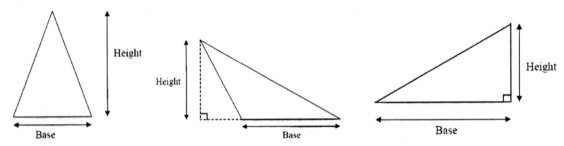

Example 1: What is the area of a triangle whose base measures 12 cm and whose height is 10 cm?

Solution: 60 cm^2.

$$A = \frac{1}{2}bh_b = \frac{1}{2} \times 12 \times 10 = 60$$

Example 2: What is the area of a right triangle whose legs measure 10 cm and 18 cm respectively?

Solution: 90 cm^2.

Since the triangle is a right triangle, any of the two legs can be the height and the other leg will be the base.

$$A = \frac{1}{2}bh_b = \frac{1}{2} \times 10 \times 18 = 90$$

Example 3: If the area of rectangle $ABCD$ is 24, find the area of $\triangle ABD$. (Mathcounts Handbooks)

Solution: 12.

The area of $\triangle ABD$ is half of the area of rectangle $ABCD$.
The answer is 24/2 = 12.

Example 4: The area of a triangle is 24 square units, and its height is 6 units. How many units are in the length of the base?

Solution: 8

$$A = \frac{1}{2}bh_b$$

$$24 = \frac{1}{2} \times 6 \times h_b \qquad\qquad \Rightarrow \qquad h_b = 8.$$

Rectangle:

Perimeter: $P = 2(L + W)$ Area: $A = L \times W$

This can be thought as the area of two triangles added together.

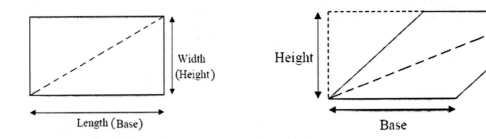

Example 5: What is the perimeter of a square whose edge measures 12 cm?

Solution: 48.

The perimeter of a square is 4 times the side length a:
$P = 4a = 4 \times 12 = 48$ cm.

Example 6: What is the area of a rectangle whose length is 9 cm and whose width is 8 cm? (Mathcounts Handbooks)

Solution: 72 cm^2.

Area: $A = L \times W = 9 \times 8 = 72$ cm^2.

Example 7: What is the perimeter of a rectangle whose length is 13 cm and whose width is 8 cm? (Mathcounts Handbooks).

Solution: 42 cm.
$P = 2(L + W) = 2(13 + 8) = 42$ cm.

Example 8: What is the area of a parallelogram whose base measures 14 cm and whose height is 9 cm? (Mathcounts Handbooks).

Solution: 126 cm^2.
Area: $A = L \times W = 14 \times 9 = 126$ cm^2.

Example 9: A rectangle is cut from the corner of a larger rectangle as shown. How many feet are in the perimeter of the shape?

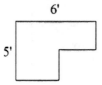

Solution: 22.

A good way to solve this problem is to move two red colored sides to each end. (Note the perimeter does not change before and after moving). After doing that, a rectangle is formed with known side lengths.

The perimeter is $P = 2(L + W) = 2(6 + 5) = 22'$.

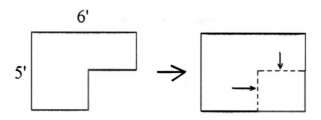

Example 10: How many square feet are there in the house with the dimensions shown in the figure?

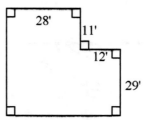

Solution: $1468(\text{ft}^2)$.

A good way to solve this problem is to move two red colored sides to each end. (Note the area does increase for the new figure by a part of $11 \times 12 = 131$ square units). After doing that, a rectangle is formed with known side lengths.

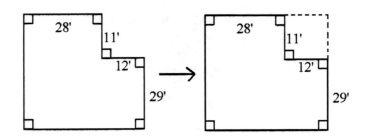

The area of new figure is $A = L \times W = (28 + 12) \times (29 + 11) = 40 \times 40 = 1600$.
The area of the original figure is then $1600 - 132 = 1468$.

Example 11: *ABCD* is a 4 × 6 rectangle formed by three 4 × 2 small rectangles. *B* and *E* are the centers of the arcs *AG* and *FC*, respectively. Find the shaded area.

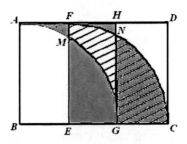

Solution: 8.
The shaded area is the same as the area of the rectangle *FHGH*, which is 4 × 2 = 8.

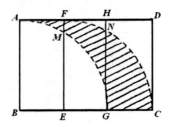

Trapezoid:

Perimeter of a trapezoid: $P = a + b + c + d$.

Area of a Trapezoid: $A = \dfrac{(b_1 + b_2)}{2}h$

This can be thought as the area of two triangles added together

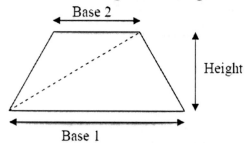

Example 12: What is the number of square centimeters in the area of the trapezoid shown? (Mathcounts Handbooks).

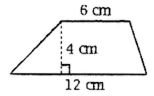

Solution: 36.

Area of a Trapezoid: $A = \dfrac{(b_1 + b_2)}{2} h = \dfrac{(6+12)}{2} \times 4 = 18 \times 2 = 36$

Example 13: If the perimeter of trapezoid ABCD is 42 cm, what is the number of square centimeters in its area?

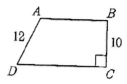

Solution: 100(cm^2).

Perimeter of a trapezoid: $P = b_1 + b_2 + c + d$ $\Rightarrow$ $42 = b_1 + b_2 + 12 + 10$

$b_1 + b_2 = 42 - 12 - 10 = 20$

So the area of the trapezoid: $A = \dfrac{(b_1 + b_2)}{2} h = \dfrac{20}{2} \times 10 = 100$

Rhombus:

Perimeter of a rhombus: $P = 4a$ (a is the side length).

Area of a rhombus: $A = \dfrac{1}{2}d_1 \times d_2$ (d_1 and d_2 are diagonals).

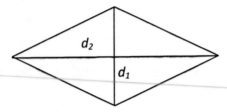

Example 14: Find the area of a rhombus whose diagonals have length 4 and 9.

Solution: 18 (units^2)

Area of a rhombus: $A = \dfrac{1}{2}d_1 \times d_2 = \dfrac{1}{2} \times 4 \times 9 = 2 \times 9 = 18$.

Circle:

Circumference (perimeter) $C = 2\pi r$

Area of a circle: $A = \pi r^2 = \dfrac{\pi}{4}d^2$

d is the diameter of the circle. $d = 2r$

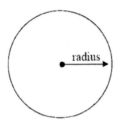
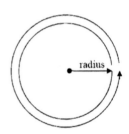

Sector:

Given a sector of a circle where l is the length of the arc and A is the area of the sector:

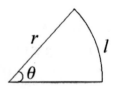

$l = 2\pi r \times \dfrac{\theta}{360}$;

$A = \pi r^2 \times \dfrac{\theta}{360}$

Example 15: What is the area of a circle whose radius measures 4 cm?

Solution: 16π cm^2.
$$A = \pi\, r^{\,2} = \pi \times 4^2 = 16\pi.$$

Example 16: What is the radius of a circle whose perimeter is 64π cm?

Solution: 32 cm.
$$C = 2\pi r \quad\Rightarrow\quad 64\pi = 2\pi \times r \quad\Rightarrow\quad 32 = r$$

Example 17: What is the radius of a circle whose area is 64π cm^2?

Solution: 8 units.
$$A = \pi\, r^{\,2} = 64\pi \quad\Rightarrow\quad 64\pi = \pi \times r^2 \quad\Rightarrow\quad 64 = r^2 \quad\Rightarrow\quad r = 8.$$

Example 18: If the circumference of a circle is 8π, what is its area?

Solution: 16π (units^2)
$$C = 2\pi r \quad\Rightarrow\quad 8\pi = 2\pi \times r \quad\Rightarrow\quad 4 = r$$
$$A = \pi\, r^{\,2} = \pi \times 4^2 = 16\pi.$$

Example 19: Find in terms of π the number of square inches in the area of the shaded region formed by the intersecting diameters of a circle with radius 6. (Mathcounts Handbooks).

Solution: 12π.
The sum of the angles of the shaded sectors is 120°. The shaded area is:
$$A = \pi\, r^{\,2} \times \frac{\theta}{360} = \pi \times 6^2 \times \frac{120}{360} = 36\pi \times \frac{1}{3} = 12\pi.$$

Ellipse

Perimeter: $P = 2\pi\sqrt{\dfrac{a^2+b^2}{2}}$

Area: $A = \pi\, ab$

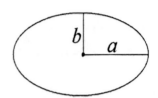

Example 20: A tennis racket is elliptical in shape. The formula for the area of an ellipse is $A = ab\pi$, where a is half of the width and b is half of the length. If the racket shown has a hitting surface of 35π square inches, find the number of inches in the width of the hitting surface. (Mathcounts Handbooks).

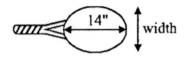

Solution: 10.

$A = ab\pi \qquad \Rightarrow \qquad 35\pi = \dfrac{14}{2}b\pi \quad \Rightarrow \quad b = 5 \qquad\qquad \Rightarrow \qquad\qquad 2b = 10.$

FURTHER KNOWLEDGE OF PERIMETERS AND AREAS:

(1) In a rectangle $ABCD$, if a, b, and c are all integers, then the area of $ABCD$ must be divisible by 12.

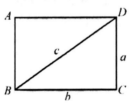

Example 21: Which one could be the area of rectangle $ABCD$ if the sides and the diagonal of the rectangle are all integers?
(a) 116   (b) 118   (c) 120   (d) 122   (e) 124

Solution: (c).
Only the answer (c) 120 is divisible by 12.

(2) Area of a triangle with sides a, b, and c (Heron Formula).

$$A = \sqrt{s(s-a)(s-b)(s-c)}$$

where $s = \dfrac{1}{2}(a+b+c)$ and a, b, and c are the three sides.

Example 22: Find the perimeter and the area of the triangle with the side lengths of 21, 28, and 35.

Solution: Perimeter $= 21 + 28 + 35 = 84$.

$s = \dfrac{84}{2} = 42$

$A = \sqrt{s(s-a)(s-b)(s-c)} = \sqrt{42(42-21)(42-28)(42-35)} = 294$

(3) Area of a quadrilateral inscribed in a circle with sides a, b, c and d.

$$A = \sqrt{s(s-a)(s-b)(s-c)(s-d)}$$

(4) Area of a rectangle with four cut areas

The rectangle is divided into four rectangles with areas as shown.

x	y
u	v

The following relationship is true: $x \times v = y \times u$

Example 23: A large rectangle is partitioned into four rectangles by two segments parallel to its sides. The areas of three of the resulting rectangles are shown. What is the area of the fourth rectangle? (AMC 1994 #2).

Solution: 15.

$6 \times 35 = 14 \times x$
$x = 15$

6	14
x	35

(5) In the parallelogram $ABCD$, T is any interior point, we have always:

$$S_{\triangle TAB} + S_{\triangle TCD} = \frac{1}{2} \times S_{ABCD}$$

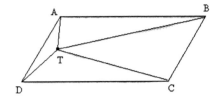

(6) For any point T on the plane of rectangle $ABCD$, we have always:

$$AT^2 + TC^2 = BT^2 + TD^2$$

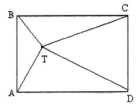

(7) Pick's law (Finding the area of the region bounded by grids)

For unit rectangular grid $Area = \frac{B}{2} + I - 1$

For unit triangular grid $Area = B + 2I - 2$

I is the number of points inside the region, not touching any of the sides. *B* is the number of points on the edges of the region.

Example 24: Find the area of each polygon.

(*a*).   (*b*).

Solution (*a*): 6.

$B = 8, I = 3, \quad A = 8/2 + 3 - 1 = 6.$

Solution (*b*): 14.

$B = 16, I = 7, \quad A = 16/2 + 7 - 1 = 14.$

EXERCISES:

Triangles

1. The perimeter of an equilateral triangle is $\dfrac{1}{27}$ units. How many units are in the length of one side?

2. In the figure shown, $AC = 4$, $CE = 5$, $DE = 3$, and angle ABC and angle CDE are right angles. Find the number of square units in the area of triangle ABC. Express your answer as a common fraction.

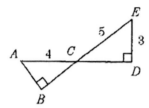

3. If $AC = 12$, $CD = 9$ and $BE = 3$, find the area of trapezoid $BCDE$.

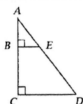

4. A and B are the midpoints of two adjacent sides of the rectangle shown, what is the area of the shaded region?

5. What is the ratio of the area of triangle ABC to that of the area of the square? Express your answer as a common fraction.

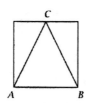

6. In $\triangle ABC$, $\angle B$ is a right angle. D is the midpoint of $\overline{AC}$, F is the midpoint of $\overline{BC}$, and E is the midpoint of $\overline{CF}$. $AB = 12$cm. $BC = 16$ cm. What is the number of square centimeters in the area of $\triangle BDE$? (Mathcounts Handbooks)

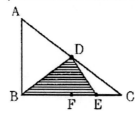

7. The area of the square is 64. C is the midpoint of $\overline{AD}$ and B is the midpoint of $\overline{AC}$. What is the area of the shaded region?

8. The point M is the midpoint of segment BE. What percent of the area of rectangle $BTRE$ is shaded?

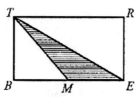

Rectangles

1. The side of a square measures 8 cm. If the perimeter of the square is decreased by 8 cm, by how many square centimeters is the area of the square decreased?

2. How many 9-inch square tiles are needed to cover the floor of a 12' × 18' rectangular room?

3. The measures of the sides of two squares are in the ratio 5: 3. What is the ratio of the area of the lesser square to the area of the greater square? Express your answer in the form $a : b$.

4. The diagonal of a square is 10. Find the area of the square.

5. What is the number of meters in the perimeter of a square which has an area of 49 square meters?

6. Find the number of square units in the area of a figure like the one shown. Right angles and dimensions are marked in the figure.   (Mathcounts Competitions)

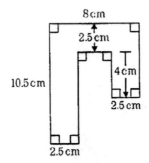

7. The sum of the lengths of the diagonals of a square is 24 cm. Find the number of square centimeters in the area of the square.

8. The length of a diagonal of a rectangle is 10. What is the maximum possible area of the rectangle?

9. What is the area of a square whose side measures 8cm?

10. The diagonal of the rectangle measures 17 cm. The height of the rectangle is 15 cm. Find the area of the rectangle.

11. A floor is completely covered with 120 tiles each 9 in. by 9 in. How many square feet are in the area of the floor? Express your answer as a mixed number. (Mathcounts Handbooks)

12. Find the perimeter of this figure, which consists of six congruent squares and has an area of 294 square units.

13. Given that all of the angles below are right angles, find the number of centimeters in the perimeter of the polygon. (Mathcounts Handbooks)

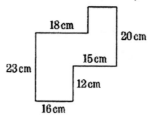

14. In the diagram, *ABCD* is a square. The area of rectangle *NFMD* is half the area of *ABCD*, and $ND = \frac{1}{2}CN$. If the area of *ABCD* is 36 square centimeters, what is the number of centimeters in the perimeter of rectangle *ABEM*?

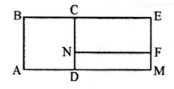

15. ABCD is a parallelogram with BC = 40, AB = 17, and AE = 8. Find the area of the parallelogram.

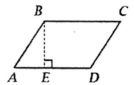

Trapezoids

1. Find the area of the shaded region within the trapezoid if $AB = 12$, $BC = 8$, $CD = 10$, and $\overline{AB}$ is perpendicular to $\overline{BC}$. (Mathcounts Competitions)

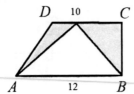

2. What is the area of a trapezoid whose bases measure 9 cm and 7 cm, respectively, and whose height is 5 cm?

3. An isosceles trapezoid has area of 24, height of 8, and one base of length 4. Find the number of units in the length of the other base.

Circles

1. If the radius of a circle is decreased by 10%, by what percent is its area decreased?

2. The diameter of a circle is 16. By what number must the radius be decreased in order to decrease the area of the circle by 48π

3. $\overline{OA}$ is the diameter of the smaller circle and the radius of the larger circle. How many square units are in the area of the shaded region?

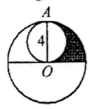

4. If the radius of the circle is 6 cm and the measure of the indicated central angle is 150^0, find the area of the shaded region. Let $\pi = 3.14$.

5. What is the number of meters in the circumference of a circle whose diameter is 6 m?

6. A square and an equilateral triangle share a side, and a circle with diameter 2 cm is centered at a vertex of the square. The radius of the circle is half the side length of the square. What is the number of centimeters in the perimeter of the shaded region? Express your answer as a decimal to the nearest tenth.

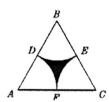

7. Equilateral triangle ABC has sides of length 2cm with midpoints $D, E,$ and F. $\overset{\frown}{DF}, \overset{\frown}{DE},$ and $\overset{\frown}{EF}$ are parts of circles with centers A, B and C, respectively. How many square centimeters are in the area of the shaded region? Express your answer in radical form in terms of π.

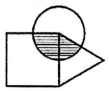

Others

1. Find the area of the shaded region if $ABCDEF$ is a regular hexagon and $BC = 6$.

2. What is the perimeter of a regular hexagon whose edge measures 9 cm?

3. What is the total surface area, in square centimeters, of a cube whose edge measures 9 centimeters?

4. The home plate used in baseball can be produced by adding two isosceles right triangles to a square as shown. What is the area of home plate in square feet?

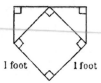

1 foot   1 foot

5. Parallelogram $ABCD$ has longer dimension 28cm as shown. $\overline{DE} \perp \overline{BC}$, and $\overline{CF} \perp \overline{AB}$ with lengths CF and DE shown. Find the number of square meters in the area of $ABCD$. (Mathcounts Handbooks)

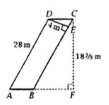

6. A, B and C lie on circle O so that $AC = BC = 1$. Find the number of square units in the area of circle O. Express your answer as a decimal in terms of π.

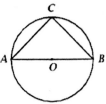

7. Find the number of square units in the area of the figure shown.

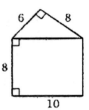

8. In right triangle *ABC*, *AB* = *BC*. What is the area of triangle *ABC*?

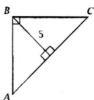

9. How many triangles in this diagram have an area equal to half the area of the rectangle?

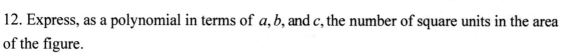

10. What is the ratio, expressed in the form $a:b$, of the area of triangle *ABC* to the area of triangle *ABD*?

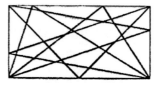

11. Figure *ABCD* is a parallelogram with diagonal $\overline{AC}$. $\overline{BE}$ is the median to side $\overline{CD}$, intersecting $\overline{AC}$ at *O*. If the area of *ABCD* is 120 units, find the number of square units in the areas of quadrilateral *AOED* and triangles *AOB*, *BOC*, and *EOC*.

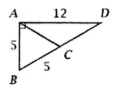

12. Express, as a polynomial in terms of a, b, and c, the number of square units in the area of the figure.

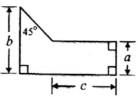

13. A stained glass window is composed of pieces of glass shaped as a semicircle, a rectangle, a square, an equilateral triangle, and two trapezoids. Find the number of square units, to the nearest tenth, of the region labeled *T*.

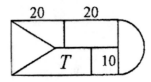

14. How many units are in the perimeter of the figure? Express your answer in simplest radical form.

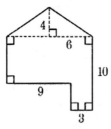

15. In the figure, how many units are in the perimeter of $\triangle ABC$ if $\overline{AP}$ ∥ $\overline{BC}$? Express your answer in simplest radical form.

16. *ABCD* and *EFGH* are congruent parallelograms. $AD = 10$ cm, $MC = 8$ cm, and the area of *ABCD* is 112 cm^2. What is the number of centimeters in $\overline{EN}$? Express your answer as a decimal to the nearest tenth.

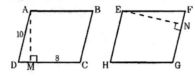

17. What is the total number of square units in the shaded regions of the 3 × 4 grid of unit squares? Express your answer as a common fraction.

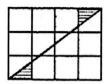

18. The vertices of square *EFGH* lie on the edges of square *ABCD*. $\dfrac{AE}{EB} = \dfrac{1}{2}$. What is the ratio of the area of square *EFGH* to the area of square *ABCD*?

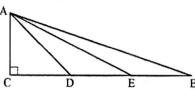

19. In the figure shown, $AC = CD = DE = EB$, and $AE = 4\sqrt{5}$ in. What is the number of square inches in the area of $\triangle ADB$?

20. *ABCD* is a square with vertex *A* at the center of the circle. *AE* = 10 in. What is the number of square inches in the area of $\triangle BCD$?

21. In the figure, $\overline{AP} \parallel \overline{BC}$. How many units are in the perimeter of $\triangle ABC$? Express your answer to the nearest whole number.

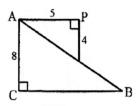

22. A square is constructed on diameter $\overline{AC}$ such that the area of the square is equal to the area of the circle. What percent of $\overline{AC}$ is $\overline{BC}$? Express your answer to the nearest whole number.

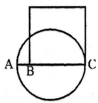

23. Square $ABCD$ has midpoints $E, F, G,$ and H. $AB = 15$ centimeters. Find the area of the shaded interior square in square centimeters.

24. Isosceles right triangle ABC has legs of length 4cm with midpoints D and E. $\overset{\frown}{DG}, \overset{\frown}{DE},$ and $\overset{\frown}{EF}$ are arcs of circles with centers A, B and C, respectively. How many square centimeters are in the area of the shaded region? Express your answer in terms of π.

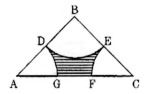

174

25.   Joe's French poodle, FooFoo, is tied to the corner of the barn which measures 40' × 30'. FooFoo's rope is 50' long In terms of π, over how many square feet can FooFoo wander? (Mathcounts Handbooks)

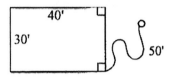

ANSWER KEYS:

Triangles

1. $\dfrac{1}{81}$ 2. $\dfrac{96}{25}$ (units^2)   3. 48 sq units   4. 3 sq units   5. 1/2
6. 36   7. 8 sq units   8. 25

Rectangles

1. 28(cm^2)   2. 384(tiles)   3. 9 : 25   4. 50(units^2)   5. 28(meters)
6. 50(units^2) 7.72(cm^2)   8. 50 (units^2) 9. 64 cm^2 10. 120 cm2
11. 67 ½ units   12. 98 units   13. 126   14.42   15. 600 sq

Trapezoids

1. 40(units^2)   2. 40 cm^2 3. 2

Circles

1. 19(%)   2.4   3. 2 π 4. 65.94 cm2   5. 6 π

6. 4.6   7.) $\sqrt{3} - \dfrac{\pi}{2}$.

Others

1. $18\sqrt{3}$ (units^2)   2. 54 cm   3. 486(cm^2)   4. 1.5 (ft^2)   5. 112
6. 0.5 π 7. 104   8. 25   9. 5   10. 5:13
11. 50, 40, 20, 10.   12. $\dfrac{1}{2}b^2 - \dfrac{1}{2}a^2 + ac$ 13. 213.4   14. $32 + 4\sqrt{13}$.
15. $18 + 2\sqrt{41}$ 16. 11.2   17.3/4   18. 5/9   19. 16

20. 25   21. 31.   22. 89   23. 45   24. $8 - 2\pi$

25. 2000 π.

BASIC KNOWLEDGE

1. Counting Using Charts

Example 1: Two dice are rolled. How many outcomes are there?

D₂ \ D₁	1	2	3	4	5	6
1	1,1	1,2	1,3	1,4	1,5	1,6
2	2,1	2,2	2,3	2,4	2,5	2,6
3	3,1	3,2	3,3	3,4	3,5	3,6
4	4,1	4,2	4,3	4,4	4,5	4,6
5	5,1	5,2	5,3	5,4	5,5	5,6
6	6,1	6,2	6,3	6,4	6,5	6,6

We have 36 outcomes.

Example 2: Two dice are rolled. How many ways are there to roll a sum of 5?

D₂ \ D₁	1	2	3	4	5	6
1	2	3	4	5	6	7
2	3	4	5	6	7	8
3	4	5	6	7	8	9
4	5	6	7	8	9	10
5	6	7	8	9	10	11
6	7	8	9	10	11	12

We have four ways of rolling a sum of 5.

Example 3: Alex, Bob, Catherine, and Debbie each makes a card. They put all four cards on a table and each person randomly takes one card. How many ways are there such that no one will pick up her or his own card?

Solution: 9.

Let *a* be the card made by Alex, *b* be the card made by Bob, *c* be the card made by Catherine, and *d* be the card made by Debbie.

First we consider the case that Alex picks up Bob's card. There are three possible ways:

A	B	C	D
b	a	d	c
b	c	d	a
b	d	a	c

 Similarly there are three ways Alex picks Catherine's card or Debbie's card.

Total 3 + 3 + 3 = 9 ways.

Try yourself:

1. A number cube has its faces numbered 1, 2, 3, 4, 5, and 6. A second cube has its faces numbered 2, 4, 6, 8, 10, and 12. If the cubes are rolled, how many ways are there that the sum of the numbers showing is 8?

Answer: 3.

2. Two different prime numbers are selected at random from among the first ten prime numbers. How many ways are there such that the sum of the two primes is 24?

Answer: 3.

3. Two standard dice are rolled and their face values multiplied. How many ways are there such that the product is a prime or ends in 6?

Answer: 12.

2. Counting Using Tree Diagram

You can use a tree diagram to list all the possible outcomes of events.

Example 4: How many possible outcomes are there if you toss a penny and a nickel at the same time?

Solution: 4.

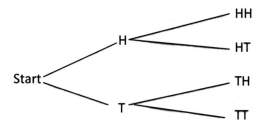

The possible outcomes are HH, HT, TH, and TT.

Example 5: A designer has 3 fabric colors he may use for a dress: red, green, and blue. Four different patterns are available for the dress. If each dress design requires one color and one pattern, how many different dress designs are possible? (Mathcounts Competitions)

Solution: 12 (designs).

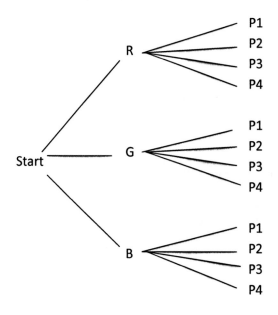

Example 6: Alex and Bob play tennis matches. The rule is that anyone who wins the first two games is the winner. If nobody wins after the first two games, then anyone who wins three games first is the winner. How many possible ways are there?

Solution: 14.

We have two cases.

Case I: Alex wins the first game.

We consider the cases where Alex wins the first game. The check mark in the chart means the winner. We have 7 possible ways of winning as shown in the chart below.

Case II: Bob wins the first game.

Similarly, we have 7 possible ways of winning.

Total possible ways is 7 + 7 = 14.

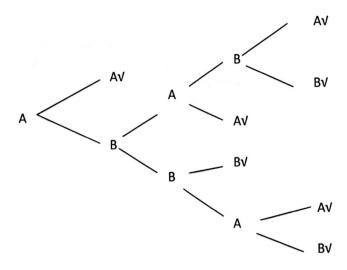

Try yourself:

1. How many 4-digit numbers can be formed by using the digits 2, 3, 4, and 5? No digit is allowed to be used twice in a number.

Answer: 24.

2. Using one kind of cheese, one kind of meat, and one kind of bread, how many different sandwiches can be made from the following:

Bread: rye, white, wheat, oatmeal
Cheese: cheddar, swiss
Meat: bologna, turkey, ham   (Mathcounts Competitions).

Answer: 24.

3. Counting using water pipes

Typical addition rule:

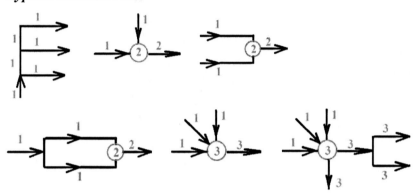

Example 7: Using only the line segments given in the indicated direction, how many paths are there from A to B?

Solution: 6.

Think about water flowing in pipes (line segments). The starting point is the source of the water. When two or more branches of water meet, they add and the addition carries to next segment.

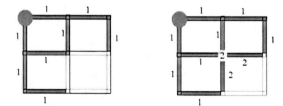
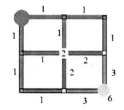

Example 8: If you must always be moving from the left toward the right, how many paths can you take from point S to point T? (Mathcounts Competitions).

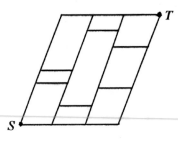

Solution: 14.

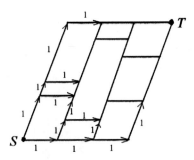   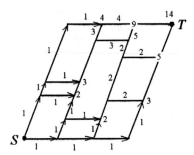

Try yourself:

1. In the plane figure, only downward motion (movement leaving you relatively lower than where you were) is allowed. Find the total number of paths from A to B.

Answer: 11.

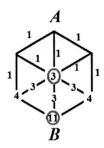

2. The configuration shown is built from 28 segments. How many paths from A to B if one can only walk from left toward right and from down to up use these segments?

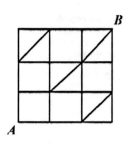

Answer: 26.

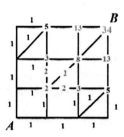

3. Using only the paths and the indicated directions, how many different routes are there from A to J? (Mathcounts Competitions).

Answer: 22 routes.

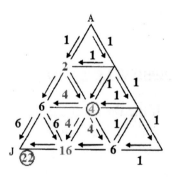

4. The Sum Rule

If an event E_1 can happen in n_1 ways, event E_2 can happen in n_2 ways, event E_k can happen in n_k ways, and if any event E_1, E_2,.. or E_k happens, the job is done, then the total ways to do the job is $n_1 + n_2 + \cdots + n_k$.

Example 9: In how many ways can one book be selected from a book shelf of 5 paperback books and 3 hardcover books?

Solution: 8.

The event is to select one book. No matter if it is hardcover or paperback, as long as we select one book, our job is done. So we can use the sum rule to get the number of ways:

$5 + 3 = 8$.

Example 10: A palindrome number is a number that is the same when written forwards or backwards. How many palindrome numbers less than 1000 are there?

Solution: 109.

There are 10 one-digit palindromes: 0, 1, 2, 3, 4, 5, 6, 7, 8, and 9.

There are 9 two-digit palindromes: 11, 22, 33, 44, 55, 66, 77, 88, 99.

There are 90 3-digit palindromes: 101, 111, 121, ...999.

Total: $10 + 9 + 90 = 109$.

Try yourself: Park Middle School's math club consists of 6 boys and 4 girls from 6th grade, 4 boys and 3 girls from 7th grade, and 5 boys and 5 girls from 8th grade. How many ways are there to select one student from the club to represent the school for a big math competition?

Answer: 27.

5. The Product Rule (Fundamental Counting Principle)

When a task consists of k separate parts, if the first part can be done in n_1 ways, the second part can be done in n_2 ways, and so on through the kth part, which can be done in n_k ways, then total number of possible results for completing the task is given by the product:

$$n_1 \times n_2 \times n_3 \times \cdots \times n_k$$

Note:

$n \times (n-1) \times (n-2) \times (n-3)...\times 1 = n!$

$n!$ is called the factorial and is the number of ways to arrange n objects in a row.

$1! = 1$ $0! = 1$.

Factorial table

Number n	Factorial $n!$
0	1
1	1
2	2
3	6
4	24
5	120
6	720
7	5040

Example 11: How many ways are there to arrange 5 people in a row of 5 seats?

Solution: 5! = 120.

Example 12: How many 3-digit positive integers are there by using the digits 3, 4 and 5? No digit is allowed to be used twice in any such 3-digit number.

Solution: 3! = 6.

Example 13: A girl has 5 shirts, 4 skirts, and 3 pairs of shoes. How many different outfits can she create? (Mathcounts Competitions).

Solution: 60(outfits).

We see three steps to finish the job (assembling an outfit). If one step is missing, the job is not done. Only when 3 parts are done, the job is done.

She has 5 ways to select a shirt, 4 ways to select a skirt, and 3 ways to select a pair of shoes.

By the product rule, we have $5 \times 4 \times 3 = 60$ outfits.

Example 14: A boy is walking along the line starting from point A to point B. Any point of intersection and line cannot be walked twice in one trip. How many ways are there?

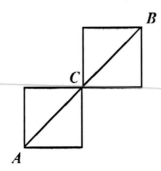

Solution: 9.

The job (walking from A to B) is done only if he finishes two steps: walking from A to C, and walking from C to B.

The boy has 3 ways from A to C, and 3 ways from C to B. The job (walking from A to B) can be done in $3 \times 3 = 9$ ways.

Example 15: Park Middle School's math club consists of 6 boys and 4 girls from 6th grade, 4 boys and 3 girls from 7th grade, and 5 boys and 5 girls from 8th grade. How many ways are there to select one student from each grade to represent the school for a big math competition?

Solution: 700

The event is to select one student from each grade. There are 10 ways to select one student from 6th grade, 7 ways from 7th grade, and 10 ways from 8th grade. Only when all steps are done, the job is finished. The number of ways is $10 \times 7 \times 10 = 700$.

<u>Try yourself:</u>

1. How many 3-digit numbers can be formed using the digits 1, 2, 3, 4, 5, 6, and 7? No digit is allowed to be used twice in any such 3-digit number.

Solution: 210.

2. The only moves allowed along the edges of the figure are to the right or down. How many different paths are there from *A* to *B*? (Mathcounts Handbooks).

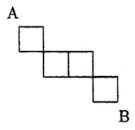

Answer: 12 paths.

3. A coin is flipped eight times, and the sequence of heads and tails occurring is recorded. How many distinct sequences are possible?

Answer: 256 (sequences).

6. Counting with restriction

Example 16: In how many ways can 5 books be arranged on a shelf if two of the books must remain together, but may be interchanged? (Mathcounts Handbooks).

Solution: 48.

We tie these two books, say book A and book B together, and treat them as one book. Our problem becomes to arrange 4 books on a shelf without restriction:

$$\underline{4} \times \underline{3} \times \underline{2} \times \underline{1} = 4! = 24.$$

Then we un-tie these two books and switch their position (AB $\Rightarrow$ BA), the answer will then be: $2 \times 24 = 48$.

Example 17: How many different even natural numbers each containing three distinct digits can be written using just the digits 0, 2, 3, 5, and 8? (Mathcounts Competitions).

Solution: 30

We know that "0" cannot be the first digit in a number, but we first pretend that it can be.

If the number is even then its last digit must be even. There are only three even digits to choose from. Then we arrange the remaining digits.

$4 \times 3 \times 3 = 36$

We now have to subtract the numbers that have "0" in the hundreds digit place. So we first put "0" in the hundreds place. Then we have 2 remaining digits that are even to choose from to put in the units digit. Lastly for the tens digit we can choose any of the remaining numbers:

$1 \times 3 \times 2 = 6$

Subtract and get 30.

Example 18: How many ways can 5 distinct paperback books and 1 hardcover book be arranged on a shelf if the hardcover must be the rightmost book on the shelf? (Mathcounts Competitions).

Solution: 120 (ways)

The rightmost book must be hardcover so there is only one way. The next five books have no restrictions so they can be any of the remaining books arranged.

$1 \times 5 \times 4 \times 3 \times 2 \times 1 = 120$

Try yourself:

1. How many different ways can 5 people be seated in a row of five seats if Alex and Bob must not be in adjacent seats?

Answer: 72.

2. How many different three-digit odd numbers can be formed using the digits 1, 2, 3, and 4 if no digit is repeated in a number?

Answer: 12(numbers).

EXERCISES:

Problem 1. A 35 mm slide is mounted in a 2 inch by 2 inch holder. How many different ways could the slide be inserted into the projector? (Mathcounts Competitions).

Problem 2. In how many ways can 7 different colors be arranged in a row if the first is always red, the last is always blue, and the middle one is always yellow?

Problem 3. A room has 5 doorways. A student enters the room and leaves through a different doorway. In how many ways can this be done?

Problem 4. How many different three-digit odd positive integers can be made using the digits 3, 4, 5, and 6 if no digit can be used more than once in a number?

Problem 5. Using only the line segments given in the indicated direction, how many paths are there from A to B? (Mathcounts Competitions).

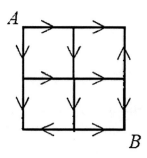

Problem 6. How many 3-digit positive integers can be formed using no zeros and at least one 7?

Problem 7. How many different 4-digit numbers can be made using the digits 1, 1, 9, and 9?

Problem 8. In how many different orders can six candidates be listed on the ballot?

Problem 9. The configuration shown is built from 27 segments. How many paths from A to B use exactly five of these segments? (Mathcounts Competitions).

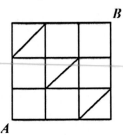

Problem 10. How many even four-digit numbers can be formed if the sum of the middle two digit must be 10?

Problem 11. How many different, positive three-digit integers can be formed using any three of the following five digits: 1, 2, 2, 3 and 3?

Problem 12. How many different line segments can be formed by marking seven distinct points on a line?

Problem 13. How many even four-digit numbers greater than 7000 can be formed using the digits 3, 4, 5, 7 and 9 when no repetition of digits is allowed in a number? (Mathcounts Competitions).

Problem 14. How many positive four-digit even positive integers can be written without using any of the digits 0, 1, 2, 3 or 4?

Problem 15. In how many different ways can three students be seated in a row of five chairs?

Problem 16. If the digits can be used more than once, how many different, even three-digit integers can be written using the digits 1, 2, 3, 5, and 7?

Problem 17. How many pairs of unit squares can be chosen on a 3 by 4 array of unit squares if sharing a common side is not permitted?

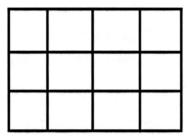

Problem 18. If the digits can be used more than once, how many positive even three-digit integers can be created using the digits 2, 3, 4, 5, 7 and 9?

Problem 19. How many even four-digit counting numbers can be formed by choosing digits from the set {1, 2, 3, 4, 5} if digits can be used more than once?

Problem 20. How many different four-digit positive integers can be obtained by using any four of the digits 2, 3, 4, 4 and 4?

Problem 21. How many different ways can six students be seated in a row of seven seats if Jim and John must be in adjacent seats?

Problem 22. Alex, Bob, Charles, and Dan are sitting in a row with the first to fourth places starting from left to right. How many ways are there if Alex does not sit in the first place, Bob does not sit in the second place, Charles does not sit in the third place, and Dan does not sit in the fourth place?

Problem 23. Four students are taking some pictures. One of the four must be the cameraperson and the rest are standing in a row when taking the picture. How many arrangements are there?

Problem 24. How many numbers are there from 1995 to 5895 that have the same tens digit and units digit?

Problem 25. Numbers 12321, 50005, and 61016 are called palindromes (a palindrome number is a number that is the same when written forwards or backwards). How many 5-digit even palindromes are there?

Problem 26. How many numbers from 1 to 400 are there that do not contain the digit 5?

Problem 27. Twenty five books of the same kind are divided into 6 groups. Each group has at least one book and each group has a different number of books. How many ways are there to divide the books?

Problem 28. There are six cards labeled 2, 3, 4, 5, 6, and 7 respectively. Take out any five cards from the six and put them in a row to form a 5-digit number. How many different 5-digit numbers can be formed?

Problem 29. Seven identical balls are put into four different boxes with each box at least one ball. How many ways are there to do so?

Problem 30. Using only the paths that follow the line segments and go downward, how many different paths go from A to Z? (Mathcounts Competitions).

ANSWER KEYS:

Problem 1. 8(ways)   **Problem** 2. 24(ways)   **Problem** 3. 20(ways)

Problem 4. 12(numbers)   **Problem** 5. 4.   **Problem** 6. 217(numbers)

Problem 7. 6(numbers)   **Problem** 8. 720   **Problem** 9. 6(paths)

Problem 10. 405(numbers) **Problem** 11. 18(numbers)   **Problem** 12. 21(segments)

Problem 13. 12(numbers)   **Problem** 14. 250(numbers) **Problem** 15. 60

Problem 16. 25   **Problem** 17. 49   **Problem** 18. 72

Problem 19. 250   **Problem** 20. 20   **Problem** 21. 1440

Problem 22. 9.   **Problem** 23. 24.   **Problem** 24. 390.

Problem 25. 400.   **Problem** 26. 324   **Problem** 27. 5.

Problem 28. 720.   **Problem** 29. 20.   **Problem** 30. 60 paths.

BASIC KNOWLEDGE

1. DEFINITION:

$$\underbrace{a \times a}_{2 \text{ a's}} = a^2 \qquad \underbrace{a \times a \times a}_{3 \text{ a's}} = a^3 \qquad \underbrace{a \times a \times a \times a}_{4 \text{ a's}} = a^4 \qquad \underbrace{a \times a \times a \times a \times a \ldots a}_{n \text{ times}} = a^n$$

a is an integer, decimal, or fraction and is called **the base.** n is any counting number and is called **the exponent**.

An exponent is used to show how many times the base is multiplied.

Exponent form	Read	General form	Value
2^2	Two to the second power or 2 squared	2×2	4
2^3	Two to the third power or 2 cubed	$2 \times 2 \times 2$	8
2^5	Two to the fifth power	$2 \times 2 \times 2 \times 2 \times 2$	32
2^{10}	Two to the tenth power	$2 \times 2 \times 2 \times 2 \times 2 \times 2 \times 2 \times 2 \times 2 \times 2$	1024

Note:

$2^4 \neq 2 \times 4$ since $2^4 = 16$ and $2 \times 4 = 8$.

$2^3 \neq 3^2$ since $2^3 = 8$ and $3^2 = 9$.

Generally $a^m \neq m^a$ but $2^4 = 4^2$ since $2^4 = 16$ and $4^2 = 16$.

2. PROPERTIES OF EXPONENTS:

Property 1: $a^0 = 1$

Examples:

1. $1^0 = 1$ 2. $0.1^0 = 1$

3. $10^0 = 1$ 4. $100^0 = 1$

5. $2012^0 = 1$ 6. $0.02^0 = 1$

7. $2.11^0 = 1$

8. $(\frac{1}{7})^0 = 1$

9. $(5\%)^0 = 1$

10. $(3^{100})^0 = 1$

Note: $(0)^0$ is not defined and $(0)^0 \neq 1$.

Property 2: $a^1 = a$

Examples:

1. $1^1 = 1$

2. $0.1^1 = 0.1$

3. $10^1 = 10$

4. $100^1 = 100$

5. $2012^1 = 2012$

6. $0.02^1 = 0.02$

7. $2.11^1 = 2.11$

8. $(\frac{1}{7})^1 = \frac{1}{7}$

9. $(5\%)^1 = 5\%$

10. $(3^{100})^1 = 3^{100}$.

Property 3: $a^m \times a^n = a^{m+n}$ $\quad\Leftrightarrow\quad$ $a^{m+n} = a^m \times a^n$ (Power rule)

Note: $a^m + a^n \neq a^{m+n}$

Examples:

1. $2^3 \times 2^7 = 2^{3+7} = 2^{10} = 1024$.

2. $3^2 \times 3^3 = 3^{2+3} = 3^5 = 243$.

3. $x^3 \times x^7 = x^{3+7} = x^{10}$.

4. $\left(\frac{1}{2}\right)^3 \times \left(\frac{1}{2}\right)^2 = \left(\frac{1}{2}\right)^{3+2} = \left(\frac{1}{2}\right)^5 = \frac{1}{2} \times \frac{1}{2} \times \frac{1}{2} \times \frac{1}{2} \times \frac{1}{2} = \frac{1}{32}$

Property 4: $\dfrac{a^m}{a^n} = a^{m-n}$ (Quotient rule).

Examples:

1. $\dfrac{2^5}{2^3} = 2^{5-3} = 2^2 = 4$.

2. $\dfrac{3^5}{3^2} = 3^{5-2} = 3^3 = 27$.

3. $\dfrac{5^5}{5} = 5^{5-1} = 5^4 = 625$.

4. $\dfrac{\left(\dfrac{1}{2}\right)^5}{\left(\dfrac{1}{2}\right)^3} = \left(\dfrac{1}{2}\right)^{5-3} = \left(\dfrac{1}{2}\right)^2 = \dfrac{1}{2} \times \dfrac{1}{2} = \dfrac{1}{4}$.

Property 5: $(a^m)^n = a^{mn}$ $(ab)^n = a^n b^n$ (Power rule)

Examples:

1. $(2^2)^5 = 2^{2\times 5} = 2^{10} = 1024$.
3. $(x^3)^7 = x^{3\times 7} = x^{21}$.

2. $(3^2)^3 = 3^{2\times 3} = 3^6 = 729$.
4. $(xy)^7 = x^7 y^7$.

Property 6: $\dfrac{a^m}{b^m} = \left(\dfrac{a}{b}\right)^m$ $\Leftrightarrow$ $\left(\dfrac{a}{b}\right)^m = \dfrac{a^m}{b^m}$ (Power rule)

Examples:

1. $\dfrac{6^5}{2^5} = \left(\dfrac{6}{2}\right)^5 = 3^5 = 243$.

2. $\dfrac{15^3}{3} = \left(\dfrac{15}{3}\right)^3 = 5^3 = 125$.

3. $\left(\dfrac{28}{15}\right)^4 \times \left(\dfrac{15}{4}\right)^4 = \dfrac{28^4}{15^4} \times \dfrac{15^4}{4^4} = \dfrac{7^4 \times 4^4}{4^4} = 7^4 = 2401$.

4. $\dfrac{2^8}{\left(\dfrac{2}{3}\right)^8} = \dfrac{2^8}{\dfrac{2^8}{3^8}} = 3^8 = 6561$.

Property 7: $a^{-n} = \dfrac{1}{a^n}$ (Negative exponents)

Examples:

1. $4^{-2} = \dfrac{1}{4^2} = \dfrac{1}{16}$.

2. $\left(\dfrac{3}{5}\right)^{-5} = \dfrac{1}{\left(\dfrac{3}{5}\right)^5} = \dfrac{1}{\dfrac{3^5}{5^5}} = \dfrac{5^5}{3^5} = \dfrac{3125}{243}$.

Property 8: $a^{\frac{m}{n}} = \left(a^{\frac{1}{n}}\right)^m$ (Rational exponents)

Examples:

1. $625^{\frac{5}{4}} = \left(5^4\right)^{\frac{5}{4}} = 5^5 = 3125$.   2. $(16)^{-\frac{3}{4}} = \dfrac{1}{(16)^{\frac{3}{4}}} = \dfrac{1}{(2^4)^{\frac{3}{4}}} = \dfrac{1}{2^3} = \dfrac{1}{8}$.

3. SOLVING EXPONENT EQUATIONS

$a^m = a^n$ if and only if $m = n$.

Example 1: Solve for x: $5^3 = 5^x$.

Solution: 3.
We know that $a^m = a^n$ if and only if $m = n$.
So $x = 3$.

Example 2: Solve for x: $3^x = 81$.

Solution: 4.
Since $81 = 3^4$, so $3^x = 3^4$ $\Rightarrow$ $x = 4$.

4. COMPARING TWO EXPONENTS

Example 3: Which number is greater: 31^{11} or 17^{14}? (Math circles).

Solution: 17^{14}.
$31^{11} < 32^{11} = (2^5)^{11} = 2^{55}$
$17^{14} > 16^{14} = (2^4)^{14} = 2^{56}$
So $17^{14} > 2^{56} > 2^{55} > 32^{11} > 31^{11}$.

Example 4: Which number is greater: 2^{300} or 3^{200}? (Math circles).

Solution:
By the power rule $(a^m)^n = a^{mn}$,
$2^{300} = (2^3)^{100}$
$= 8^{100}$
$3^{200} = (3^2)^{100} = 9^{100}$
Clearly $8^{100} < 9^{100}$, that is, 2^{300} is smaller than 3^{200}.

Example 5: Which number is greater: 2^{40} or 3^{28}? (Math circles).

Solution:
By the power rule $(a^m)^n = a^{mn}$,
$2^{40} = (2^{10})^4$ and $3^{28} = (3^7)^4$.
$2^{10} = 1024$ and $3^7 = 2187$
Since $2187 > 1024$, 2^{40} is smaller than 3^{28}.

Example 6: Which number is greater: 5^{44} or 4^{53}? (Math circles).

Solution:
By the power rule $(a^m)^n = a^{mn}$,
$4^{53} = 2^{106} > 2^{105} = (2^7)^{15}$.
$5^{44} < 5^{45} = (5^3)^{15}$.
Since $2^7 = 128 > 5^3 = 125$
4^{53} is greater than 5^{44}.

Example 7: Which number is greater: 100^{100} or $50^{50} \times 150^{50}$? (Math circles).

Solution:
$100^{100} = (100^2)^{50} = 10000^{50}$ and $50^{50} \times 150^{50} = (50 \times 150)^{50} = (7500)^{50}$
Since $10000 > 7500$, 100^{100} is greater than $50^{50} \times 150^{50}$.

EXERCISES

Problem 1. What is the base in the expression $(2a)^4$. (Mathcounts Handbooks).

Problem 2. Simplify: $(3^5 - 2^2)^2$.

Problem 3. Simplify: $(\frac{3}{2})^0 (\frac{2}{3})^3$.

Problem 4. Express in simplest form: $(2^3 \cdot 3^2)^2$.

Problem 5. What is the value of $(324^{\frac{1}{2}} \times 2)^2$?

Problem 6. Express as a decimal: $(1)^3 + (3)^{-1} - 0.\overline{6}$

Problem 7. Simplify $8^0 + 8^{\frac{1}{3}} + 8^{\frac{2}{3}} + 8^1$.

Problem 8. Express as a common fraction: $(\frac{1}{2} + (\frac{1}{3})^{-1})^{-1}$.

Problem 9. Arrange the numbers $a = 2^{88}$, $b = 3^{55}$, $c = 5^{44}$, and $d = 7^{33}$ in order form least to greatest. (Mathcounts Handbooks).

Problem 10. If m and n are positive integers, find the value of $m + n$ if $3^m + 2^n$ is the largest three-digit number of this form. (Mathcounts Handbooks).

Problem 11. Express one–third of 9^{30} as a power of 3. (Mathcounts Handbooks).

Problem 12. Solve for x: $3^{4x-2} = 27^{x+1}$

Problem 13. $3^7 - 3^6 = N \cdot 3^6$. Find N.

Problem 14. Express $(4)^{-\frac{1}{2}}$ as a common fraction.

Problem 15. What is the integer M such that $M \times 2^3 \times 3^7 = 6^7$?

Problem 16. Simplify: $(2^2)^3$.

Problem 17. Given $(81)^{\frac{1}{n}} = 3$, find n^2.

Problem 18. Solve for x: $3^{2x} = \sqrt{27}$. Express your answer as a common fraction. (Mathcounts Handbooks).

Problem 19. Calculate the value of $\dfrac{3^{12} - 3^{10}}{3^{10} - 3^8}$.

Problem 20. What is the sum of the digits of the decimal representation of 11^5? (Mathcounts Handbooks).

Problem 21. Compute the value of $(\dfrac{2}{3} + \dfrac{1}{2})^{-3}$. Express your answer as a common fraction.

Problem 22. How many digits are in the number $25^{21} \times 2^{48}$?

Problem 23. One trillion is 10^n times one-trillionth. What is the value of n? (Mathcounts Handbooks).

Problem 24. What is the value of $(11^{10})(11^5 + 11^5)^{-1}$? Express your answer as a decimal to the nearest tenth.   (Mathcounts Handbooks).

Problem 25. How many digits are in the value of the following expression? $(2^{2001} \times 5^{1950}) \div 4^{27}$

Problem 26. Determine the number of digits in the value of $2^{12} \times 5^8$.

Problem 27. Simplify: $(4^3 - 2^3)^2$

Problem 28. Express as a common fraction: $\left((\frac{1}{2})^{-1} + (\frac{1}{3})^{-1} + (\frac{1}{5})^{-1} + (\frac{1}{7})^{-1} \right)^{-1}$.

Problem 29. Simplify: $3^{-1} + 2^{-2}$.

Problem 30. Express $16^{-\frac{3}{4}}$ as a common faction.

Problem 31. What positive number squared is equal to 2^6?

Problem 32. Evaluate: $(1)^{5^2} + 1^{2^5}$.

Problem 33. Express as a single power of 2: $2^{20} - 2^{19} - 2^{18}$.

Problem 34. What is one-half of 8^{50} expressed as a power of 2? (Mathcounts Competitions).

Problem 35. Of the numbers $3^{\frac{1}{3}}$, $4^{\frac{1}{4}}$, $5^{\frac{1}{5}}$, and $6^{\frac{1}{6}}$, which is the greatest? (Mathcounts Competitions).

Problem 36. Evaluate $(3^5)(2^3) - (2^4)(3^4)$.

Problem 37. Find the product of $(\frac{1}{4})^{-3}$ $(8)^{-2}$.

Problem 38. Evaluate $7^0 + 7^1 + 7^2$.

Problem 39. Find x such that $5^3 + 5^3 + 5^3 + 5^3 + 5^3 = 5^x$.

Problem 40. Which is the largest, 4^{16}, 2^{33}, $(\frac{1}{8})^{-11}$, $(2)^{34}$, or 16^8?

Problem 41. Which of the following is the largest number?

(a) 2^{3^4} (b) 2^{4^3} (c) 3^{4^2} (d) 4^{3^2} (e) 4^{2^3}

Problem 42. Find the value of 5^{3x+1} if $5^{x+1} = 30$.

Problem 43. Express the value of $(16/625)^{(1/4)}$ as a common fraction.

Problem 44. Find the value of $8n^0 \times (8n)^0$ for $n \neq 0$.

Problem 45. Compute: $(5 + 0.5)^2 - (5 - 0.5)^2$.

Problem 46. For what value of n does $(5{,}000{,}000)^2 \times (2{,}000{,}000)^2 = 10^n$? (Mathcounts Competitions).

Problem 47. For what value of x does $3^{18} = x^x$?

Problem 48. Write $\left(\dfrac{16}{25}\right)^{-0.5} + 2^0 + 81^{0.75}$ as a mixed number.

Problem 49. Give the letter of the expression with the greatest value:

a) $(3.14)^3$ b) $(3)^{3.14}$ c) π^π d) $(1/3)^{-4}$

Problem 50. Which number is greater: 7^{92} or 8^{91}?

ANSWER KEYS:

Problem 1. 2a   **Problem** 2. 57121   **Problem** 3. 8/27

Problem 4. 5184   **Problem** 5. 1296   **Problem** 6. $0.\overline{6}$

Problem 7. 15   **Problem** 8. 2/7   **Problem** 9. badc

Problem 10. 14   **Problem** 11. 3^{59}.   **Problem** 12. 5

Problem 13. 2   **Problem** 14. ½   **Problem** 15. 16

Problem 16. 64   **Problem** 17. 16   **Problem** 18. ¾

Problem 19. 9   **Problem** 20. 14   **Problem** 21. 216/343

Problem 22. 44   **Problem** 23. 24   **Problem** 24. 80,525.5

Problem 25. 1950   **Problem** 26. 10   **Problem** 27. 3136

Problem 28. 1/17   **Problem** 29. 7/12   **Problem** 30. 1/8

Problem 31. 8   **Problem** 32. 2   **Problem** 33. 2^{18}

Problem 34. 2^{149}.   **Problem** 35. $3^{\frac{1}{3}}$ **Problem** 36. 648

Problem 37. 1   **Problem** 38. 57   **Problem** 39. 4

Problem 40. $(2)^{34}$ **Problem** 41. a   **Problem** 42. 1080.

Problem 43. 2/5   **Problem** 44. 8   **Problem** 45. 10

Problem 46. 26   **Problem** 47. 9.   **Problem** 48. 29 1/4.

Problem 49. d   **Problem** 50. 8^{91}. [$8^6 = 262144$ and $7^6 = 117649$. $8^6/7^6 > 2$ and $(8/7)^{18} > 8$. $8^{91}/7^{92} = (8^{91}/7^{91})\cdot(1/7) = (8/7)^{73}\cdot(8/7)^{18}\cdot(1/7) > 1)$. So $8^{91} > 7^{92}$]

BASIC KNOWLEDGE

1. TERMS:

The symbol $\sqrt[n]{}$ is called a radical sign. An expression like $\sqrt[n]{a}$ is a **radical**. The number a is called the radicand. n is **the index** of the radical $\sqrt[n]{a}$.

When $n = 2$, $\sqrt[2]{}$ is called **the square root**. It is customary to use the notation $\sqrt{}$ instead of $\sqrt[2]{}$ for the square root.

$\sqrt{2} \approx 1.414$, $\sqrt{3} \approx 1.732$, and $\sqrt{5} \approx 2.236$.

$\sqrt[3]{2} \approx 1.26$, $\sqrt[3]{3} \approx 1.44$, and $\sqrt[3]{5} \approx 1.71$.

2. OPERATIONS:

What number multiplied by itself is 25?

Let the number be a. We want to find out $a \times a$ or a^2, that is, we square the number:

$5 \times 5 = 5^2 = 25$.

What number is the square root of 25?

To find a square root of a number, you take its square root:

$\sqrt{25} = \sqrt{5^2} = 5$.

Note the inverse of squaring a number is taking its square root.

The radical symbol $\sqrt{}$ is used to represent the positive, or principal, square root.

3. DEFINITION OF THE PRINCIPAL SQUARE ROOT:

If x is a whole number, the principal square root of x is the nonnegative number y such that $y^2 = x$.

204

Examples:

(1). Find $\sqrt{1}$ (2). Find $\sqrt{4}$ (3). Find $\sqrt{9}$ (4). Find $\sqrt{16}$

(5). Find $\sqrt{25}$ (6). Find $\sqrt{36}$ (7). Find $\sqrt{49}$ (8). Find $\sqrt{64}$

(9). Find $\sqrt{81}$ (10). Find $\sqrt{100}$ (11). Find $\sqrt{121}$ (12). Find $\sqrt{144}$

(13). Find $\sqrt{169}$ (14). Find $\sqrt{196}$ (15). Find $\sqrt{225}$ (16). Find $\sqrt{256}$

4. RADICAL NOTATION FOR $\sqrt[n]{a}$:

$$\sqrt[n]{a} = a^{\frac{1}{n}}$$

Examples:

(1). $\sqrt{16} = 16^{\frac{1}{2}} = (4^2)^{\frac{1}{2}} = 4^{2 \times \frac{1}{2}} = 4^1 = 4$

(2). $\sqrt[3]{27} = 27^{\frac{1}{3}} = (3^3)^{\frac{1}{3}} = 3^{3 \times \frac{1}{3}} = 3^1 = 3$

(3). $\sqrt[4]{81} = 81^{\frac{1}{4}} = (3^4)^{\frac{1}{4}} = 3^{4 \times \frac{1}{4}} = 3^1 = 3$

(4). $\sqrt[3]{\dfrac{8}{27}} = \left(\dfrac{8}{27}\right)^{\frac{1}{3}} = \left(\dfrac{2^3}{3^3}\right)^{\frac{1}{3}} = \left(\dfrac{2}{3}\right)^{3 \times \frac{1}{3}} = \left(\dfrac{2}{3}\right)^1 = \dfrac{2}{3}$

5. RADICAL NOTATION FOR $\sqrt[n]{a^m}$:

$$\sqrt[n]{a^m} = \left(\sqrt[n]{a}\right)^m = a^{\frac{m}{n}} \qquad \Rightarrow \qquad \sqrt[n]{a^n} = \left(\sqrt[n]{a}\right)^n = a^{\frac{n}{n}} = a^1 = a$$

Examples:

(1). $\sqrt[3]{64} = \sqrt[3]{4^3} = \left(\sqrt[3]{4}\right)^3 = 4^{3 \times \frac{1}{3}} = 4^1 = 4$

(2). $\sqrt[3]{27} = \sqrt[3]{3^3} = (\sqrt[3]{3})^3 = 3^{3\times\frac{1}{3}} = 3^1 = 3$

(3). $\sqrt[4]{81} = \sqrt[4]{3^4} = (\sqrt[4]{3})^4 = 3^{4\times\frac{1}{4}} = 3^1 = 3$

(4). $\sqrt[3]{\dfrac{8}{27}} = \left(\sqrt[3]{\dfrac{2^3}{3^3}}\right) = \left(\sqrt[3]{\left(\dfrac{2}{3}\right)^3}\right) = \left(\sqrt[3]{\left(\dfrac{2}{3}\right)}\right)^3 = \left(\dfrac{2}{3}\right)^{3\times\frac{1}{3}} = \left(\dfrac{2}{3}\right)^1 = \dfrac{2}{3}$

6. MORE EXPONENT PROPERTIES OF RADICALS:

$\sqrt[n]{a} \times \sqrt[n]{b} = a^{\frac{1}{n}} \times b^{\frac{1}{n}} = (ab)^{\frac{1}{n}} = \sqrt[n]{ab}$ $\Rightarrow$ $\sqrt{ab} = \sqrt{a} \times \sqrt{b}$ $(a > 0, \text{ and } b > 0)$

$\dfrac{\sqrt[n]{a}}{\sqrt[n]{b}} = \dfrac{a^{\frac{1}{n}}}{b^{\frac{1}{n}}} = \left(\dfrac{a}{b}\right)^{\frac{1}{n}} = \sqrt[n]{\dfrac{a}{b}}$ $\Rightarrow$ $\dfrac{\sqrt{a}}{\sqrt{b}} = \sqrt{\dfrac{a}{b}}$ $(a > 0, \text{ and } b > 0)$

$\sqrt[n]{\sqrt[m]{a}} = \left(a^{\frac{1}{m}}\right)^{\frac{1}{n}} = a^{\frac{1}{n}\times\frac{1}{m}} = a^{\frac{1}{nm}} = \sqrt[nm]{a}$

$m\sqrt{a} \pm n\sqrt{a} = (m \pm n)\sqrt{a}$

Examples:

(1). $\sqrt{125} = \sqrt{25 \times 5} = \sqrt{25} \times \sqrt{5} = 5\sqrt{5}$

(2). $\dfrac{\sqrt[3]{32}}{\sqrt[3]{4}} = \sqrt[3]{\dfrac{32}{4}} = \sqrt[3]{8} = 2$

(3). $\sqrt[3]{\sqrt{729}} = \sqrt[6]{729} = 3$

(4). $\sqrt{125} + \sqrt{45} = \sqrt{25} \times \sqrt{5} + \sqrt{9 \times 5} = 5\sqrt{5} + 3\sqrt{5} = 8\sqrt{5}$

7. SIMPLIFYING RADICALS:

Simplifying a radical is to write the radical in the simplest form.

A radical is in its simplest form if

(a) The power of the radicand is less than the index.

Example: $\sqrt{125}$ is not the simplest form since $\sqrt{125} = \sqrt{5^2 \times 5} = 5\sqrt{5}$.

(b). The radicand is not in a fraction form.

Example: $\sqrt{\dfrac{1}{2}}$ is not in the simplest form. $\Rightarrow$ $\sqrt{\dfrac{1}{2}} = \sqrt{\dfrac{1}{2} \times \dfrac{2}{2}} = \sqrt{\dfrac{2}{2^2}} = \dfrac{\sqrt{2}}{2}$

(c). No denominator contains a radical.

Example: $\dfrac{\sqrt{2}}{\sqrt{3}}$ is not in the simplest form. $\Rightarrow$ $\dfrac{\sqrt{2}}{\sqrt{3}} = \dfrac{\sqrt{2} \times \sqrt{3}}{\sqrt{3} \times \sqrt{3}} = \dfrac{\sqrt{2 \times 3}}{3} = \dfrac{\sqrt{6}}{3}$

(d). All possible operations should be performed.

Examples:

(1). Calculate: $\sqrt{120} \times \sqrt{30}$ (Mathcounts Competitions).

$$\sqrt{120} \times \sqrt{30} = \sqrt{120 \times 30} = \sqrt{2^2 \times 30^2} = \sqrt{60^2} = 60$$

(2). Express in simplest form: $\sqrt{12} \times \sqrt{3}$ (Mathcounts Handbooks).

$$\sqrt{12} \times \sqrt{3} = \sqrt{12 \times 3} = \sqrt{4 \times 3 \times 3} = \sqrt{6^2} = 6$$

(3). Simplify: $\sqrt{128} + \sqrt{72}$ (Mathcounts Competitions).

$$\sqrt{128} + \sqrt{72} = \sqrt{64 \times 2} + \sqrt{36 \times 2} = 8\sqrt{2} + 6\sqrt{2} = 14\sqrt{2}$$

(4). Multiply: $\sqrt{54} \cdot \sqrt{32} \cdot \sqrt{6}$ (Mathcounts Handbooks).

$$\sqrt{54} \cdot \sqrt{32} \cdot \sqrt{6} = \sqrt{6 \times 9} \cdot \sqrt{2 \times 16} \cdot \sqrt{6} = 3\sqrt{6} \cdot 4\sqrt{2} \cdot \sqrt{6} = 72\sqrt{2}$$

(5). Express in simplest form: $\sqrt{3^4 \cdot 4^2}$ (Mathcounts Handbooks)

$$\sqrt{3^4 \cdot 4^2} = \sqrt{12^2 \times 3^2} = \sqrt{36^2} = 36$$

(6). Simplify and express your answer as a common fraction: $\sqrt{0.16}$ (Mathcounts Handbooks).

$$\sqrt{0.16} = \sqrt{(0.4)^2} = 0.4 = \frac{4}{10} = \frac{2}{5} .$$

(7). Express in simplest form: $\sqrt{5^6 + 5^6 + 5^6 + 5^6}$. (Mathcounts Competitions).

$$\sqrt{5^6 + 5^6 + 5^6 + 5^6} = \sqrt{4 \times 5^6} = \sqrt{2^2 \times (5^3)^2} = \sqrt{(2 \times 5^3)^2} = 2 \times 5^3 = 250 .$$

8. RATIONALIZING THE DENOMINATOR:

When we simplify a radical, we want to get rid of the radical sign in the denominator. The process of achieving this is called **rationalizing the denominator**.

$$\frac{\sqrt{a}}{\sqrt{b}} = \frac{\sqrt{ab}}{b}$$

Examples:

(1). $\sqrt{\dfrac{3}{4}} = \dfrac{\sqrt{3}}{\sqrt{4}} = \dfrac{\sqrt{3}}{2}$

(2). $\sqrt{\dfrac{3}{2}} = \sqrt{\dfrac{3 \times 2}{2 \times 2}} = \dfrac{\sqrt{6}}{2}$

(3). $\sqrt[4]{\dfrac{3}{2}} = \dfrac{\sqrt[4]{3}}{\sqrt[4]{2}} = \dfrac{\sqrt[4]{3} \times \sqrt[4]{2^3}}{\sqrt[4]{2} \times \sqrt[4]{2^3}} = \dfrac{\sqrt[4]{3 \times 2^3}}{\sqrt[4]{2^4}} = \dfrac{\sqrt[4]{24}}{2}$

(3). $\dfrac{1}{\sqrt{3}+\sqrt{2}} = \dfrac{1}{\sqrt{3}+\sqrt{2}} \times \dfrac{\sqrt{3}-\sqrt{2}}{\sqrt{3}-\sqrt{2}} = \dfrac{\sqrt{3}-\sqrt{2}}{(\sqrt{3}+\sqrt{2})\sqrt{3}-\sqrt{2})} = \dfrac{\sqrt{3}-\sqrt{2}}{3-2} = \sqrt{3}-\sqrt{2}$

Note: $(a+b)(a-b) = a^2 - b^2$

(4). $\dfrac{1}{\sqrt{3}-\sqrt{2}} = \dfrac{1}{\sqrt{3}-\sqrt{2}} \times \dfrac{\sqrt{3}+\sqrt{2}}{\sqrt{3}+\sqrt{2}} = \dfrac{\sqrt{3}+\sqrt{2}}{(\sqrt{3}-\sqrt{2})\sqrt{3}+\sqrt{2})} = \dfrac{\sqrt{3}+\sqrt{2}}{1} = \sqrt{3}+\sqrt{2}$

9. EVALUATING RADICALS:

The following formulas are often used in this procedure:

$a^2 + 2ab + b^2 = (a+b)^2$ (1)

$a^2 - 2ab + b^2 = (a-b)^2$ (2)

$\sqrt{a \pm \sqrt{b}} = \sqrt{\dfrac{a+\sqrt{a^2-b}}{2}} \pm \sqrt{\dfrac{a-\sqrt{a^2-b}}{2}}$ (3)

Examples:

(1). Simplify $\sqrt{3+2\sqrt{2}}$

Method 1: $\sqrt{3+2\sqrt{2}} = \sqrt{2+2\sqrt{2}+1} = \sqrt{(\sqrt{2})^2 + 2\sqrt{2}\times1 + 1^2} = \sqrt{(\sqrt{2}+1)^2} = \sqrt{2}+1$

Method 2: $\sqrt{3+2\sqrt{2}} = \sqrt{3+\sqrt{8}} = \sqrt{\dfrac{3+\sqrt{3^2-8}}{2}} + \sqrt{\dfrac{3-\sqrt{3^2-8}}{2}} = \sqrt{\dfrac{4}{2}} + \sqrt{\dfrac{2}{2}} = \sqrt{2}+1$

(2). Simplify $\sqrt{3-2\sqrt{2}}$

$\sqrt{3-2\sqrt{2}} = \sqrt{2-2\sqrt{2}+1} = \sqrt{(\sqrt{2})^2 - 2\sqrt{2}\times1 + 1^2} = \sqrt{(\sqrt{2}-1)^2} = \sqrt{2}-1$

(3). Simplify $\sqrt{7+\sqrt{24}}$

$$\sqrt{7+\sqrt{24}} = \sqrt{7+2\sqrt{6}} = \sqrt{6+2\sqrt{6}+1} = \sqrt{(\sqrt{6})^2 + 2\sqrt{6}\times1+1^2} = \sqrt{(\sqrt{6}+1)^2} = \sqrt{6}+1$$

(4). Simplify $\sqrt{7-\sqrt{24}}$

$$\sqrt{7-\sqrt{24}} = \sqrt{7-2\sqrt{6}} = \sqrt{6-2\sqrt{6}+1} = \sqrt{(\sqrt{6})^2 - 2\sqrt{6}\times1+1^2} = \sqrt{(\sqrt{6}-1)^2} = \sqrt{6}-1$$

10. TAKING THE SQUARE ROOT MANUALLY:

Calculate: $\sqrt{1156}$

Theoretical basis:

Since $30^2 = 900$ and $35^2 = 1225$, We know that $\sqrt{1156}$ is greater than 30 and less than 35. We can write 1156 as the following:

$1156 = (30 + a)^2 = 30^2 + 2 \times 30a + a^2$.

$1156 - 30^2 = 2 \times 30a + a^2$

The following relationship is used to complete the job:

$$\frac{1156 - 30^2}{20 \times 3 + a} = a$$

Detailed steps:

(1). Group the digits of the radicand by two, starting from the units digit, to the left.

For example, $\sqrt{1156} \Rightarrow 11'56$. The number of groups indicate the number of digits of the square root.

(2). Find the most left digit of the square root by doing the following division.

```
                    3
        3 ⌡   11 ′ 56
                 9
        ─────────────
                 2
```

(2). Move the next group down

$$
\begin{array}{r}
3 \\
3\,\overline{)\,11\,'\,56} \\
\underline{9} \\
2\quad 56
\end{array}
$$

(3). Multiply 3 by 20 to get 60. Use 60 as the divisor for 256.

$$
\begin{array}{r}
3 \\
3\,\overline{)\,11\,'\,56} \\
\underline{9} \\
20\times3=60\,\big|\,2\quad 56
\end{array}
$$

(4). Get the testing quotient "4"

$$
\begin{array}{r}
3\quad ? \\
3\,\overline{)\,11\,'\,56} \\
\underline{9} \\
20\times3=60\,\big|\,2\quad 56
\end{array}
\quad\Rightarrow.\quad
\begin{array}{r}
3\quad 4 \\
3\,\overline{)\,11\,'\,56} \\
\underline{9} \\
20\times3=60\,\big|\,2\quad 56
\end{array}
$$

(5). Get the real divisor "64" :

$$
\begin{array}{r}
3\quad x \\
3\,\overline{)\,11\,'\,56} \\
\underline{9} \\
20\times3=60\,\big|\,2\quad 56 \\
+4\,\big| \\
\hline
64\,\big|
\end{array}
$$

(6). Try the quotient "4" to get the result.

$$
\begin{array}{r|lll}
 & 3 & & 4 \\
3 & 11 & ' & 56 \\
 & 9 & & \\
\hline
20\times 3=60 & 2 & & 56 \\
+ \qquad 4 & & & \\
\hline
64 & 2 & & 56 \\
 & & & 0
\end{array}
$$

Examples:

(1). Find the square root of 1024.

Solution: $\sqrt{1024} = 32$

$$
\begin{array}{r|lll}
 & 3 & & 2 \\
3 & 10 & ' & 24 \\
 & 9 & & \\
\hline
20\times 3=60 & 1 & & 24 \\
+ \qquad 2 & & & \\
\hline
62 & 1 & & 24 \\
 & & & 0
\end{array}
$$

(2). To which integer is $\sqrt{175}$ closest?   (Mathcounts Handbooks)

Solution: 13.

$$
\begin{array}{r|lll}
 & 1 & & 3 \\
1 & 1 & ' & 75 \\
 & 1 & & \\
\hline
20\times 1=20 & 0 & & 75 \\
+ \qquad 3 & & & \\
\hline
23 & & & 69 \\
 & & & 6
\end{array}
$$

(3). Find the square root of 85264.

Solution:

$\sqrt{85264}\ \ = 292$

212

$$
\begin{array}{r}
2 \quad\ 9 \quad\ 2 \\
2\,\overline{)8\,'\,52\,'\,64}
\end{array}
$$

$$
\begin{array}{r}
\underline{4}
\end{array}
$$

$$
\begin{array}{r}
(20\times2+9)\ \ 49\ \big|\ \ 4\quad 52 \\
4\quad 41
\end{array}
$$

$$
\begin{array}{r}
(20\times29+2)\ \ 582\ \big|\ \ 11\quad 64 \\
11\quad 64 \\
\hline
0
\end{array}
$$

11. OTHER PROBLEMS WITH RADICALS:

Example 1: Which of the following is larger, $\sqrt{5}+\sqrt{6}$ or $\sqrt{3}+\sqrt{8}$?

Solution: $\sqrt{5}+\sqrt{6}$.

Since $\sqrt{5}+\sqrt{6} = \sqrt{(\sqrt{5}+\sqrt{6})^2} = \sqrt{11+2\sqrt{30}}$ and

$\sqrt{3}+\sqrt{8} = \sqrt{(\sqrt{3}+\sqrt{8})^2} = \sqrt{11+2\sqrt{24}}$, so $\sqrt{5}+\sqrt{6} > \sqrt{3}+\sqrt{8}$.

Example 2: Which of the following is larger, $\dfrac{3}{2}\sqrt{48}$ or $\dfrac{5}{7}\sqrt{147}$?

Solution: $\dfrac{3}{2}\sqrt{48}$.

Since $\dfrac{3}{2}\sqrt{48} = 6\sqrt{3}$ and $\dfrac{5}{7}\sqrt{147} = 5\sqrt{3}$, so $\dfrac{3}{2}\sqrt{48} > \dfrac{5}{7}\sqrt{147}$

Example 3: Which of the following is larger, $\sqrt{19}$ or $6-\sqrt{3}$?

Solution: $\sqrt{19}$.

Since $(\sqrt{19})^2 = 19 = 39-20 = 39-\sqrt{400}$ and $(6-\sqrt{3})^2 = 39-12\sqrt{3} = 39-\sqrt{432}$, so

$\sqrt{19} > 6-\sqrt{3}$.

Example 4: If $\sqrt{5} = a$ and the decimal part of a is b, find the value of or $\dfrac{1}{b} - a$.

Solution: 2.

The integer part of $\sqrt{5}$ is 2 and the decimal part $b = \sqrt{5} - 2$.

$$\frac{1}{b} - a = \frac{1}{\sqrt{5} - 2} - \sqrt{5} = \sqrt{5} + 2 - \sqrt{5} = 2.$$

Example 5: If the decimal part of $5 + \sqrt{7}$ is a and the decimal part of $5 - \sqrt{7}$ is b, find the value of $ab - 2a + 3b + 12$.

Solution: 12.

Since $2 < \sqrt{7} < 3$, so $7 < 5 + \sqrt{7} < 8$ and $2 < 5 - \sqrt{7} < 3$.

$$a = (5 + \sqrt{7}) - 7 = \sqrt{7} - 2, \quad b = (5 - \sqrt{7}) - 2 = 3 - \sqrt{7}$$

$$ab - 2a + 3b$$

$$= (\sqrt{7} - 2)(3 - \sqrt{7}) - 2(\sqrt{7} - 2) + 3(3 - \sqrt{7}) + 12 = 12.$$

Example 6: How many pairs of integer solutions are there for the equation $\sqrt{x} + \sqrt{y} = \sqrt{99}$?

Solution: 4 pairs.

Since x and y are integers,

$$\sqrt{99} = 3\sqrt{11} = \sqrt{0} + 3\sqrt{11} = \sqrt{0} + \sqrt{99}$$

$$\sqrt{99} = 3\sqrt{11} = \sqrt{11} + 2\sqrt{11} = \sqrt{11} + \sqrt{44}$$

$$\sqrt{99} = 3\sqrt{11} = 2\sqrt{11} + \sqrt{11} = \sqrt{44} + \sqrt{11}$$

$$\sqrt{99} = 3\sqrt{11} = 3\sqrt{11} + \sqrt{0} = \sqrt{99} + \sqrt{0}.$$

There are four pairs of (x, y).

Example 7. Find all a such that $\dfrac{3}{1-\sqrt{a-2}} + \dfrac{3}{1+\sqrt{a-2}} = 6$.

Solution: 2.

First we divide both sides by 3 to simplify the process:

$$\dfrac{1}{1-\sqrt{a-2}} + \dfrac{1}{1+\sqrt{a-2}} = 2 \qquad \Rightarrow \qquad \dfrac{1+\sqrt{a-2}+1-\sqrt{a-2}}{(1-\sqrt{a-2})(1+\sqrt{a-2})} = 2 \qquad \Rightarrow$$

$$\dfrac{2}{1-(a-2)} = 2 \qquad \Rightarrow \qquad \dfrac{1}{1-(a-2)} = 1 \qquad \Rightarrow \qquad 1-(a-2)=1$$

So $a = 2$ is the solution.

Example 8: How many pairs of positive integer solutions are there for the equation

$$\sqrt{x} + 3\sqrt{y} = \sqrt{300} ?$$

Solution: 3 pairs.

We know that $\sqrt{300} = 10\sqrt{3}$ and x and y are all positive integers, the simplest forms of $\sqrt{x}$ and $\sqrt{y}$ should contain $\sqrt{3}$.

All the possible cases are:

$$\sqrt{x} + 3\sqrt{y} = \sqrt{3} + 9\sqrt{3} = 4\sqrt{3} + 6\sqrt{3} = 7\sqrt{3} + 3\sqrt{3} = 10\sqrt{3}.$$

There are three pairs of solutions:

$$\begin{cases} x_1 = 3 \\ y_1 = 27 \end{cases}; \qquad \begin{cases} x_2 = 48 \\ y_2 = 12 \end{cases}; \quad \text{and} \quad \begin{cases} x_3 = 147 \\ y_3 = 3 \end{cases}$$

EXERCISES:

Problem 1. Find $\sqrt{5}$ to the nearest tenth.

Problem 2. Express in simplest form: $\sqrt{12} \times \sqrt{3}$.

Problem 3. Find the positive-valued difference between $\sqrt{\dfrac{9}{16}}$ and $(1.1)^2$. Express your answer as a decimal. (Mathcounts Handbooks)

Problem 4. Simplify and express your answer as a common fraction: $\sqrt{6\dfrac{1}{4}}$.

Problem 5. Simplify $\sqrt{91-3^3}$.

Problem 6. Express the product in simplest form: $\sqrt{49} \cdot \sqrt{196}$.

Problem 7. Express as a decimal: $\sqrt{0.000016}$.

Problem 8. Simplify $\sqrt{5\dfrac{11}{49}}$ and express your answer as a common fraction. (Mathcounts Handbooks)

Problem 9. Simplify: $\sqrt{162-3^4}$.

Problem 10. Simplify: $\sqrt{3^3+3^3+3^3}$.

Problem 11. Simplify: $\sqrt{3\sqrt{3\sqrt{3}}}$.

Problem 12. Find the digit in the tenths place when $\sqrt{\dfrac{27}{48}}$ is written as a decimal numeral. (Mathcounts Handbooks)

Problem 13. Simplify: $\sqrt{6} \times \sqrt{15} \times \sqrt{10}$.

Problem 14. Simplify: $\sqrt{2} \times \sqrt[3]{4}$.

Problem 15. On a number line, the point X that corresponds to $\sqrt{9} + \sqrt{10} + \sqrt{11}$ would be located between what two consecutive integers? (Mathcounts Handbooks).

Problem 16. What is the smallest positive integer x such that $x\sqrt{115}$ will be greater than 115?

Problem 17. Write the following as a common fraction: $\sqrt[3]{4} \div 13.5$

Problem 18. Simplify: $\sqrt{\sqrt{\sqrt{256}}}$.

Problem 19. What is the square root of the cube root of 64?

Problem 20. Express the following as a simplified common fraction:
$\dfrac{1^2 + 2^2 + 3^2 + 4^2 + 5^2}{\sqrt{1^2} \cdot \sqrt{2^2} \cdot \sqrt{3^2} \sqrt{4^2} \cdot \sqrt{5^2}}$ (Mathcounts Handbooks)

Problem 21. Calculate $\sqrt{0.64} - \sqrt[3]{-0.008} + \sqrt[4]{\dfrac{4}{20.25}} + \sqrt[5]{(16 \div \dfrac{1}{2})}$.

Problem 22. Simplify: $\sqrt[3]{270} - \sqrt[3]{80}$.

Problem 23. The numbers a and b are consecutive positive integers, and $a < \sqrt{200} < b$. what is the value of the product ab? (Mathcounts Handbooks)

Problem 24. What is the value of the following expression? Express your answer as a common fraction.   (Mathcounts Handbooks)

$$\sqrt{11(0.\overline{14}+0.\overline{41}+0.\overline{15}+0.\overline{51})}$$

Problem 25. Find the largest positive integer whose square is less than 1,439,979. (Mathcounts Competitions).

Problem 26. Simplify: $\sqrt{2}\cdot\sqrt[3]{4}\cdot\sqrt[6]{32}$.

Problem 27. Simplify: $\sqrt{18}$ - $\sqrt{8}$ + $\sqrt{\dfrac{1}{2}}$.

Problem 28. The square root of 127 is between what two whole numbers?

Problem 29. Express the following as a mixed number:

$$\left(\sqrt{2\frac{1}{4}}\right)\ \left(\sqrt[3]{3\frac{3}{8}}\right)\ \left(\sqrt[4]{5\frac{1}{16}}\right)$$

Problem 30. Calculate $\sqrt{0.49}+\sqrt[3]{0.216}-\sqrt[5]{0.00032}$.

Problem 31. What is $\sqrt{200}$ to the nearest tenth?

Problem 32. Find the value of $\sqrt{\sqrt{2,560,000}}$.

Problem 33. Express as a common fraction: $\sqrt{\dfrac{1}{9}+\dfrac{1}{16}}$.

Problem 34. Find the value of $\sqrt{5^5+5^5+5^5+5^5+5^5}$.

Problem 35. $\sqrt{50}+\sqrt{75}$ lies between two consecutive integers, a and b, where $a < b$. What is the value of b? (Mathcounts Competitions).

Problem 36. Express in simplest form: $\sqrt{5\frac{4}{9}}$.

Problem 37. Round $\sqrt{390}$ to the nearest whole number.

Problem 38. Multiply: $\sqrt{24} \cdot \sqrt{18} \cdot \sqrt{12}$.

Problem 39. Simplify $\sqrt{2^6 + 2^6 + 2^6 + 2^6}$.

Problem 40. Express $\sqrt[3]{2(\sqrt{2})}$ in simplest radical form.

Problem 41. Find the smallest integer greater than $\sqrt{300}$.

Problem 42. Write $2^{\frac{1}{2}} + 2^{\frac{1}{2}}$ in simplest radical form.

Problem 43. Find the smallest whole number greater than $\sqrt{30} + \sqrt{56} + \sqrt{110}$.

ANSWER KEYS:

Problem 1. 2.2   **Problem 2.** 6   **Problem 3.** 0.46   **Problem 4.** 5/2

Problem 5. 8   **Problem 6.** 98   **Problem 7.** 0.004   **Problem 8.** 16/7

Problem 9. 9   **Problem 10.** 9   **Problem 11.** $\sqrt[8]{3^7}$ **Problem 12.** 7

Problem 13. 30   **Problem 14.** $2\sqrt[6]{2}$ **Problem 15.** 9 and 10.

Problem 16. 11   **Problem 17.** 2/3   **Problem 18.** 2   **Problem 19.** 2

Problem 20. 11/24   **Problem 21.** 3 2/3   **Problem 22.** $\sqrt[3]{10}$ **Problem 23.** 210.

Problem 24. 11/3   **Problem 25.** 1199.   **Problem 26.** 4   **Problem 27.** $\dfrac{3\sqrt{2}}{2}$

Problem 28. 11 and 12.

Problem 29. 3 3/8   **Problem 30.** 1.1   **Problem 31.** 14.1

Problem 32. 40   **Problem 33.** 5/12   **Problem 34.** 125   **Problem 35.** 16

Problem 36. 7/3   **Problem 37.** 20   **Problem 38.** 72   **Problem 39.** 16

Problem 40. $\sqrt{2}$ **Problem 41.** 18   **Problem 42.** $2\sqrt{2}$ **Problem 43.** 24

BASIC KNOWLEDGE

SCIENTIFIC NOTATION

A number is written in scientific notation when it is expressed in the form
$$a \times 10^n \qquad \text{where } 1 \leq |a| \leq 10 \text{ and } n \text{ is an integer.}$$

Converting to scientific notation

Step 1 Place a caret, $\wedge$, to the right of the first nonzero digit.

Step 2 Count the number of digits from the caret to the decimal point. This number gives the absolute value of exponent on 10.

Step 3 Decide whether multiplying by 10^n should make the number larger or smaller. The exponent should be positive to make the product larger; it should be negative to make the product smaller.

Example 1: Write the number 820,000 in scientific notation.

Solution: 8.2×10^5
Place a caret to the right of the digit 8 (the first nonzero digit)
$$8 \wedge 20,000$$

Count from the caret to the decimal point, which is understood to be after the last 0.
$8 \wedge 20,000. \leftarrow$ Decimal point
Count 5 places.

Since the number 8.2 is to be made larger, the exponent on 10 is positive.
$820,000 = 8.2 \times 10^5$

Example 2: Write the number 0.000072 in scientific notation.

Solution: 7.2×10^{-5}
Place a caret to the right of the digit 7 (the first nonzero digit)

Count from right to left.   0.00007˄2   5 places

Since the number 7.2 is to be made smaller, the exponent on 10 is negative.

$0.000072 = 7.2 \times 10^{-5}$

Try it yourself:

(1). Write scientific notation for 32500.

Answer: 3.25×10^{4}

(2). Write scientific notation for 0.000489. (Mathcounts Handbooks)

Answer: 4.89×10^{-4}

(3). Write scientific notation for the number of millimeters in 3.2 kilometers?
(Mathcounts Handbooks)

Answer: 3.2×10^{6}

(4). Express in scientific notation: 3600.

Answer: 3.6×10^{3}

(5). Write 240 divided by 0.015 in scientific notation.

Answer: 1.6×10^{4}

(6). Write 0.007×0.00033 in scientific notation.

Answer: 2.31×10^{-6}

(7). Write scientific notation for 2160000.

Answer: 2.16×10^{6}

SIGNIFICANT DIGIT (SIGNIFICANT FIGURE)

Count from left, first non-zero digit to the rest digit.

Example 3: The following numbers have three significant digits:

4.15;   41.5;   0.0415;   0.0000415.

Note: 41.50 is a four-digit significant figure.

Rules for Counting Significant Figures

1. Always count nonzero digits

    Example 4: 22 has two significant figures, while 8.925 has four

2. Never count leading zeros

    Example 5: 022 and 0.022 both have two significant figures

3. Always count zeros which fall somewhere between two nonzero digits

    Example 6: 20.2 has three significant figures, while 0.00104002 has six

4. Count trailing zeros if and only if the number contains a decimal point

    Example 7: 220 and 220000 both have two significant figures, while 220. has three and 220.00 has five

5. For numbers expressed in scientific notation, ignore the exponent and apply Rules 1-4.

    Example 8: 4.2010×10^{28} has five significant figures

More examples:

(1). Round 642,396 to four, three, and two significant digits:
642,400 (four significant digits)
642,000 (three significant digits)

640,000 (two significant digits)

(2). Round 0.06284 to four, three, and two significant digits:

0.06284 (four significant digits)
0.0628   (three significant digits)
0.063   (two significant digits)

(3). Round 631.45 to four, three, and two significant digits:

631.5 (four significant digits)
631   (three significant digits)
630   (two significant digits)

SOME ROUNDING RULES

a. When adding or subtracting numbers, find the number which has the fewest decimal places, then round the result to that decimal place.

Example 9: $21.398 + 605 - 2.9 = 623$

(The number 605 has only an ones place, so the result must be rounded to the ones place.)

b. When multiplying or dividing numbers, find the number with the fewest significant figures, then round the result to that many significant figures.

Example 10: $0.049623 \times 32.0 / 478.8 = 0.00332$ (0.003316491)

(The number 32.0 is only known to three significant figures, so the result must be rounded to three significant figures.)

c. When raising a number to some power which isn't very large or very small -- say, squaring it (power = 2) or taking the square root (power = ½) , count the number's significant figures, then round the result to that many significant figures.

Example 11: $(5.8)^2 = 34$ (33.64)
(The number 5.8 is known to two significant figures, so the result must be rounded to two significant figures.)

More examples:

(1). Add:

43.112233	(6 places after the decimal point)
1.3324	(4 places after the decimal point)
+ 0.25	(2 places after the decimal point)
44.694633	(on calculator)

44.69 (rounded to 2 places in the answer)

(2). Multiplication:

33.123123	(8 significant figures)
× 1.3344	(5 significant figures)
44.199495	(on calculator)

44.199   (rounded to 5 significant figures)

Round to a certain named place

For the counting numbers:

...(ten-thousands) (thousands) (hundreds) (tens) (ones)

For decimal places:

(decimal point) (tenths) (hundredths) (thousandths) (ten-thousandths)....

Example 12: Round π to the nearest thousandth.

"The nearest thousandth" means that we need to count off three decimal places (tenths, hundredths, thousandths), and then round:

3.141 | 59265...
Then π, rounded to the nearest thousandth, is 3.142.

Example 13: Round 2.796 to the hundredths place.

The hundredths place is two decimal places, so we count off two decimal places, and round according to the third decimal place:
2.79 | 6

Since the third decimal place contains a 6, which is greater than 5, we have to round up. But rounding up a 9 gives a 10. In this case, we round the 79 up to an 80: 2.80

Note: "2.8" is incorrect.

More Examples:

0.14159 is accurate to the hundred-thousandths place

2000 is accurate to the thousands place

2000.0 is accurate to the tenths place

0.00045 is accurate to the hundred-thousandths place

0.000450 is accurate to the millionths place (note the extra zero)

2006 is accurate to the units place

660 is accurate to the tens place

660. is accurate to the units place (note the decimal point)

660.0 is accurate to the tenths place.

Try it yourself:

(1). Round to the nearest hundredth: 7.20631.

Answer: 7.21

(2). Round to the nearest whole number: 38.498.

Answer: 38

(3). Round 28.2508 to the nearest tenth.
Answer: 28.3

(4). Round 72.4983 to the nearest whole number.

Answer: 72

(5). Round to the nearest thousandth: 7.47075.

Answer: 7.471

(6). Round to the nearest hundred: 4329.829

Answer: 4300

(7). Round 26.9953 to the nearest hundredth.

Answer: 27.00

(8). Round 68.47982 to the nearest thousandth.

Answer: 68.480

(9). Round to the nearest hundredth: 18.4851.

Answer: 18.49

EXERCISES

Problem 1. Write the standard numeral for 7.5×10^5.

Problem 2. Simplify: $(2.4)(2.4 \times 10^3) \div 1000$.

Problem 3. Write the standard numeral for 2.45×10^{-3}.

Problem 4. Calculate: $(3.2 \times 10^3) \div (1.6 \times 10^2)$

Problem 5. Write as a decimal number: 0.12×10^3.

Problem 6. A googol is written with 1 followed by one hundred zeros. Write a googol in scientific notation. (Mathcounts Handbooks)

Problem 7. Write 0.007×0.00033 as scientific notation.

Problem 8. Write as scientific notation: $\dfrac{3.64 \times 10^{12}}{0.04 \times 10^6}$.

Problem 9. Write the quotient below as a number in scientific notation: $\dfrac{1.96 \times 10^9}{0.07 \times 10^4}$.

Problem 10. Write $\dfrac{3}{5} \times 10^3 \times 38.9 \times 10^4$ as scientific notation.

Problem 11. Express $3.21 \times 10^4 + 2.71 \times 10^5$ in scientific notation.

Problem 12. Express $2.65 \times 10^3 + 3.5 \times 10^4$ in scientific notation. Round your answer to two significant digits.

Problem 13. Simplify, expressing your answer in scientific notation:
$\dfrac{3.5 \times 10^{-3}}{1.75 \times 10^{-3}} \cdot \dfrac{1.44 \times 10^6}{1.2 \times 10^{-4}}$ (Mathcounts Handbooks)

Problem 14. Simplify and express the result in scientific notation:

$$\frac{(0.0000009)^3(9\times10^4)^2}{(3,000,000)^2(0.00243)}$$ (Mathcounts Handbooks)

Problem 15. During one season from May to September, a pair of mosquitoes can become parents and ancestors to 1.7×10^{21} mosquitoes. If a large swamp in Florida contains 10^{10} pairs of mosquitoes, how many mosquitoes can be produced in one season? Express your answer in scientific notation. (Mathcounts Handbooks)

Problem 16. Divide and express your answer in scientific notation: $\dfrac{2\times10^{13}}{4\times10^{10}}$.

Problem 17. The distance from Pluto to the sun is about 3.67×10^9 mi, and from. Neptune to the sun is about 2.79×10^9 mi. How many miles further from the sun is Pluto than Neptune? Express your answer in scientific notation. (Mathcounts Handbooks)

Problem 18. The sun has a mass of 1.989×10^{30} kilograms and a radius of 6.96×10^9 meters. How many kilograms per cubic meter are in the density (mass per unit volume) of the Sun? Express your answer as a decimal rounded to the nearest hundredth. (Mathcounts Handbooks)

Problem 19. The speed of light is 186,000 miles per second. How many miles per hour is the speed of light? Express your answer in scientific notation to one decimal place. (Mathcounts Handbooks)

Problem 20. Which one represents the greater number? $\dfrac{2}{7}$ or 0.2857 .

Problem 21. Which is closer to $\dfrac{5}{6}$? $\dfrac{9}{10}$ or $\dfrac{3}{4}$.

Problem 22. Which one represents the greater number? $(\dfrac{2}{3})^2$ or 47%.

Problem 23. Which one is closer to $\sqrt{10}$? 3.0 or 3.5.

Problem 24. Which one represents the greater number? $\sqrt{2\frac{1}{4}}$ or $(1.2)^2$.

Problem 25. Which one represents the greater number? $(1.25)^2$ or 150%.

Problem 26. Which one represents the greater number?

$$\sqrt{\frac{1}{9}+\frac{1}{6}} \text{ or } \sqrt{\frac{1}{2}+\frac{1}{8}}$$

Problem 27. Which one is closer to $37\frac{1}{2}\%$? $\frac{1}{3}$ or $\frac{9}{20}$.

Problem 28. Round to the nearest thousandth: 3.60209.

Problem 29. Round the product of 5.37 and 9.67 to the nearest hundredth. (Mathcounts Handbooks)

Problem 30. Which one represents the greatest number?

$$\sqrt{\frac{1}{4}+\frac{1}{8}} \text{ or } \sqrt{\frac{1}{3}+\frac{1}{9}} \text{ or } \sqrt{\frac{1}{5}+\frac{1}{6}}$$

Problem 31. A certain three-digit number has all of its digits distinct. When its digits are reversed, the new three-digit number is less than the original number. When this new number is subtracted from the original, what is the tens digit of the difference? (Mathcounts Handbooks)

Problem 32. Express as a decimal rounded to the nearest hundredth: 3694.8572.

Problem 33. Give the decimal equivalent to: $3 \times \frac{1}{1000} + 2 \times \frac{1}{10}$.

Problem 34. In a certain set of base-ten addition problems, when a two-digit number $\underline{AB}$ is added to a one-digit number B, the result is a three-digit number $C\square\square$. How many different ordered triples (A, B, C) satisfy these conditions? (Mathcounts Handbooks)

Problem 35. What is the sum of all of the digits in the first 99 natural numbers?

Problem 36. It took 3001 digits to number the pages in a book beginning with page 1. How many pages does the book have? (Mathcounts Handbooks)

Problem 37. If the product $1,001,001,001 \times 999 \times 1,000,000,000,001$ is computed, how many 9's are in the product? (Mathcounts Handbooks)

Problem 38. Let $a = 1.234$, $b = 2.34$, and $c = 3.4$. Find the value $a + b + c$ to the nearest hundredth.

Problem 39. Calculate the following to the nearest ten: $\dfrac{0.5 \times 0.12 \times 2500}{31 \times 0.09}$.

Problem 40. How many times does the digit 1 appear in the page numbers of a 500-page book?

Problem 41. Which of the following three numbers is the largest? 20^{30}, 40^{20}, 50^{10}.

ANSWER KEYS

Problem 1. 750,000   **Problem 2.** 5.76   **Problem 3.** 0.00245

Problem 4. 20   **Problem 5.** 120   **Problem 6.** 1×10^{100}

Problem 7. 2.31×10^{-6} **Problem 8.** 9.1×10^{7} **Problem 9.** 2.8×10^{6}.

Problem 10. 2.334×10^{8} **Problem 11.** 3.031×10^{5} **Problem 12.** 3.8×10^{4}

Problem 13. 2.4×10^{10}.   **Problem 14.** 2.7×10^{-19} **Problem 15.** 1.7×10^{31}

Problem 16. 5×10^{2} **Problem 17.** 8.8×10^{8} **Problem 18.** 1.41

Problem 19. 6.7×10^{8} **Problem 20.** $\dfrac{2}{7}$ **Problem 21.** $\dfrac{9}{10}$

Problem 22. 47%.   **Problem 23.** 3.0   **Problem 24.** $\sqrt{2\dfrac{1}{4}}$

Problem 25. $(1.25)^{2}$ **Problem 26.** $\sqrt{\dfrac{1}{2}+\dfrac{1}{8}}$ **Problem 27.** $\dfrac{1}{3}$

Problem 28. (3.602)   **Problem 29.** 51.93   **Problem 30.** $\sqrt{\dfrac{1}{3}+\dfrac{1}{9}}$

Problem 31. 9   **Problem 32.** 3694.86   **Problem 33.** 0.203

Problem 34. 5   **Problem 35.** 900   **Problem 36.** 1027

Problem 37. 24 estimate   **Problem 38.** 6.97   **Problem 39.** 50 is a good

Problem 40. 200   **Problem 41.** 20^{30}

BASIC KNOWLEDGE

Definition

The absolute value of a number x is $|x|$. It is the distance the number is from the zero point on the number line.

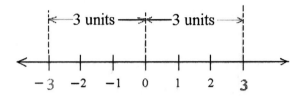

Say: The absolute value of 3 is 3

Write: $|3| = 3$

Say: The absolute value of -3 is 3

Write: $|-3| = 3$

Example:

$$|-3| + |3| = 3 + 3 = 6$$

Properties of Absolute Value:

(1). $|x| = \begin{cases} x & \text{if } x > 0 \\ 0 & \text{if } x = 0 \\ -x & \text{if } x < 0 \end{cases}$ or $|x| = \begin{cases} x & \text{if } x \geq 0 \\ -x & \text{if } x < 0 \end{cases}$ or $|x| = \begin{cases} x & \text{if } x > 0 \\ -x & \text{if } x \leq 0 \end{cases}$

(2). For any real numbers x and y:

$|x| = |y|$ if and only if $x = y$ or $x = -y$.

(3). $|x| \geq 0$. The equality holds if and only if $x = 0$.

(4). $|-x| = |x|$

(5). $|x - y| = |y - x|$

(6). $|xy| = |x| \cdot |y|$, and $\left|\dfrac{x}{y}\right| = \dfrac{|x|}{|y|}$ $y \neq 0$.

Theorem: The solutions to the equation

$$\left|f_1(x)\right| \pm \left|f_2(x)\right| = g(x) \tag{1}$$

are among the solutions to the system of equations:

$$\left.\begin{array}{l}
f_1(x) + f_2(x) + g(x) = 0 \\
f_1(x) + f_2(x) - g(x) = 0 \\
f_1(x) - f_2(x) + g(x) = 0 \\
f_1(x) - f_2(x) - g(x) = 0
\end{array}\right\} \tag{2}$$

Proof:

To solve the equation $\left|f_1(x)\right| + \left|f_2(x)\right| = g(x)$, we need to deal with four cases:

Case 1: $f_1(x) < 0$ and $f_2(x) < 0$

$\left|f_1(x)\right| \pm \left|f_2(x)\right| = g(x) \Rightarrow \quad -f_1(x) - f_2(x) = g(x) \Rightarrow$

$$f_1(x) + f_2(x) + g(x) = 0 \tag{3}$$

Case 2: $f_1(x) < 0$ and $f_2(x) \geq 0$

$\left|f_1(x)\right| \pm \left|f_2(x)\right| = g(x) \Rightarrow \quad -f_1(x) + f_2(x) = g(x) \Rightarrow$

$$f_1(x) - f_2(x) + g(x) = 0 \tag{4}$$

Case 3: $f_1(x) \geq 0$ and $f_2(x) < 0$

$\left|f_1(x)\right| \pm \left|f_2(x)\right| = g(x) \Rightarrow \quad f_1(x) - f_2(x) = g(x) \Rightarrow$

$$f_1(x) - f_2(x) - g(x) = 0 \tag{5}$$

Case 4: $f_1(x) \geq 0$ and $f_2(x) \geq 0$

$\left|f_1(x)\right| \pm \left|f_2(x)\right| = g(x) \Rightarrow \quad f_1(x) + f_2(x) = g(x) \Rightarrow$

$f_1(x) + f_2(x) - g(x) = 0$ (6)

Similarly, we get (2) for $|f_1(x)| - |f_2(x)| = g(x)$.

After we get the solutions to the equation (2), we need to check them for equation (1).

Example 1: Find all values of $a + b$ if $|a| = 1$ and $|b| = 2$.

Solution: $1, 3, -1, -3$.

We need to get rid of the absolute value signs

$|a| = 1 \qquad \Rightarrow \qquad a = \pm 1$

$|b| = 2 \qquad \Rightarrow \qquad b = \pm 2$

When $a = 1$ and $b = 2$, $a + b = 3$

When $a = -1$ and $b = 2$, $a + b = 1$

When $a = 1$ and $b = -2$, $a + b = -1$

When $a = -1$ and $b = -2$, $a + b = -3$

Example 2: Simplify $2 - \left|2 - |x - 2|\right|$ if $x < -1$.

Solution: $2 + x$

Since $x < -1$, $x - 2 < 0$.

$2 - \left|2 - |x - 2|\right| = 2 - |2 + (x - 2)| = 2 - |x| = 2 + x$

Example 3: Simplify $|6 - x| + |x - 10|$ if $|5 - x| = 5 - x$ and $|3 - x| = x - 3$

Solution: $16 - 2x$

Since $|5 - x| = 5 - x$, $5 - x \geq 0 \qquad \Rightarrow \qquad x \leq 5$

Since $|3 - x| = x - 3$, $x - 3 \geq 0 \qquad \Rightarrow \qquad x \geq 3$

$|6 - x| + |x - 10| = 6 - x + (10 - x) = 16 - 2x$

Example 4: Simplify $|b - a| + |a + c| + |c - b|$. The coordinates of a, b, and c are shown on the number line below.

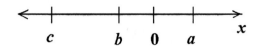

Solution: $-2c$

From the number line we know that $a > 0$, $b < 0$, $c < 0$, and $|c| > |a| > |b| > 0$.

$|b - a| + |a + c| + |c - b| = (a - b) - (a + c) + (b - c) = -2c$

Example 5: Simplify $|a| + |b| + |a + b| + |b - c|$. The coordinates of a, b, and c are shown on the number line below.

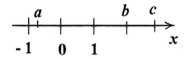

Solution: $b + c$

Since $a < 0$, $b > 0$, $c > b$. $b > a$.

$|a| + |b| + |a + b| + |b - c| = (-a) + b + (b + a) + c - b = b + c$.

Example 6: Calculate: $\left| \dfrac{1}{1992} - \dfrac{1}{1991} \right| + \left| \dfrac{1}{1993} - \dfrac{1}{1992} \right| - \left| \dfrac{1}{1993} - \dfrac{1}{1991} \right|$.

Solution: 0

$$\left| \frac{1}{1992} - \frac{1}{1991} \right| + \left| \frac{1}{1993} - \frac{1}{1992} \right| - \left| \frac{1}{1993} - \frac{1}{1991} \right| =$$

$$-\left(\frac{1}{1992} - \frac{1}{1991} \right) - \left(\frac{1}{1993} - \frac{1}{1992} \right) - \left[-\left(\frac{1}{1993} - \frac{1}{1991} \right) \right]$$

$$= -\frac{1}{1992} + \frac{1}{1991} - \frac{1}{1993} + \frac{1}{1992} + \frac{1}{1993} - \frac{1}{1991} = 0$$

Example 7: Evaluate $a^2 - 2ab$ if $|a - 2| + |3 + b| = 0$.

Solution: 16.

Since $|a - 2| \geq 0$ and $|3 + b| \geq 0$ and $|a - 2| + |3 + b| = 0$, so $|a - 2| = 0$ and $|3 + b| = 0$

$a = 2$ and $b = -3$

$a^2 - 2ab = 2^2 - 2 \times 2 \times (-3) = 16$

Example 8: What is the sum of all values of x for which $|x-3|+|3-x|-1=3$?
(Mathcounts Competitions)

Solution: 6.

Method 1: $|x-3|+|3-x|-1=3 \quad\Rightarrow\quad |x-3|+|3-x|=4$

$(x-3+3-x+4)(x-3+3-x-4)[x-3-(3-x)+4][x-3-(3-x)-4]=0 \Rightarrow$

$4\times(-4)(2x-2)(2x-10)=0 \qquad \Rightarrow (2x-2)(2x-10)=0$

$x=1$ and $x=5$

We check both values and know that they are the solutions. The sum is $1+5=6$.

Method 2: $|x-3|+|3-x|-1=3 \Rightarrow |x-3|+|x-3|=4 \qquad\Rightarrow\qquad 2|x-3|=4$

$\Rightarrow \qquad |x-3|=2$

$x=1$ and $x=5$

The sum is $1+5=6$.

Example 9: Find the integer solutions of $|x^2-x|-|5-2x|=1$.

Solution: 2 or -3.

$|x^2-x|-|5-2x|=1 \quad\Rightarrow$

$x^2-x+5-2x+1=0$	$\Rightarrow$ $x^2-3x+6=0$	(no integer solutions)
$x^2-x+5-2x-1=0$	$\Rightarrow$ $x^2-3x+4=0$	(no integer solutions)
$x^2-x-(5-2x)-1=0$	$\Rightarrow$ $x^2+x-4=0$	(no integer solutions)
$x^2-x-(5-2x)+1=0$	$\Rightarrow$ $x^2+x-6=0$	$x=2$ or $x=-3$ (checked)

Example 10: Solve the equation $|x+1|+\frac{1}{2}|2x-3|=5x+2$.

Solution: $x=\dfrac{1}{10}$

$x+1+x-\dfrac{3}{2}+5x+2=0 \quad\Rightarrow\quad 7x+\dfrac{3}{2}=0 \quad\Rightarrow\quad x=-\dfrac{3}{14}$ (Checked no)

$x+1+x-\dfrac{3}{2}-(5x+2)=0 \Rightarrow \quad -3x-\dfrac{5}{2}=0\Rightarrow \quad x=-\dfrac{5}{6}$ (Checked no)

$$x + 1 - (x - \frac{3}{2}) + 5x + 2 = 0 \Rightarrow 5x + \frac{9}{2} = 0 \Rightarrow x = -\frac{9}{10} \text{(Checked no)}$$

$$x + 1 - (x - \frac{3}{2}) - (5x + 2) = 0 \Rightarrow -5x + \frac{1}{2} = 0 \Rightarrow x = \frac{1}{10} \text{ (Checked yes)}$$

The only solution is $x = \dfrac{1}{10}$.

Try it yourself.

(1). Simplify: $-2 + |-2 + (-2)| + (-2)$.

Answer: 0.

(2). If $a < b$, what is the value of $|a - b| + a + b$?

Answer: 2b.

(3). Simplify: $|-3^2 + 4|$.

Answer: 5.

(4). Given that $x < 5$, rewrite $5x - |x - 5|$ without using absolute value signs. (Mathcounts Handbooks)

Answer: $6x - 5$.

(5). Find all values of n for which the following is true: $|n + 3| = 8$ (Mathcounts Handbooks)

Answer: 5, – 11.

(6). Solve for b: $|b + 4| = |-15|$.

Answer: – 19, 11.

(7). If $a = b - 1$, then what is the value of $|a - b| + |b - a|$?

Answer: 2.

(8). Given that $a^2 + 2ab + b^2 = 144$, what is the greatest possible value for $a + b$? (Mathcounts Competitions)

Answer: 12.

(9). Express as a decimal: $|6.3| - |-6.15|$.

Answer: 0.15.

(10). Express in simplest form: $-(2+6)^2 - |-2-6|^3$.

Answer: -576.

(11). Evaluate: $|-10-(-7)|$.

Answer: 3.

(12). Simplify $|a-b| + |b-c| - |c-a|$. The coordinates of a, b, and c are shown on the number line below.

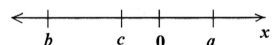

Answer: $2c - 2b$.

(13). Evaluate $\frac{1}{4}a^{2b-1} - (a^3 + \frac{1}{2}a^b + 4)$ if $2|3a-2b| + (4b-12)^2 = 0$.

Answer: -8 ($a = 2$ and $b = 3$).

EXERCISES

Problem 1. If $M(x,y) = \frac{1}{2}(|y-x|+y+x)$, what is the value of $M(-1,4)$? (Mathcounts Handbooks)

Problem 2. Find all values of w for which the following is true: $|w| = 7$.

Problem 3. Find the value(s) of m for which the following is true: $|2m+6| = 10$

Problem 4. Find the value(s) of n for which $|2n+1| = 9$.

Problem 5. Find the value(s) of x for which $|2x-3| = 5$.

Problem 6. What is the value of x which will yield the minimum value of y in the equation $y = |x-2| - 2$?

Problem 7. Find the value(s) of x for which $|x+1| = |x-1|$.

Problem 8. If $a \times b = 42$ and $a - b = 11$, find $|a+b|$.

Problem 9. Find the sum of the members of the solution set of $|2x+5| = 5$.

Problem 10. Find the product of the solutions of $|y| = 2(|y|-1)$.

Problem 11. Find the two values of x for which $|x-1|+|x|+|x+1| = \frac{5}{2}$. (Mathcounts Handbooks)

Problem 12. Find the solution to the equation $x|x| = 2x+1$ which has the smallest value. (Mathcounts Handbooks)

Problem 13. Find the sum of all values of x such that $|x-1|=7$.

Problem 14. Find the arithmetic mean of all solutions to $|x-2|=2$.

Problem 15. Find the arithmetic mean, expressed as a common fraction, of all solutions to $|4x|-\sqrt{4x}=0$. (Mathcounts Handbooks)

Problem 16. What value of x makes the equation true? $2x+4=|-17+3|$.

Problem 17. What is the sum of the solutions to $|4x-6|=4$?

Problem 18. If $x\in\{-3,-2,-1,0,1,2\}$, what is the maximum value for $|x-8|$?
 (Mathcounts Competitions)

Problem 19. Evaluate: $|-2-(-5)|$.

Problem 20. Simplify completely: $-2(4-1)(-1-2^2)+|-3+5|$.

Problem 21. Find all values of x for which $|x+2|+2=20$.

Problem 22. Find all values of n for which $|n-1|=5$ is true.

Problem 23. Find all values of x which satisfy $|x-3|=|x+5|$.

Problem 24. Find all real numbers n for which $|n+2|=|n-4|$.

Problem 25. Find all possible values of n which make the following true: $|n-1|+5=10$.

Problem 26. Find all possible values of y for which $|3y+7|=|2y-1|$.

241

Problem 27. Find all values of x which satisfy $|x| = |x+1|$.

Problem 28. Find all real values of x for which $x + |x| = 0$.

Problem 29. If $X > 3$, find Y for which $Y = |X| - |3 - X|$.

Problem 30. $|x+2| + |y-3| = 1$ is an equation for a square. How many units are in the lengths of its diagonals?

Problem 31. Find the positive difference between the solutions of $|x+3| = 6$.

Problem 32. For what value of x less than zero will $|x-1| = 23$?

Problem 33. Find the sum of all solutions of the equation $|2 - x| = 3$.

Problem 34. Find the sum of the solutions for $|2x| = 127$.

Problem 35. What is the product of all solutions to the equation $|2x - 5| = 7$?

Problem 36. What is the product of all real numbers n for which $|n^2 - 9n + 20| = |16 - n^2|$?

Problem 37. Find the least value of x that is a solution of $|-x+3| = 7$.

Problem 38. What is the sum of the values of x that satisfy the equation $|x+3| - 5 = 2$?

Problem 39. Given that $a = b + 5$, what is the value of $|a - b| + |b - a|$?

Problem 40. For how many values of x does $|3x - 2| - 4 = 0$?

Problem 41. Find the smallest value of x such that $|5x - 1| = |3x + 2|$? Express your answer as a common fraction.

Problem 42. Find the number of solutions of the equation $|x + 2| = 2x$.

Problem 43. Find the positive difference between the solutions to $\left|\dfrac{x}{2} - 6\right| = 20$.

Problem 44. Find the value(s) of T for which $|T + 4| = |2T - 6|$. Express your answer(s) as whole number(s) or as common fraction(s).

Problem 45. If x and y are prime numbers and $x + y = 100$, find the smallest possible value of $|x - y|$.

Problem 46. Find x such that $|x + 2| = |x - 3|$.

ANSWER KEYS

Problem 1. 4

Problem 2.$- 7, 7$

Problem 3. $2, - 8$

Problem 4. 4 and $- 5$

Problem 5.$- 1$ and 4

Problem 6. 2

Problem 7. 0

Problem 8. 17

Problem 9.$- 5$

Problem 10. $- 4$

Problem 11. 1/2 and $- 1/2$

Problem 12. $- 1$

Problem 13. 2

Problem 14. 2

Problem 15. 1/8

Problem 16. 5

Problem 17. 3

Problem 18. 11

Problem 19. 3

Problem 20. 32

Problem 21. $16, - 20$

Problem 22. $- 4, 6$

Problem 23. $- 1$

Problem 24. 1

Problem 25. $6, - 4$

Problem 26. $\{-\dfrac{6}{5}, - 8\}$

Problem 27. $-\dfrac{1}{2}$

Problem 28. $x \le 0$

Problem 29. 3

Problem 30. 2 (units)

Problem 31. 12

Problem 32. $- 22$

Problem 33. 4

Problem 34. 0

Problem 35. $- 6$

Problem 36. 2

Problem 37. $- 4$

Problem 38. $- 6$

Problem 39. 10

Problem 40. 2 (values)

Problem 41. $-\dfrac{1}{8}$

Problem 42. 1 (solution)

Problem 43. 80

Problem 44. $10, \dfrac{2}{3}$

Problem 45. 6

Problem 46. $\dfrac{1}{2}$.

BASIC KNOWLEDGE

Order of operations

The order of operations is a rule (convention) telling you which operations should be performed first in a given expression.

PEMDAS

A common technique for remembering the order of operations is the abbreviation "PEMDAS" (Please Excuse My Dear Aunt Sally). It stands for "Parentheses, Exponents, Multiplication and Division, and Addition and Subtraction". This tells you the ranks of the operations.

P: Parentheses
E: Exponents (Powers and Square Roots, etc.)
MD: Multiplication and Division (left-to-right)
AS: Addition and Subtraction (left-to-right)

You should do what is possible within parentheses first, then exponents, then multiplication and division (from left to right), and then addition and subtraction (from left to right). If parentheses are enclosed within other parentheses, work from the inside out.

Notes:

A raised dot or parentheses can be used to indicate multiplication.

$3 \cdot 2$ means 3×2

3(4), (3)4, or (3)(4)   means 3×4.

A fraction bar can be used to indicate division.

$$\frac{24-2}{4+8}$$ means $(24 - 2) \div (4 + 8)$

Example 1: Calculate: $5 + 3 \times 7$

Solution: 26.

Steps:

(1). multiply 3 and 7
(2). add 5 and 21

$5 + 3 \times 7 = 5 + 21 = 26$

Example 2: Calculate: $9 \div 3 + 4 \times 7 - 20 \div 4$

Solution: 26.

Steps:

(1). divided 9 by 3
(2). multiply 4 and 7
(3). divide 20 by 4
(4). add 3 and 28
(5). subtract 5 from 31

$9 \div 3 + 4 \times 7 - 20 \div 4$

$= 3 + 28 - 5 = 31 - 5 = 26.$

Example 3: Calculate: $2(3 + 5) - 3 \cdot 4$

Solution: 4.

Steps:

(1). Add 3 and 5
(2). multiply 2 and 8
(3). multiply 3 and 4
(4). subtract 12 from 16

$2(3 + 5) - 3 \cdot 4$

$= 2(8) - 12 = 16 - 12 = 4$

Example 4: Simplify $5 + 3^2$.

Solution: 14.

We need to simplify the term with the exponent before trying to add in the 5:

$5 + 3^2 = 5 + 9 = 14$

Example 5: Simplify $5 + (2 + 1)^2$.

Solution: 14.

We have to simplify inside the parentheses before we can take the exponent. Then we do the addition of the 5.

$5 + (2 + 1)^2 = 5 + (3)^2 = 5 + 9 = 14$

Example 6: Simplify $1976 + [5 + (7 - 6)]^2$.

Solution: 2012.

Steps:

(1). simplify inside the parentheses
(2). simplify inside the square brackets
(3). take care of the squaring
(4). add in the 1976

$1976 + [5 + (7 - 6)]^2 \;\; = 1976 + [5 + 1]^2 = 1976 + [6]^2 = 1976 + 36 = 2012$

Example 7: Simplify $100 - 3[8 - 2(6 - 3)] \div 2$.

Solution: 97.

Steps:
(1). the parentheses
(2). the square brackets
(3). do the division

(4). add in the 100.

$$100 - 3[8 - 2(6 - 3)] \div 2 = 100 - 3[8 - 2(3)] \div 2 = 100 - 3[8 - 6] \div 2$$
$$= 100 - 3[2] \div 2 = 100 - 6 \div 2 = 100 - 3 = 97.$$

Example 8: Simplify $19 - 3(8 - 3)^2 \div 5$.

Solution: 4.

$$19 - 3(8 - 3)^2 \div 5 = 19 - 3(5)^2 \div 5 = 19 - 3(25) \div 5 = 19 - 75 \div 5 = 19 - 15 = 4$$

Example 9: Simplify $60 \div 2[8 - 3(4 - 2)] + 1$.

Solution: 16.

$$60 \div 2[8 - 3(4 - 2)] + 1 = 60 \div 2[8 - 3(2)] + 1 = 60 \div 2[8 - 6] + 1 = 60 \div 2[2] + 1$$
$$= 60 \div 4 + 1 = 15 + 1 = 16.$$

Note: Even though multiplication and division are at the same level (the left-to-right rule should apply), parentheses outrank division. So the first 2 goes with the [2], rather than with the "60 divided by". That is, multiplication/division that is indicated by placement against parentheses (or brackets, etc) is "stronger" than "regular" multiplication/division.

Example 10: Evaluate: $\dfrac{3[8 + 2(5 - 3)]}{2}$ (Mathcounts Competitions)

Solution: 18

$$\frac{3[8 + 2(5 - 3)]}{2} = \frac{3[8 + 2(2)]}{2} = \frac{3[8 + 4]}{2} = \frac{3 \times 12}{2} = 3 \times 6 = 18$$

Remember to reduce fractions when you're done.

Example 11: Calculate: $\dfrac{8 + 3 \times 4 \times 50 + 4^3}{(7 - 5)(5 - 1)}$.

Solution: 84.

$$\frac{8+3\times4\times50+4^3}{(7-5)(5-1)}=\frac{8+600+64}{2\times4}=\frac{672}{8}=84$$

Example 12: Calculate: $\dfrac{4+8}{2+1}-(3-2)+2$

Solution: 5

$$\frac{4+8}{2+1}-(3-2)+2=\frac{12}{3}-1+2=4-1+2=5$$

Example 13: Calculate: $8+\dfrac{16-4}{2^2+2}-2$

Solution: 8.

$$8+\frac{16-4}{2^2+2}-2=8+\frac{12}{4+2}-2=8+\frac{12}{6}-2=8-2+2=8$$

Example 14: Calculate: $5^2+(\sqrt{121}-3^2)^{10}-10^3$

Solution: 49

$$5^2+(\sqrt{121}-3^2)^{10}-10^3=25+(11-9)^{10}-1000=25+1024-1000=25+24=49$$

Example 15: If $a = 1 \div 2 \div 3 \div 4$, $b = 1 \div (2 \div 3 \div 4)$, $c = 1 \div (2 \div 3) \div 4$, and $d = 1 \div 2 \div (3 \div 4)$, find the value of $(b \div a) \div (c \div d)$.

Solution: 256.

$$a=1\times\frac{1}{2}\times\frac{1}{3}\times\frac{1}{4}=\frac{1}{24}. \quad b=\frac{1}{2\times\frac{1}{3}\times\frac{1}{4}}=6. \quad c=1\times\frac{3}{2}\times\frac{1}{4}=\frac{3}{8}. \quad d=\frac{1}{2}\div\frac{3}{4}=\frac{1}{2}\times\frac{4}{3}=\frac{2}{3}.$$

$$(b\div a)\div(c\div d)=(6\div\frac{1}{24})\div(\frac{3}{8}\div\frac{2}{3})=6\times24\div\frac{9}{16}=6\times24\times\frac{16}{9}=256.$$

EXERCISES

Problem 1. Simplify: $3 + 4 \cdot 7 - 9$.

Problem 2. Simplify: $-3 \cdot (5 - 8 \cdot 4) + 4$.

Problem 3. Simplify: $-5 \cdot (-4 + 9) \div 4 + 6$.

Problem 4. Simplify: $9 - 4(3 - 2.4)^2$.

Problem 5. Express in simplest form: $-6 \div 2 \cdot 3$.

Problem 6. Simplify: $30 - 4 \div 2 + 3 \cdot 5$.

Problem 7. Compute: $2 + 5 \cdot 7 - 7$.

Problem 8. Calculate $7 + 3^2 \cdot 4 - 2(14 - 8 \div 2)$.

Problem 9. Express in simplest form: $15 \div 5 \div 3 \times 2 \times 5 \times \dfrac{1}{2}$.

Problem 10. Express in simplest form: $8 + 18 \div 3 \div 6 \times (18 - 5 - 4)$

Problem 11. Express in the simplest form $3 + 3 \div 3 + 3 \times 3 - 3$.

Problem 12. Simplify: $-2 + |-2 + (-2)| + (-2)$.

Problem 13. Express $\left(-13 - (-42)\right) \div \left(46 + 3(-2)^2\right)$ as a fraction in simplest form.

Problem 14. Simplify: $4 + 6 \div 2 \times 8 - 3$.

Problem 15. Simplify: $9 + 9 \div 9 \times 9 - 9$.

Problem 16. Simplify: $(67 + 7 \times 2) - \left[(29+52) \div 2\frac{1}{4} \right]$.

Problem 17. Simplify: $1 - 7(3 - 4) \div (-3 + 1)$.

Problem 18. Simply: $5 \bullet 11^2 - 3(2^4 \div 2 \bullet 3)$.

Problem 19. What is the value of $5 \div 5 \div 5 \div \frac{1}{5} \div \frac{1}{5}$?

Problem 20. Using each operation symbol only once, insert +, −, ×, and ÷ in the correct order to get the desired result.

      $11 \square\ 3\ \square\ 2\ \square\ 4\ \square\ 1 = 9$ (Mathcounts Handbooks)

Problem 21. The value of the expression $1 \div 2 \div 3 \div 5 \div 7 \div 11 \div 13$ can be altered by including parentheses. If we are allowed to place as many parentheses as we want, how many distinct values can be obtained for this expression?   (Mathcounts Handbooks)

Problem 22. What is the maximum value that can be attained from the following expression when grouping symbols are added? (Mathcounts Handbooks)

      $4 + 5 \times 8 + 4 - 2 \times 3$

Problem 23. How many distinct values can be obtained for the expression $1 \div 2 \div 3 \div 5 \div 7 \div 11 \div 13 \div 17$ if an unlimited number of parentheses may be placed in the expression? (Mathcounts Handbooks)

Problem 24. Simplify: $\sqrt{1\frac{1}{2} + 1\frac{1}{2} \div 1\frac{1}{2} - (1\frac{1}{2})(1\frac{1}{2})}$.

Problem 25. Fill in addition signs to produce the sum. (Example: $1 + 23 + 4 = 28$) (Mathcounts Competitions)

      $1\ 2\ 3\ 4\ 5\ 6\ 7\ 8\ 9 = 3564$

Problem 26. What is the value of $\dfrac{6 + \dfrac{4}{3} - 3 \div (2 + 2^2)}{1 + 2 \times 3}$?

Problem 27. Simplify: $3 + 3(3) - 3 \div 3$.

Problem 28. Find the value of $8[6^2 - 3(11)] \div 8 + 3$.

Problem 29. Evaluate: $5 - 7(8 - 3^2)4$.

Problem 30. Express in simplest form: $3^3 \bullet 3 + 7^0 - 2(16 - 8 \div 4)$.

Problem 31. Simplify: $2^{-1} \bullet (3 - 5)^{-2} + (1 - \dfrac{1}{3})$.

Problem 32. Simplify: $4 - 8[3^2 - 4(-3)]$.

Problem 33. Compute: $5 - 7(5^2 - 3^3)^4$.

ANSWER KEYS:

Problem 1. 22   **Problem 2.** 85   **Problem 3.** $-\dfrac{1}{4}$

Problem 4. 7.56   **Problem 5.** -9   **Problem 6.** 43

Problem 7. 30   **Problem 8.** 23   **Problem 9.** 5

Problem 10. 17   **Problem 11.** 10   **Problem 12.** 0

Problem 13. $\dfrac{1}{2}$ **Problem 14.** 25   **Problem 15.** 9

Problem 16. 45   **Problem 17.** $-\dfrac{5}{2}$ **Problem 18.** 533

Problem 19. 5   **Problem 20.** $-, \times, +, \div$ **Problem 21.** 32

Problem 22. $[(4+5) \times (8+4) - 2 \times 3 = 318$ **Problem 23.** 64

Problem 24. 1/2

Problem 25. $12 + 3456 + 7 + 89$ **Problem 26.** 41/42

Problem 27. 11   **Problem 28.** 6   **Problem 29.** 33

Problem 30. 54   **Problem 31.** 19/24   **Problem 32.** -164

Problem 33. -107

BASIC KNOWLEDGE

TERMS

Variable: A letter (the most popular letter is x) acts as a placeholder in an algebraic expression. It is called a variable because the value can change.

Like terms: The algebraic expression $3x + 2x$ has two terms with the same variable x. $3x$ and $2x$ are called the like terms. Like terms can be combined together. $3x + 2x = 5x$.

Integers: The set of all integers: $\{....... -3, \ -2, \ -1, \ 0, \ +1, +2, +3,.....\}$, shown on a number line:

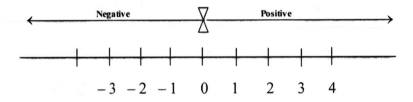

The symbol for the positive integer 4 is called the sign and is written as $+4$ or 4.

The symbol for the negative four is written as -4.

RULES FOR MULTIPLYING AND DIVIDING INTEGERS

The product or quotient of two integers with the same sign is positive.

Examples:

(1). Calculate: 11×27
Solution:
$11 \times 27 = 297$

(2) Calculate: $(-11) \times (-27)$
Solution:
$(-11) \times (-27) = 297$

Two negative signs cancel each other.

<u>Note: It is incorrect to write this way: -11×-27.</u>

Remember: two signs are never added, subtracted, multiplied, divided, etc. together without parentheses or brackets

Examples: How would you express the product of negative five multiplied by negative seven?

Incorrect: -5×-7
Incorrect: $(-5) \times -7$
Correct: $(-5) \times (-7)$
Correct: $-5 \times (-7)$

The product or quotient of two integers with different signs is always negative.

> **Examples**:
>
> (1). Calculate: -11×27
> Solution:
> $-11 \times 27 = -297$
>
> (2) Calculate: $11 \times (-27)$
> Solution:
> $11 \times (-27) = -297$

RULES FOR ADDING AND SUBTRACTING INTEGERS

> *To add integers with the same sign, add their values. Give the result the same sign as the integers.*
>
> **Examples:**
>
> (1). Calculate: $18 + 12$
> Solution: $18 + 12 = 30$.
>
> (2). Calculate: $-18 - 12$
> Solution:

Step 1: Ignore the signs. Just add $18 + 12 = 30$

Step 2: Put the sign back to the result $\Rightarrow$ -30

   The answer: $-18 - 12 = -30$.

To add integers with different signs, ignore the signs first, subtract the smaller one from the greater one. Give the result the same sign as the integer with the greater value without the sign.

Examples:

(1). Calculate: $18 - 12$

Solution:

Step 1: Ignore the signs. Subtract the smaller number from the greater number:
$18 - 12 = 6$

Step 2: Put the sign of the greater number to the result: 6.
The answer: $18 - 12 = 6$.

(2) Calculate: $-18 + 12$
Solution:
Step 1: Ignore the signs. Subtract the smaller number from the greater number:
$18 - 12 = 6$

Step 2: Put the sign of the greater number to the result: $\Rightarrow$ -6
The answer: $-18 + 12 = -6$.

RULES FOR REMOVING PARENTHESES

If the sign before the parentheses is positive, there is no sign change in each term inside the parentheses when the parentheses are removed.

Example 1: Find the sum of 84 and $(-a + b - 3c)$

   Solution:

$$84 + (-a + b - 3c) = 84 - a + b - 3c$$

If the sign before the parentheses is negative, each term inside the parentheses changes its sign from positive to negative or vice versa when the parentheses are removed.

Example 2: Find the difference of 84 and -48

> **Solution:** 132.
> $$84 - (-48) = 84 + 48 = 132 \qquad \Rightarrow \qquad 84 - (-48) = 84 + 48 = 132$$

Note 1: It is incorrect to write the expression this way: $84 - -48$.

Note 2: Two negative signs cancel each other.
Ignore 84 and deal with the rest first:
$$-(-48) = -(-1 \times 48) = -(-1) \times 48 = (-1) \times (-1) \times 48 = 1 \times 48 = 48$$

So $84 - (-48) = 84 + 48 = 132.$

Example 3: Find the difference of 84 and $(-a + b - 3c)$

> **Solution:**
>
> $$84 - (-a + b - 3c) = 84 + a - b + 3c$$

RULES FOR ADDING PARENTHESES

If the sign before the parenthesis is positive, there is no sign change in the terms when the parentheses are added around them.

Example 4: Find the sum of 84 and $(a + b - 3c)$

> **Solution:** The following expressions are equivalent:
>
> $$84 + a + b - 3c$$

$$= 84 + (a + b - 3c)$$

$$= 84 + (a + b) - 3c$$

$$= (84 + a + b) - 3c$$

$$= 84 + a + (b - 3c)$$

If the sign before the parenthesis is negative, there is sign change for these terms when the parentheses are added around them.

Example 4: The following expressions are equivalent:

$84 - a - b - 3c + 4d$

$$= 84 - (a + b + 3c - 4d)$$

$$= 84 - a - (b + 3c - 4d)$$

$$= -(-84 + a + b + 3c - 4d)$$

Try it yourself:

Add parentheses to the last two terms of following expressions in two different ways:

(1). $3a - 2b - 6c + 4$

(2). $3a - 2b + 6c - 4$

(3). $3a + 2b - 6c - 4$

RULES FOR COMBINING THE LIKE TERMS

The expression $3x^2 + 4x - 6$ consists of three terms: $3x^2, 4x$, and -6. The coefficient of the term $3x^2$ is 3, and the degree about x is 2. The coefficient of the term $4x$ is 4, and the degree about x is 1. The coefficient of the term -6 is itself, and the degree about x is 0.

Like terms are terms with (1) the same variable and (2) the same degree about the variable.

To combine like terms is to add the coefficients but to keep the variable and the degree unchanged.

 Examples:

(1). Express in simplest form : $8(3n + 2) - 7$

Answer: $24n + 9$

(2). Express in simplest form: $7(4 - n) - 4n + 2$

Answer: $-11n + 30$

(3). Express in simplest form: $2(3n + 4) - (5n + 2)$

Answer: $n + 6$

(4). Simplify the expression: $3(5n - 4) + 9(n + 1)$

Answer: $24n - 3$

(5). Simplify the expression: $-3(n + 4) + 7(n - 1) + 20$

Answer: $4n + 1$

(6). Simplify the expression: $-(7n - 5)^2 - 4(2 - 8n)$

Answer: $-49n^2 + 102n - 33$

(7). Express in simplest form: $5a^2b(2ab)^2$

Answer: $20a^4b^3$

(8). Which of the following terms are like terms?

      (A) $\dfrac{3}{m}$ and $\dfrac{5}{m}$ (B) $\dfrac{1}{2}xy^2$ and $0.5yx^2$ (C) $7ab^5c^3$ and $-\dfrac{1}{5}ac^3b^5$

      (D) $\dfrac{1}{2a^2b}$ and $\dfrac{1}{3ba^2}$

Solution: (A), (C), and (D).

For (A), if we let x be $\dfrac{1}{m}$, we get $3x + 5x = 8x$ or $\dfrac{8}{m}$.

For (B), the exponents are different for x and y.

For (C), two terms have the same variables raised to the same power. The order of the variables does not matter.

(D) is similar to (C).

ALGEBRA EXPRESSIONS

An algebraic expression is a combination of variables, numbers, and operation signs. To evaluate an expression, you just replace variables with numbers and find the value.

Examples: Use an algebraic expression to represent each of the following:

(1). The amount of money Alex has (in cents) if he has 6 more dimes than the number of dimes Bob has.

Solution: $10(x + 6)$ cents.
Let x be the number of dimes Bob has.
Then $x + 6$ is the number of dimes Alex has.
So, Alex has $10(x + 6)$ cents.

(2). The sum of three unknown numbers.

Solution: $x + y + z$ (or $a + b + c$)

(3) An odd positive integer

Solution: $2n + 1$ where n is a nonnegative integer.
or $2n - 1$ where n is a positive integer.

(4). The sum of the product of four consecutive positive integers and 1.

Solution: $n(n + 1)(n + 2)(n + 3) + 1$

(5). Ten less than 8 times a number.

Solution: $8x - 10$.

(6). The sum of a number, its square, and its square root is 2457.

Solution: $x + x^2 + \sqrt{x} = 2457$.

(7). Two times the smallest of three consecutive odd integers is 9 more than three times the middle integer.

Solution:
Let the three consecutive odd integers be $2n + 1$, $2n + 3$, and $2n + 5$.
Answer is: $2(2n + 1) = 9 + 3(2n + 3)$.

(8). The shaded area in the figure below:

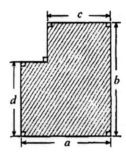

Solution: $ad + (b - d)c$

(9). The area of $\triangle ABC$. a and b are the side lengths of two squares shown in the figure.

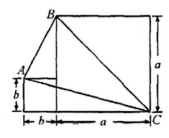

Solution:

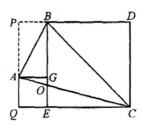

$$(a+b)\times a - \frac{1}{2}(a+b)\times b - \frac{1}{2}a^2 - \frac{1}{2}b(a-b)$$

$$= a^2 + ab - \frac{1}{2}ab - \frac{1}{2}b^2 - \frac{1}{2}a^2 - \frac{1}{2}ab + \frac{1}{2}b^2 = \frac{1}{2}a^2$$

(10). The area of the larger square by two different ways

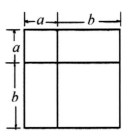

Solution: (1) The area $= (a + b)^2$.

  (2) The area $= a^2 + 2ab + b^2$

It is seen that $(a + b)^2 = a^2 + 2ab + b^2$

TRY IT YOURSELF

(1). Two times the sum of three unknown numbers.
Answer: $2(x + y + z)$

(2). The difference between $\frac{4}{5}$ of x and $\frac{1}{3}$.

Answer: $\frac{4}{5}x - \frac{1}{3}$.

(3). The number that is divisible by 3 with the quotient of n.
Answer: $3n$.

(4). Twice the difference between a number and 7.

Answer: $2(x - 7)$.

(5). Four times the sum of a number and 1001.

Answer: $4(x + 1001)$.

(6). Twice the difference between a number and 1024.

Answer: $2(x - 1024)$.

(7). The square of the sum of two numbers.

Answer: $(x + y)^2$.

(8). The quotient of a number and 2 less than the number.

Answer: $\dfrac{x}{x - 2}$

(9). The area of the shaded region.

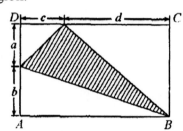

Answer:

$$(a+b)(c+d) - \frac{1}{2}ac - \frac{1}{2}b(c+d) - \frac{1}{2}d(a+b)$$

$$= \frac{1}{2}(ac + bc + ad)$$

(10). The area of the shaded region.

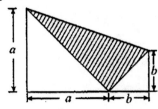

263

Answer:

$$\frac{(a+b)}{2} \cdot (a+b) - \frac{1}{2}a^2 - \frac{1}{2}b^2$$

$$= \frac{1}{2}a^2 + \frac{1}{2}b^2 + ab - \frac{1}{2}a^2 - \frac{1}{2}b^2 = ab$$

EXERCISES

Problem 1. Simplify: $3(n + 7)$.

Problem 2. Simplify: $a^2b \cdot 3ab^3c$.

Problem 3. Simplify: $(2ab^2)^3$.

Problem 4. Express in simplest form: $\dfrac{2a^3b}{2ab}$.

Problem 5. Simplify and express the result using only positive exponents: $\dfrac{(6a^2b)^2}{3a^2b^3}$.

Problem 6. Express in simplest form and without negative exponents:

$$\cfrac{1}{1 - \cfrac{1}{1 - \cfrac{1}{1 - \cfrac{1}{x}}}}$$

Problem 7. If p is the product of $(x + 1)$ and $(x^2 - x + 1)$ and q is the product of $(x - 1)$ and $(x^2 + x + 1)$, find the value of $p - q$. (Mathcounts Competitions)

Problem 8. Simplify: $\dfrac{\dfrac{x-2}{2x} + \dfrac{1}{x+2}}{\dfrac{3}{2} - \dfrac{6}{x^2 + 2x}}$.

Problem 9. Express the quotient in simplest form using only positive exponents:
$\dfrac{(8a^3b^2)^2}{4a^4b^6}$.

Problem 10. Simplify: $(x^4y^{-2})(x^{-1}y^5)$.

Problem 11. Simplify: $\dfrac{\dfrac{1}{x-1}+\dfrac{1}{x+1}}{\dfrac{2}{x+1}-\dfrac{1}{x-1}}$.

Problem 12. Simplify: $\dfrac{\dfrac{1}{a}-\dfrac{1}{b}}{\dfrac{1}{b}-\dfrac{1}{a}}$.

Problem 13. Find the value of $a + b$ for $\sqrt{\dfrac{3}{2}\times\dfrac{4}{3}\times\dfrac{5}{4}\times\dfrac{6}{5}\times\cdots\times\dfrac{a}{b}}=3$.

Problem 14. Given $x = 3$ and $y = 2$, find the value of the expression $\dfrac{4x^2}{9y^2}$.

Problem 15. Find the quotient when $6x^{2a+b-c}$ is divided by $3x^{a+2b+3c}$.

Problem 16. If $(x + 2)(3x^2 - x + 5) = Ax^3 + Bx^2 + Cx + D$, what is the value of $A + B + C + D$?   (Mathcounts Competitions)

Problem 17. Simplify: $\dfrac{(1-x^{-1})^{-1}+1}{(1-x^{-1})^{-1}-1}$, $x \neq \{0, 1\}$

Problem 18. Simplify: $\dfrac{ab^3c^3 - a^3b^2c}{a^2b^2c^2}$.

Problem 19. Simplify: $\dfrac{(xy - y^2)}{(xy - x^2)}$.

Problem 20. Simplify the following and express the result without using negative exponents.

$$\frac{(3a^{-2}b^3c^{-1})^2}{2} \cdot \frac{\sqrt{2}ab^{-1}c^2}{3}$$ (Mathcounts Competitions)

Problem 21. Simplify: $\dfrac{(n+1)!(n+3)(n+2)}{(n+4)!}$

Problem 22. Given that $7x - 14 = 35$, what is the value of $x - 2$?

Problem 23. Simplify: $\dfrac{(5x)^3}{25x^2}$.

Problem 24. Express in simplest form: $6\pi - 2\pi$.

Problem 25. If $n! = 1 \cdot 2 \cdot 3 \ldots (n-1)(n)$, find $\dfrac{7!}{4!}$.

Problem 26. Simplify: $\dfrac{4!5!}{6!}$

Problem 27. Simplify: $56^2 - 44^2$.

Problem 28. Simplify: $(\dfrac{1}{a} + \dfrac{1}{b} + \dfrac{1}{c})^{-1}$

Problem 29. Find y if the expression $(2x + 1)^2 + (2x + 1)(2x - 1)$ is written in the form y $(2x + 1)$.

Problem 30. Simplify: $\dfrac{x^{-2} - y^{-2}}{x^{-1} - y^{-1}}$

Problem 31. Express the following in simplest form: $(-2)^{4x+2}(2)^{6x-5}(8)^x$.   (Mathcounts Handbooks)

Problem 32. Given $x \neq -2, -1, 0$, write as a common fraction: $\dfrac{\dfrac{1}{x+1} - 1}{\dfrac{x}{x+1} + x}$.

Problem 33. Simplify: $\dfrac{(37037 \times 15) + (37037 \times 9)}{37037 \times 3}$

Problem 34. For $x \neq \dfrac{3}{2}$, what is the value of $\dfrac{3}{2x-3} - \dfrac{2x}{2x-3}$?   (Mathcounts Handbooks)

Problem 35. The expression $(x^3 + 1)^2(x^2 + 2)^3$ can be written as a polynomial. Find the degree of this polynomial.

ANSWER KEYS

Problem 1. $3n + 21$ **Problem 2.** $3a^3b^4c$ **Problem 3.** $8a^3b^6$

Problem 4. a^2 **Problem 5.** $\dfrac{12a^2}{b}$ **Problem 6.** $\dfrac{1}{x}$

Problem 7. 2 **Problem 8.** $\dfrac{1}{3}$ **Problem 9.** $\dfrac{16a^2}{b^2}$

Problem 10. x^3y^3 **Problem 11.** $\dfrac{2x}{x-3}$ **Problem 12.** -1

Problem 13. 35 **Problem 14.** 1 **Problem 15.** $2x^{a-b-4c}$

Problem 16. 21 **Problem 17.** $2x - 1$ **Problem 18.** $\dfrac{bc^2 - a^2}{ac}$

Problem 19. $-\dfrac{y}{x}$ **Problem 20.** $\dfrac{3\sqrt{2}b^5}{2a^3}$ **Problem 21.** $\dfrac{1}{n+4}$

Problem 22. 5 **Problem 23.** $5x$ **Problem 24.** 4π

Problem 25. 210 **Problem 26.** 4 **Problem 27.** 1200

Problem 28. $\dfrac{abc}{ac + ab + bc}$ or equivalent   **Problem 29.** $4x$

Problem 30. $\dfrac{x+y}{xy}$ **Problem 31.** 2^{13x-3} **Problem 32.** $\dfrac{-1}{x+2}$ or $\dfrac{1}{-x-2}$

Problem 33. 8 **Problem 34.** -1 **Problem 35.** 12

H

hexagon, 169

I

improper fraction, 62
integer, 10, 26, 40, 47, 48, 49, 50, 58, 60, 61, 65, 66,
    67, 68, 70, 81, 84, 87, 113, 118, 125, 194, 200, 212,
    214, 215, 217, 218, 219, 237, 254, 256, 260, 261
integers, 19, 20, 47, 48, 49, 50, 51, 57, 58, 60, 61, 67,
    70, 83, 86, 101, 116, 118, 120, 123, 134, 160, 185,
    189, 190, 191, 199, 214, 215, 217, 218, 254, 255,
    256, 260, 261
intersection, 186
inverse, 2, 204
isosceles, 168, 170

L

least common multiple, 90
line, 6, 7, 11, 36, 39, 82, 83, 148, 181, 186, 189, 190,
    192
line segment, 181, 189, 190, 192
lowest terms, 63, 74, 85, 86, 136

M

median, 171
midpoint, 165
mixed number, 62, 70, 74, 75, 132, 135, 138, 167,
    202, 218
multiple, 21, 61, 118, 123

N

natural number, 26, 57, 120, 122, 187, 231
natural numbers, 26, 57, 120, 122, 187, 231
negative number, 57
number line, 78, 81, 217, 233, 235, 236, 239, 254
numerator, 62, 63, 64, 65, 81

O

odd number, 47, 49, 50, 51, 53, 54, 55, 56, 60, 61,
    123, 188
operation, 51, 60, 96, 251, 260

P

palindrome, 184, 192
parallel, 162
parallelogram, 154, 162, 167, 171
percent, 96, 97, 98, 99, 100, 102, 104, 106, 108, 109,
    110, 125, 126, 130, 133, 135, 140, 165, 168, 174
perimeter, 154, 155, 157, 158, 159, 161, 164, 165,
    166, 167, 169, 172, 174
perpendicular, 168
plane, 162, 182
point, 81, 82, 83, 84, 125, 126, 149, 162, 165, 181,
    182, 186, 217, 221, 223, 225, 226, 233
polygon, 152, 163, 167
polynomial, 171, 268
positive number, 144, 201
power, 86, 87, 194, 198, 199, 201, 207, 224, 260
prime number, 12, 14, 178, 243
principal square root, 204
product, 11, 30, 31, 33, 34, 35, 36, 39, 40, 43, 44, 45,
    47, 48, 57, 60, 64, 74, 75, 76, 77, 78, 83, 92, 93,
    120, 123, 131, 133, 138, 178, 184, 186, 201, 216,
    217, 221, 230, 231, 240, 242, 254, 255, 260, 265
proportion, 143

Q

quadrilateral, 119, 161, 171
quotient, 30, 45, 62, 75, 84, 93, 211, 228, 254, 255,
    262, 263, 265, 266

R

radius, 159, 168, 169, 229
random, 114, 115, 116, 121, 178
rate, 103, 142, 148
ratio, 96, 101, 107, 136, 140, 141, 142, 144, 145, 146,
    147, 149, 150, 164, 166, 171, 173
rational number, 85, 86